THE BEAUTIFUL ORNAMENT OF
THE THREE VISIONS

THREE VISIONS
Fundamental Teachings of the Sakya Lineage of Tibetan Buddhism

A translation of the Tibetan text
*The Beautiful Ornament of the Three Visions:
An exposition of the preliminary practices of the path which
extensively explains the instructions of the "Path Including Its Result"
in accordance with the Root Treatise of the Vajra Verses of Virūpa*

by
Ngorchen Konchog Lhundrub

Foreword by
H. H. Sakya Trizin

Translated by
Lobsang Dagpa and
Jay Goldberg

Snow Lion
Boulder

Snow Lion
An imprint of Shambhala Publications, Inc.
4720 Walnut Street
Boulder, Colorado 80301
www.shambhala.com

© 1991, 2002 by Jay Goldberg

This book was originally published as *The Beautiful Ornament of the Three Visions* (Snow Lion, 1991).

All rights reserved. No part of this book may be reproduced in any form or by any means, electronic or mechanical, including photocopying, recording, or by any information storage and retrieval system, without permission in writing from the publisher.

9 8 7 6 5 4 3

Printed in the United States of America

♾This edition is printed on acid-free paper that meets the American National Standards Institute Z39.48 Standard.
✪Shambhala Publications makes every effort to print on recycled paper. For more information please visit www.shambhala.com.
Snow Lion is distributed worldwide by Penguin Random House, Inc., and its subsidiaries.

The Library of Congress catalogues the previous edition of this book as follows:

Dkon-mchog-lhun-grub, Ṅor-chen, 1497–1557.
[Lam 'bras sñon 'gro'i khrid yig snaṅ gsum mdzes rgyan. English]
The beautiful ornament of the three visions / by Ngorchen Konchog Lhundrub; foreword by H. H. Sakya Trizin; translated by Lobsang Dagpa and Jay Goldberg.
p. cm.
Translation of: Lam 'bras sñon 'gro'i khrid yig snaṅ gsum mdzes rgyan
Subtitle: An exposition of the preliminary practices of the path which extensively explains the instructions of the "Path including its result" in accordance with the root treatise of the Vajra verses of Virūpa.
Includes bibliographical references and index.
ISBN 978-0-937938-99-7 (1st ed.)
ISBN 978-1-55939-177-1 (2nd ed.)
1. Lam-'bras (Sa-skya-pa)—Early works to 1800. I. Lobsang Dagpa. II. Goldberg, Jay. III. Title. IV. Title: Three visions.
BQ7672.4.D5413 1991
294.3'44—dc20
91-26446
CIP

Contents

Foreword — X
Preface — XI

The Preliminaries — 1

Introduction — 2
Faith — 4
Refuge — 9

The Main Teaching — 19

The instructions on the impure vision — 20
A. The instructions on the faults of worldly existence — 20
  1. The suffering of suffering — 21
    a. The suffering of the hells — 22
    b. The suffering of the hungry ghosts — 33
    c. The suffering of the animals — 36
  2. The suffering of change — 38
    a. The general suffering of change — 38
    b. The suffering of human change — 39
    c. The suffering of gods' and demigods' change — 45
  3. The suffering of conditional phenomena — 48
    a. The suffering that activities are never ending — 49
    b. The suffering of not being satisfied by desire — 50
    c. The suffering of never being wearied of birth and death — 52

B. The instructions on the difficulty of obtaining the prerequisites — 55
  1. The difficulty to obtain this human body endowed with the prerequisites — 56
  2. The great benefit of this body that has been obtained — 63

3. The prerequisites obtained will not last long	67
a. The inconceivable benefits of reflecting on impermanence	67
b. Contemplating impermanence	68
C. The instructions on virtuous and nonvirtuous deeds and their results	87
1. Producing the desire to discard nonvirtue	88
2. Producing the desire to practise virtue	95
3. Transforming neutral deeds into virtues	104
The instructions on the vision of experience	112
A. Meditating until the common experience arises in one's mindstream	112
1. Loving kindness	116
2. Compassion	125
3. The thought of enlightenment	131
a. The wishing enlightenment thought	135
b. The entering enlightenment thought	138
c. The ultimate enlightenment thought	156
B. Meditating on the unshakable understanding that an extraordinary experience in the Vajrayāna path will arise	196
The instructions on the pure vision	201
A. The enlightened body	201
B. The enlightened voice	202
C. The enlightened mind	202
Colophon	206
Notes to the preface	208
Notes to the text	210
Outline of the text	221
Bibliography	227
Index	228

Dedication

*This work is dedicated to
His Holiness Sakya Trizin,
head of the Sakyapa Tradition,
His Eminence Chogay Trichen Rinpoche,
head of the Tsarpa Tradition,
His Eminence Luding Khen Rinpoche,
head of the Ngorpa Tradition,
and all the others who preserve the teaching of
the precious "Path Including Its Result".*

His Holiness Sakya Trizin
Forty-first Patriarch of the Sakyapa Tradition

His Holiness
Sakya Trizin

**HEAD OF THE SAKYAPA ORDER
OF TIBETAN BUDDHISM**

192, RAJPUR ROAD
P.O. RAJPUR
DEHRA DUN, U.P., INDIA

༄༅། །ཡོངས་རྫོགས་བསྟན་པའི་མངའ་བདག་ལ་ཆེན་པོ་གོང་མ་ལྔ་ཡིས་ཐུན་མིན་བཞེད་སྲོལ་
རྗེ་བཙུན་བཀྱས་པ་ལ་འཇུག་པའི་ལྔ་ཕམས་ཏད་དང་རུལ་བ་རྗེ་བཙུན་གྲགས་པའི་དབང་དོ་
དོར་ཆེན་དཀོན་མཆོག་ལྷུན་གྲུབ་ཤེས་མཚན་རྒྱ་ཀྱི་བདེན་བྱེད་རྫེའི་ཤོན་ཡངས་ཀུན་ཏུ་རྒྱ་
རྒྱལ་ཏུ་གཡོ་བ་གངས་ཡིས་མཛད་པའི་གསུང་ངག་རིན་པོ་ཆེ་ལམ་འབྲས་བུ་དང་བཅས་པའི་ཆོས་
བགྲོའི་སྐྱིད་ཡིག་ཉང་གསུམ་མཇོག་པ་ར་བྱེད་པའི་ཕྱིན་ཤེས་རྒྱུ་བའི་ནི། ཕ་རྒྱལ་བའི་གསུང་
རབ་ཀུན་གྱི་ཟབ་དོན་མ་ལུས་པ་ཕྱོགས་གཅིག་ཏུ་འདུས་པ་ར་འཛིན་བྱུང་ཆེ་ཞིང་ དོན་བྱེད་
ཕུལ་ལྱུམ་ཚོགས་པས་དང་པོ་མཆོག་དགེན་ཀུན་གྱི་གོ་རྟོགས་ལྷབ་ཤོགས་གཞུར་གཉས་གམས་
དབང་འབྲུམ་ཕུག་ཏུ་མས་བཞུགས་འོ། གལ་ཅན་བར་དོའི་ལོངས་ཀྱི་ཟིམ་གས་ བགྲོ་བའི་
གདུང་བ་ཤེས་བའི་མཐུ་མཆོག་ ཡིད་བཞིན་གྱི་ནོར་བུ་ལས་ཀྱང་ཆས་རྒྱགས་པ་འདི་བཞིན་ད་
ལམ་ཁ་རིས་རྒྱལ་ཁབ་ནས་ལུ་པར་སྙན་རྗོ་བཟང་གྲགས་རྟ་དང་ ཨ་རི་ར་དགེ་སློང་དགེ་
དབང་བསམ་གཏན་དང་ ཨ་རི་བཟ་རྗོ་རྗེ་ར་ཏ་རོ་སོན་བཅས་ནས་རྒྱག་བསམ་རྣམ་པར་
དགར་བ་འདྲིས་ནད་དུ་ཡབ་བསྒྲུབ་མཛད་པ་འདིས། དེ་གབས་འདི་ཆོས་ལ་དོན་གཉེར་
ཅན་གྱི་རྒྱལ་མི་རིགས་རྣམས་ཀྱིས་མཆོན་རིགས་ལུགས་ཆད་པའི་འཇམ་དབྱངས་ཀྱི་རྒྱ་ཡོངས་ཀྱི་མཛོན་
མཆོག་དང་ དེས་ཤིག་ཀྱི་ཡམ་བཟང་བའི་རྒྱག་ཏུ་བགྲོད་པའི་བོ་གྲོས་ཀྱི་ཤིག་གསར་བ་ཙོ་
ཞེ། བཞུལ་དང་ཡུན་གྱི་ཞི་བདེ་ལྷན་ན་མཆོ་ལ་པའི་དགར་གནས་རྒྱས་འཕེལ་བའི་ཡིད་ཆེས་
དང་རེ་སྨོན་བཅས་ ཞབ་གསུམ་ལ་རྫོ་རྒྱར་དང་གནས་ན་ཆི་མེད་རྗོ་རྗེའི་ཞིང་ཁང་ནས་
དཔལ་ལ་སྐྱའི་ཁྱི་འཛིན་པས ༤༢ ཟླ་བ་ ༧ ཚེས་ ༡༤ དགེ་བ་།།

༄ ཟླ་བ་ ༧ ཚེས་ ༡༤ དགེ་བ་།།

Foreword
by His Holiness Sakya Trizin

The master and lord of scholars, Ngorchen Konchog Lhundrub, is unequaled in authentically explaining the extraordinary tradition of the 'foremost father-son gurus' of Sakya who are the great owners of the entire teaching of the Buddha. His pleasing name is a streamer that waves and flutters right up to the summit of this world. The work known as *The Beautiful Ornament of the Three Visions*, which is an explanation of "The Precious Word of the Path Including Its Result," was composed by him. As this text completely includes the profound essence of all the teachings of the Victorious One, its subject matter is vast. Since the style of its writing is perfect in every way, it is easy to be understood by all—whether of superior or inferior intelligence. Therefore, this work has been rightly praised by many impartial scholars and wise men.

This text which is like a staircase for those fortunate practitioners who desire liberation, an excellent medicine that dispels the suffering of sentient beings, and a valuable article that even surpasses a wish-fulfilling gem, was recently translated with pure intentions into English in America by the Sakya Acharya Lobsang Dagpa and the American practitioner Jay Goldberg.

It is my belief and hope that by the translation of this work at this present time all foreigners who are interested in the teaching of the Buddha and generally all the people of this world will obtain the new eye of wisdom that easily traverses the path to liberation, and that they will greatly increase their celebration of temporary and long term peace and happiness.

This was written by the head of the Śhrī Sakya order at the Amar Vajra residence in Rajpur, India on July 18, 1985.

Preface

Since the time of the Buddha Śākyamuni, the Buddhist religion has undergone progressive and continuous development, reaching out into many countries throughout the world. In every land where it took root firmly, it transformed the thinking and way of life of the people, encouraging and leading them into mature modes of existence that result in ultimate happiness. One of the most distinguished examples of this is found in Tibet, the Land of Snows, which only recently opened its doors, allowing outsiders a view of the intricate and elaborate system of Buddhist thought and practice that developed there.

Of the four main traditions that arose in Tibet, the Sakyapa (Sa.skya.pa) is the least known today. The Sakyapa tradition was a major force in the development and spread of the new tantras that came to Tibet in the eleventh century, as well as the principal political power that ruled Tibet during parts of the thirteenth and fourteenth centuries, but its political stature remained on a low level over the succeeding centuries even though great scholars, practitioners, and saints continued to appear among its ranks.

The history of the Sakyapas is found within the lineage of the Khon ('Khon), a noble family whose members frequently proved to be outstanding adepts of the Buddhist path and who also took part in shaping Tibet into what it is today. During the eighth century, Khon Lu'i Wangpo ('Khon kLui'i dbang.po) and others of the family became disciples of the renowned Indian master Guru Padmasambhava, and for the next three centuries the Khon family remained staunch supporters and followers of the old school, the Nyingmapa (rNying.ma.pa). However, during the eleventh century, when the new tantras began trickling into Tibet and the pure practice of the old school had declined in that part of Tsang Province, Khon Konchog Gyalpo ('Khon dKon.mchog rGyal.po), 1034-1102, decided that the Khon family should seek out the new tantras. Under his leadership, a monastery was begun in south-central Tibet, at a place that came to be called Sakya. This monastery quickly became a leading center for the study, practice and dissemination of the new tantras, as well as for the Mahāyāna teachings of ethics, philosophy, metaphysics, logic, and other branches of Buddhist and Indian thought. It was under the leadership of Khon Konchog Gyalpo's son, Sachen Kunga Nyingpo (Sa.chen Kun.dga' sNying.po), 1092-1158, and his sons and grandsons (who became known as the Five Founding Lamas of the Sakyapa tradition[1]) that this center took form as a major sect.

Throughout its history, members of the Sakyapa tradition who have been considered masters have been those who brought the aspects of study and practice into a proper balance. Although these masters taught and practiced the various teachings found in both the Mahāyāna sūtras and the tantras of various lineages, the heart of the Sakyapa tradition—that which makes it a distinct entity and which has sustained its vitality over the centuries—is the teaching known as the "Path Including Its Result" (Lam Dre).[2]

The Lam Dre teaching originated in India with one of the great mahāsiddhas, known as Virūpa (in Tibet, he is commonly known as Birwapa). Although the date of his birth is uncertain, Virūpa was born into a royal family in the eastern part of India. At a fairly early age, he entered the Buddhist monastic university at Nalanda, where he was given the name Śrī Dharmapāla. Being very intelligent, he was able to master the various branches of Buddhist knowledge and eventually became one of the abbots and leading teachers of the university. It was his custom to teach the different subjects found within the Hīnayāna and Mahāyāna schools of thought during the day, while secretly practicing the meditation techniques of the Vajrayāna at night. At the age of seventy-one, after having practiced in this manner for many years, he found that not only was he not making any progress but that he was even experiencing many obstacles in the form of sickness, bad omens, and bad dreams. Thoroughly discouraged by the course of his spiritual development, he threw his rosary into a urinal and resolved to abandon his Vajrayāna meditation and to apply himself solely to the meditation practices of the Hīnayāna and Mahāyāna. However, that very evening, he beheld in a pure vision a blue-colored lady who chided him for having abandoned the Vajrayāna path. Requesting him to retrieve his rosary and scent it with perfume, she then manifested herself in the form of the sixteen-deity maṇḍala of Vajra Nairātmyā and bestowed upon him the tantric initiation and empowerment. During that ceremony, he gained a realization into the true nature of all phenomena and attained the first stage (bhūmi) of spiritual attainment on the Bodhisattva's path. During the following five evenings, he received further instructions from Vajra Nairātmyā and consequently attained another stage of attainment of each of those evenings. Having thus arrived at the sixth stage of spiritual attainment on the Bodhisattva's path, his outward behavior and deportment underwent a drastic change. Always an exemplary monk, he was now seen to be constantly drinking intoxicants, and women were found in his room every night. Not understanding his behavior and thinking it a bad influence on the other monks, the authorities of the monastery requested him to leave. Returning his robes to the monastic community and donning rags and flowers, he left Nalanda, giving himself the new name Virūpa, which means "the ugly one." From that point on, many stories abounded of his uncivilized behavior and miraculous powers as he roamed the countryside subduing evil forces, bringing others into the Buddhist path, and reaching higher stages of attainment himself.

The quintessence of his attainment was formulated in a short oral teaching based upon the *Hevajra Tantra* and known as the *Root Treatise of the Vajra Verses* (rDo.rje'i tshig.rkang, *Vajragāthā*).[3] This treatise is the basis of the Lam Dre, the "Path Including Its Result." Although transmitted orally for several generations, it was eventually written down, and vast commentarial literature was composed to explain the theoretical and practical apsects of the teaching. The *Root Treatise of the Vajra Verses* consists of only twelve Tibetan folios comprising the entire path of enlightenment, starting from the point where the beginner first enters the path and extending right up to the teaching of the attainment of full and perfect enlightenment. It encompasses the teachings of all the schools of Buddhist thought--the Hīnayāna, Mahāyāna, and Vajrayāna—though in a very pithy fashion. The commentarial literature divided the root text into two parts. The first part (which covers only one side of a folio of the Tibetan text), called the "Three Visions," deals with teachings common to the Hīnayāna and Mahāyāna paths and acts as a preparation for entering into the Vajrayāna path; the second part, "Three Tantras," deals with the various aspects of the entire Vajrayāna path.

From Virūpa, this teaching was transmitted through four successive Indian masters before arriving in Tibet, where the great translator Dromi Lotsawa Śakya Yeshe ('Brog.mi Lo.tsa.ba Sha.kya Ye.shes), 993-1077, rendered it into the Tibetan language. However, it was not until the time of Sachen Kunga Nyingpo that the written commentarial tradition began to grow around the Lam Dre, the "Path Including Its Result" teaching. Sachen himself wrote eleven commentaries on various aspects of the teaching, and his third son, Jetsun Dagpa Gyaltshen (rJe.btsun Grags.pa rGyal.mtshan), wrote extensive commentaries, instructions, and treatises concerning the Lam Dre.

In the beginning, this teaching was given to only one disciple at a time, but as it passed into Tibet the number of people receiving it began to increase. Depending upon the time and conditions, the Lam Dre teaching would be given in either a brief or an extensive form. Sachen Kunga Nyingpo remained with his teacher, Zhangton Chobar (Zhang.ston Chos.'bar), for eight years. During that time, he received the teaching in a gradual manner, meditating and gaining an understanding of each part of the teaching before receiving the next section. Over the years, however, the teaching became more formalized and was given to large groups. As the teaching became more diffused, some felt that it had lost some of its vitality and profundity. To counteract this, when Muchen Sempa Chenpo Konchog Gyaltshen (Mu.chen sema.dpa' chen.po dKon.mchog rGyal.mtshan), 1388-1469, was bestowing the "Path Including Its Result" teaching to a gathering of monks at Ngor Evam Choden Monastery, each evening he took his foremost disciple, Dagchen Lodo Gyaltshen (bDag.chen bLo.gros rGal.mtshan), 1444-1495, into his own room in order to bestow a more profound and experiential form of the teaching to him individually. In this way, the transmission of Lam Dre became split into two traditions: the more common, exoteric form of the teaching given to large gatherings and known as Lam Dre Tshog Shed (Lam.'bras 'tshog.bshad), and the uncommon, esoteric form of the teaching given to one individual or to a few and known as Lam Dre Lob Shed (Lam.'bras sLob.bshad).

Though a vast amount of literature concerning the various aspects of this teaching was written by the five founding lamas of the Sakyapa tradition as well as by later scholars and meditators, it was Lama Dampa Sonam Gyaltshen (bLa.ma dam.pa bSod.nam rGyal.mtshan), 1312-1375, who gave shape to the format in which the written form of the Lam Dre teaching has been transmitted to the present day. In his system, a separate text was written for the "three visions" and for the "three tantras." Based on this format, Ngorchen Konchog Lhundrub (Ngor.chen dKon.mchog Lhun.grub), 1497-1557, the author of the present text, wrote an extensive treatise on both texts in reference to the Lam Dre Tshog Shed division of the Lam Dre teaching. A later condensation of this was written by Ngawang Chodag (Nga.dbang Chos.grags), 1572-1641. In regard to the Lam Dre Lob Shed division, authoritative texts were written by Jamyang Khyentse Wangchug ('Jam.dbyang mKhyen.btse dbang.phyug), 1524-1568, and Mangtho Ludrub Gyatsho (Mang.thos Klu.grub rGya.mtsho), 1523-?, both of whom were disciples of Tsarchen Losal Gyatso (Tsar.chen bLo.gsal rGya.mtsho), 1502-1566. A later synthesis of these two works was composed by Jamyang Loter Wangpo ('Jam.dbyang bLo.ter dbang.po), 1847-1914.

The Three Visions

The *Root Treatise of the Vajra Verses* succinctly states the "three visions" as follows:

> For sentient beings with the afflictions
> is the impure vision.
> For the meditator with transic absorption
> is the vision of experience.
> For the ornamental wheel of the Sugata's inexhaustible
> enlightened body, voice and mind is the pure vision.

In Ngorchen Konchog Lhundrub's *The Beautiful Ornament of the Three Visions*, the full implications of this verse are thoroughly treated. The first three words of the first line of the verse, *For sentient beings,* serves to demonstrate the various types of sufferings that sentient beings must endure within the six realms of worldly existence, from those of the hells up to the sufferings of the celestial states. The next three words of the first line, *with the afflictions,* is taken as a starting point for explaining the great opportunity a person has obtained in gaining this precious human body and the need to practice the holy Dharma in order to make this life fruitful. As a complement to this, the teaching of death and impermanence is given to show the need to practice Dharma quickly and diligently. The final four words of the first line, *is the impure vision,* illustrates that sentient beings under the influence of the afflictions of desire, hatred and ignorance continue to perform deeds (karma) that bind them within this world of existence. The teachings found within this section are commonly shared by both the Hīnayāna and the Mahāyāna paths.

The second line of the verse, *For the meditator with transic absorption is the vision of experience,* is categorized in two ways. The first is described as the common path, which includes the practices of loving kindness, compassion, and the enlightenment thought, which in turn includes the meditations on calm abiding and insight wisdom. This section of the teaching shares the methods found within the various traditions of the Mahāyāna's Bodhisattva's path. The second refers to the extraordinary path of the Vajrayāna teaching; here the practitioner is urged to seek out, study, and engage in its methods of practice. The purpose of this vision of experinece is to bring the practitioner's mind to maturity withing the spiritual path, so as to become qualified and prepared to enter the profound teachings of the Vajrayāna. Vajrayāna commences with the ripening experience of receiving the tantric empowerment and is accomplished through receiving and employing the methodical training, as found in teachings such as the "three tantras."[4]

The final line of the verse, *For the ornamental wheel of the Sugata's inexhaustible enlightened body, voice and mind is the pure vision,* describes the result of full and perfect Buddhahood for the sake of ultimate happiness for the benefit of both the practitioner and others.

The text is introduced with an exposition of faith and taking refuge in the Three Jewels of Buddha, Dharma, and Sangha (i.e., the Enlightened One, His Teaching, and the Community of Followers). Each section of the teaching is presented in three parts: a general summary, quotations from sūtras and scriptures to authenticate it, and the manner in which it is to be contemplated and meditated upon. The primary purpose of this text is to act as a meditation manual that will enable one gradually, step by step, to turn toward the path of Dharma, enter the path, traverse it, and realize the goal of the ultimate happiness and omniscience of Buddhahood.

Ngorchen Konchog Lhundrub

The author of this text, Ngorchen Konchog Lhundrub, was born in Sakya in 1497. Having entered the monastery as a novice monk at the age of thirteen, he began his studies of the different traditions of Buddhist teachings. Under his three principal teachers, Konchog Phel (dKon.mchog 'Phel), Muchen Sangye Rinchen (Mu.chen sang.rgyas Rin.chen), and Salo Jampa'i Dorje (Sa.lo 'Jam.dpa'i rDo.rje), he received and mastered the Lam Dre teaching as well as other Vajrayāna instructions. Having performed many meditation retreats, he realized the special view of the Lam Dre known as "the non-differentiation of worldly existence (samsāra) and liberation (nirvāna)." In this way, being able to conduct his daily life in accordance with this philosophical view of reality, all of his activities were maintained at a pure and enlightened level.

At the age of thirty-eight, he became the tenth abbot of

Ngor Evam Choden Monastery, which had been founded by the great master Ngorchen Kunga Zangpo (Ngor.chen Kun.dga' bZang.po), 1382-1456. Maintaining the strict moral discipline of a fully ordained monk and keeping to a pure vegetarian diet, Ngorchen Konchog Lhundrub held the throne of abbotship for twenty-four years. During this time, he bestowed the Lam Dre teaching on thirty-five occasions, as well as giving instructions on other aspects of the sutras and tantras. He was also a prolific writer, the best known of his writings being the *sNang.gsum mdzes rgyan, rGyud.gsum mdzes rgyan, lJon.shing mdzes rgyan, tshul.gsum gsal.byed, Legs.bshad gong.ma'i dgongs rgyan*, and the *dGag.len tshang.pa'i rigs sngags*.[5] Being a consummate master, many disciples gathered around him, so that his teaching and disciples spread throughout Tibet. Having realized the goal of the path of enlightenment, he passed away in 1557.

The Translation

Because this text is an excellent guide for beginners as well as for knowledgeable practitioners of the Dharma path, it has been the purpose of the translators to render it into vernacular English that is both easily accessible to the modern reader and faithful to the original Tibetan text. To simplify the Tibetan names found in the text, the first time a name appears it is given in its transliterated form in accordance with pronunciation and then followed by the exact spelling of the name as it is found in the Tibetan language. If the name appears later in the text, only the form in accordance with its pronunciation is given. The names of all scriptural texts and treatises are first given with their Tibetan titles, followed by the title in the original Sanskrit. The full titles for these books appear in the notes.

As Buddhist texts are becoming more readily available and Buddhist technical terms are becoming more familiar and can even be found in English dictionaries, certain terms, such as karma, nirvāna, and the like, have been left in their original Sanskrit form.

Acknowledgements

Though there are many people to whom we would like to express our thanks and gratitude, we shall limit it to just a few. First and foremost, we wish to sincerely thank the most venerable Dezhung Rinpoche, abbot of Tharlam Monastery, for clearing up many doubts we had concerning various points of the text, as well as for expanding our knowledge of the Buddha's teaching and the path. Deep gratitude is also extended to Geshe Lozang Jamspal and Jared Rhoton for kindly assisting during various stages of the translation. Profound thanks are extended to all who lent financial and moral support to make this translation possible. Special thanks are also due to Cyrus Stearns for historical notes, Victoria Scott for editing, and to Julia Regala for typing this text several times during its various stages of development. Finally, we wish to thank the Los Angeles County Museum of Art, Gift of Paul E. Manheim, for allowing us to use the photo of Ngorchen Konchog Lhundrub, which is a detail from the museum's seventeenth-century thanka (Tibetan painting) entitled "A Shaka-Pa Monk."

In conclusion, we wish to dedicate the merits arising from this undertaking to all the living beings of this world, that each one may gain happiness, freedom from all sufferings, and full and perfect enlightenment.

Sakya Thubten Dhondrup Ling
Center for Buddhist Studies and Meditation
Los Angeles, California
May 31, 1985

Om Swasti Siddham

With devotion I bow at the feet of the holy preceptors,
revered and endowed with great compassion.
May the Master, the jewel of the sky, who, having
mounted the chariot of the two virtuous accumulations,
ascends high into the vast sky of cognizable things,
and is skilled in diffusing the rays of his boundless deeds,
keep watch over me.

May the incomparable Victorious Ones, who
have cleansed all illusory, impure visions
through the vision of meditative experience,
keep watch over all these living beings
by their unceasing, all-pervasive pure vision.

Reverently I salute the feet of that Lord of Yogīs,[1]
ever reveling in the wine of the great bliss of nectar,
who stopped the great flood of worldly existence, the afflictions,
and arrested in space the immaculate sun.

Give heed, for this is the exposition of his words on basic
practice which are the essence of all sūtras and tantras,
comprising the sole path traversed by the Enlightened Ones
and the method followed by the holy sages of Sakya.

The Mahasiddha Virūpa,
The Master of Great Spiritual Attainments

THE PRELIMINARIES

Introduction

The teachings that are to be explained and practiced here are: (i) The instructions of the "Path Including Its Result", the jewel of the holy teachings, the only way traversed by all the Tathāgatas of the three times; the extracted essence of the meaning of all collections of sūtras and tantras containing the Enlightened One's profound discourses; the precepts taught by the fearless Shrī Dharmapāla,[2] that great and reverent lord of meditators; the instructions found worthy to be traversed by the wise; the true nature of the transic absorption of emptiness, excellent in every way; a lamp that illuminates all sūtras and tantras; and that which is difficult to understand by the meritless, but a stairway for those who set out for the city of liberation. (ii) The instruction on the result that includes the path. (iii) The instruction that through knowing one thing, one will know many. (iv) The instruction on transforming faults into virtues. (v) The instruction on accepting obstacles as spiritual attainments. (vi) The instruction on removing the obstacles of concentrative meditation by recognizing the transic absorptions. (vii) The instruction on removing the hindrances of Māra[3] through recognizing these obstacles for what they are. (viii) The instruction on knowing how to transform faults into virtues and accept obstacles as spiritual attainments. (ix) The instruction on unerringly knowing the true essence of the Tripiṭaka.[4] (x) The instruction that is like the philosopher's stone (which changes all that it touches into gold). (xi) The instruction on the *Root Treatise, The Vajra Verses*,[5] which is like a wish-fulfilling gem.

Involved in its explanation and practice are: first, an explanation through the method of instructions; second, the method of practicing according to these instructions; and third, sealing the meditator who practices them with the ten secrets, and also imparting instructions beneficial to fortunate disciples.

The first reference has three parts: subject matter, the means for its elucidation, and the manner of its elucidation. The subject matter consists of instructions on the "Path Including Its Result" comprising eleven profound methods. The means for its elucidation are the four authenticities and the four oral transmissions. The manner of its elucidation is : The meaning of the entire Precious Oral Teaching of the "Path Including Its Result" and all the paths of the Vajrayāna which are a specialty of the four oral transmissions are established by the four authenticities. As these are expounded at length in the *Lam 'bras khog Phub*[6], one should also consult it.

The second reference is the manner of their practice according to these instructions. This refers to the four ways in which a disciple may be guided: the guidance according to the complete teaching, the guidance according to the six essentials, the guidance according to the eleven essentials, and the guidance according to the three types of intellect — superior, mediocre, and inferior.

Here the disciples will be guided along the perfect path by the first method, that is, according to the complete teachings. In regard to this, it was taught by the Great Sakyapa (Sachen Kunga Nyingpo) in his *Lam 'bras Don bsDus Ma*,[7] that the path consist of:

> Establishing the foundation, the actual path,
> removal of conceptions, stages, to expand one's
> realization, dispelling obstacles, and the furthest
> limit of realization along with its result.

Otherwise, the great saint (Jetsun Dagpa Gyaltshen)[8] thought to further abridge all those teachings into two parts: the preliminary and the actual practice of the path. He said,

> If you wish to guide a faithful disciple, who heeds
> whatever his preceptor says according to the complete
> teachings of the Path Including Its Result, then first
> lead him according to the Three Visions,[9] and then according
> to the Three Tantras,[10] for all the teachings
> (of Vajrayāna) are compiled into these Three Tantras.
> So one should practice according to these two levels.

Therefore we shall present them here also in this manner.

Faith

First, the disciple who is to be guided according to these "three visions" is one who is endowed with faith, for as it was said in the *Chos.bcu.pa'i mDo (Daśadharma Sūtra)*,[11]

> Just as a green sprout never springs from seeds
> that have been scorched by fire, so no virtues
> will arise in people who have no faith.

If one lacks faith, then the very foundation of virtue does not exist and, as a result, one will not seek the path to liberation. For such a one, the good qualities of the Noble Ones will not be gained, nor will one obtain the blessing of the Preceptor and the Three Jewels. Thus faith is truly of utmost importance for the practice of Dharma. As it was said in the *dKon.mchog sGron.ma'i mDo (Ratna pradīpa Sūtra)*,

> Faith goes before and, like a mother, gives birth.
> It causes all virtues to arise and grow.
> Clearing away doubts and crossing the rivers,
> faith symbolizes the city of happiness.
> Faith makes the mind unsullied and pure.
> It casts off pride and is the root of reverence.
> Faith is a treasure, it is wealth, the most excellent feet,
> and, like hands, the chief means of gathering virtues.

If it is asked, what exactly faith is, the *Chos mngon.pa (Abhidharmakośa)*[12] explains,

> If it is asked, what is faith? Faith is
> full confidence in the efficacy of deeds
> (karma) and their result, in the truths and

in the Three Jewels; it is also an aspiration (for spiritual attainment) and clearminded (appreciation of the truth).

A person endowed with these three kinds of faith — clearminded appreciation, aspiration, and confidence — will not forsake religion due to the four usual causes of leaving it. These four causes of leaving religion are: desire, anger, fear, and ignorance. One who does not forsake religion through these four is one whose faith is unbroken by Māra's deeds. Not to forsake religion through desire means that, through knowing the faults of attachment, one will not renounce religion even though one knows one can gain a kingdom, or the like. As Lord Maitreya taught:

> Though they win them not, the greatly deluded
> seek worldly ephemeral pleasures.
> Steadfast seekers of liberation renounce such,
> though they might gain the riches of a perfect kingdom.

Not to forsake religion through anger means that, as was said in the *sPyod.'jug (Bodhicaryāvatāra)*,[13]

> By a single fit of anger, all the merits of
> thousands of aeons gathered through good deeds,
> such as generosity, worshiping the Sugatas,
> and the like, are destroyed.
>
> No sin is there like anger,
> no penance is there like patience;
> strive, therefore, in various ways
> to become practiced in forbearance.

Through knowing the faults of anger, one will not renounce religion because, by giving up religion through anger, one is harmed rather than harm being done to one's enemy.

Not to forsake religion through fear means that even though someone might say, "I shall kill you if you practice in accordance with religion" or "I shall rob you of all your possessions", still one would not forsake religion, knowing that the terrors and sufferings of this life hardly amount to a fraction of the anguish of the hells and other states. As it was said in the *sPyod.'jug (Bodhicaryāvatāra)*,

> Were all gods and demigods my foes they could not lead
> me into Unceasing Hell's flames united with which not
> even the ashes of Mount Sumeru would remain; yet there
> I am hurled in a moment by this mighty foe, the afflictions.

Not to forsake religion through ignorance means that as was said in the *sPyod.'jug (Bodhicaryāvatāra)*,

> Even as a man afflicted by illness
> is helpless in all his actions,
> so, too, a mind afflicted by ignorance
> is powerless in all spheres.

Realizing that ignorance of what should be accepted as wholesome and what should be rejected as unwholesome is a cause of downfall, then for the sake of learning the respective areas of acceptance and rejection, one should rely upon spiritual friends after the manner of those stories which the youth, Shrīsambhava, and the maiden, Shrīmati, narrated to Sudhana.[14] Further, by studying the sūtras and in other ways, one should comprehend the whole range of good and bad deeds in order to avoid forsaking religion. As it was said in the *sPyod.'jug (Bodhicaryāvatāra)*,

> One should learn how to rely upon preceptors
> according to the story of Shrīsambhava;
> the way is to be known by reading this and
> other discourses of the Enlightened One.

In brief, a person — who is not caused to forsake religion through these four factors that are antagonistic to it — is a worthy vessel of this doctrine of liberation. Hence, it was said in the *Rin.chen phreng.ba (Ratnāvalī)*[15], that

> One is called faithful and the excellent
> vessel of the teachings of emancipation
> who does not relinquish religion through
> desire, anger, fear, or ignorance.

Therefore understanding that faith is the root of all good qualities, one should pray to the Preceptors and the Three Jewels so that faith will grow and not be wasted.

Also, through reflecting on the practice and inspirational deeds of holy persons, reading the pure sūtras, abandoning sinful companions, and associating with religious friends who practice self-restraint, one should train oneself in methods that cause the field of faith to become extremely fertile. Therefore, as it was taught in the *bsLab.bTus, (Śikṣā Samuccaya)*,[16]

> One who longs to put an end to sorrow
> and to reach the sublimity of happiness
> must make firm the root of faith and
> steady one's mind for enlightenment.

Therefore, to help the faithless to gain faith and to strengthen the faculty of faith in those who already possess it, one ought to study carefully the biographies of (one's own) lineage of spiritual Preceptors. One should also practice devotion, meditate, and pray with diligence to them. In conjunction with this, one should recite any prayer to the lineage of Preceptors for which one has obtained oral transmission. One should read and encourage others, too, to recite them.

A person who is endowed with faith as explained above should cultivate it in a place like the one described in the *mDo.sde rgyan (Sūtrālankāra)*:[17]

> The place where the wise practice is an auspicious site,
> with abundant provisions, well surrounded
> with noble companions, and endowed with the
> requisites of the practitioner's well-being.

Abundant provisions means that essentials, such as alms and the like, are easily available. **An auspicious site** is one unfrequented by thieves, bandits, and the like. **With noble companions** means that one's friends do not contribute to the increase of afflictions and sin. **Endowed with the requisites of the practitioner's well-being** means that the place is free from crowds of people by day and from noisy sounds at night.

A beginner, it is taught, should dwell in such a place as this. How should he dwell there? He should be seated in the Vajra position or any of the other meditative postures, without reclining, slumping forward, leaning, or the like. As it was explained in the *bsBom.rim, (Bhāvanākrama)*, [18]

> Placing before oneself an image or drawing
> of the Enlightened One, the Bodhisattvas,
> or any others, one should perform whatever
> offerings and the like one can while being
> seated upon a very soft and comfortable mat,
> with feet crossed according to the way in
> which the holy Vairocana sits, or else in
> the half-lotus position.

Refuge

The meditation to be practiced is said to consist of the preparation through seeking refuge and offering prayers, the main meditation on one's chosen object, and the completion through sharing merit and recollection. According to this arrangement, the preparation and completion should be added at the beginning and the end of all the sessions of meditation described in this book. Though refuge is usually considered to be the preparation, here at the time of explaining refuge itself, it will be treated as the main meditation and a detailed description of its parts will be given. Refuge is said to consist of five topics: (A) cause, (B) object, (C) procedure, (D) benefit, (E) precepts.

The Cause of Taking Refuge

To begin, the three causes of seeking refuge are fear, faith, and compassion. Seeking refuge through fear means that, being alarmed by the miseries of worldly existence experienced by others or oneself, one seeks refuge from them. As it was said in the *sPyod.'jug, (Bodhicaryāvatāra)*,

> Formerly I disobeyed your words but now,
> having seen great terror, in dismay I
> seek refuge in you. Quickly dispel my fears.

One undertakes to rely upon this refuge, which completely saves oneself and all others who are afflicted by the sufferings of worldly existence.

Seeking refuge through faith means that in seeking refuge one is motivated by any of the three kinds of faith. Faith of clear appreciation signifies that one discerns clearly the value of refuge, which has the ability to shield one from those fears of suffering; faith of aspiration signifies that one wishes to attain the stage of the refuge itself; and faith of confidence means that one trusts in the profound teaching of interdependent origination.

Seeking refuge through compassion refers to a person who has awakened into the Mahāyāna race. Being moved by unbearable compassion for others who are afflicted by sufferings, which one infers from one's own sufferings, one seeks refuge in order to shelter them entirely.

In brief, it is most important to seek refuge with a clear recollection of the causes just described, for the action of taking refuge without reflection does not achieve any merit. As it was said in the *sPyod.'jug (Bodhicaryāvatāra)*,

> The Omniscient One has taught that, though
> they be practiced for a long time, all
> repetitions of austerities and mantras
> are useless if the mind be distracted elsewhere.

The Object of Taking Refuge

There are many different views concerning the object of refuge, due both to variance between the Mahāyāna and Hīnayāna traditions and to variations within Mahāyāna and Hīnayāna themselves. Here the object — the place of refuge — is the Master and his lineage of Preceptors who have revealed to one the transcendentally exalted path. The Jewel of the Enlightened One, the Buddha, is the one who has accomplished the Body of Reality (Dharmakāya), which is the most excellent condition for one's own self and which is endowed with every kind of virtue and free from every kind of imperfection. Further, the Enlightened One attained the Form Body (Rūpakāya), which accomplishes the excellent condition in order to benefit others and which acts solely for the welfare of beings for as long as worldly existence lasts. The Jewel of Teaching, the Dharma, is the precepts, which consist of (i) the doctrine of the three collections of scripture, or the twelve categories[19] of the Enlightened One's speech; and (ii) the realization, which consists of the three trainings[20] or the two aspects of cessation and the path. The Jewel of Assembly, the Sangha, comprises the noble ones who dwell on the stages of irreversibility and those ordinary beings who have entered the doctrine prior to oneself.

The Procedure for Taking Refuge

Having prostrated, worshiped, and made offerings before the Preceptors and image of the Three Jewels as described above, be seated on a comfortable cushion in the meditative posture. Visualize that one's Preceptors, the Buddhas, and their spiritual sons, the Bodhisattvas, are all actually present and seated in the space in front of oneself. Next, imagine that oneself, one's friends, and all living beings in the six realms of existence ranging throughout space are assembled in front of the holy ones. These beings all experience their devotion by bodily clasping their palms, by vocally reciting the formula of refuge, and by mentally arousing intense faith and devotion. Consider the significance of this act of taking refuge by thinking, "Throughout a multitude of former lifetimes, I did not act in accordance with the words of spiritual friends. By not holding to the Three Jewels as my refuge, I had become terribly distressed by many sufferings in worldly existence. Now, indeed, no matter what befalls me, whether good or evil, I shall rely upon the compassion of my Preceptors and the Three Jewels as my guide until I have attained enlightenment, confidently trusting in the Three Jewels and earnestly wishing for their help."

Hold the mind in single-pointed devotion to one's Preceptors and the Enlightened One as the illuminators who will show one the path of total liberation; to the teaching as the actual path itself; and to the assembly as one's helpers who assist one in completing that path. Then pray, "May the Preceptors and the Three Jewels see to it that all actions of body, speech, and mind of all beings and myself be directed along the path of enlightenment."

Just as oneself takes refuge, so visualize that all beings throughout space are taking refuge the same way, and perform the fourfold refuge many times with heartfelt sincerity. Finally, prostrate and go for refuge in the Preceptors and Three Precious Jewels, and request their blessings by reciting,

> Please bestow your blessings upon me in all my lifetimes;
> bless me that my mind may become attuned to the teachings;
> bless me that I may traverse the path;
> bless me that errors on the path may be allayed;
> bless me that illusions may appear to me as transcendental wisdom;
> bless me that irreligious thoughts may not arise within my mind even for a single moment;
> bless me that uncontrived love, compassion, and aspiration to enlightenment may be aroused; and
> bless me that I may quickly attain the state of omniscience, perfect enlightenment.

If one wishes to recite the refuge in verse form, then:

> In the most holy Preceptor who is the essence
> of the qualities and deeds of the body, voice,
> and mind of all the Tathāgatas abiding in the
> ten directions and three times, the source of
> the eighty-four thousand teachings of the
> Doctrine and the Master of all the noble
> assemblies, I and all sentient beings equal
> to the ends of space from this time forth
> until the essence of enlightenment is reached
> steadfastly:
>
> With great devotion of body, voice, and mind
> we take refuge in the holy root and lineage Preceptors;
> With great devotion of body, voice, and mind
> we take refuge in the Enlightened Ones, the teachers, who
> have reached the end of renunciation and realization;
> With great devotion of body, voice and mind

> we take refuge in the holy Doctrine, the teaching,
> which is the essence of the precepts and realizations;
> With great devotion of body, voice, and mind
> we take refuge in the Noble Assembly of holy beings,
> the Bodhisattvas, who uphold the teaching.

Thus recite this as many times as one can. Then recite the following prayer three times or more:

> We prostrate and take refuge in the most excellent Preceptor and Three Jewels. Please bestow your blessings upon the body, voice, and mind of myself and all living beings;
> bless us that our minds may become attuned to the Dharma;
> bless us that we may traverse the path of religion;
> bless us that the way may be cleared of all errors;
> bless us that the illusory visions may appear as transcendental wisdom;
> bless us that irreligious thoughts may never arise;
> bless us to accomplish the two kinds of enlightenment thought;[21]
> bless us quickly to attain Buddhahood.

For a short while, in the manner of meditating and visualizing, think further that due to one's prayer the objects of refuge "see me through the transcendental wisdom of omniscience, heed me through the compassion of love, cherish me through the activities of transcendental deeds, protect me through the power of shielding, and bless and keep watch over me."

The conclusion of the procedure is to direct the merit one has earned through the taking of refuge for the enlightenment of all beings and to be mindful. When one rises from the session of meditation, reflect, "In this way, by whatever merit I have accumulated, may my parents and all other beings attain the state of enlightenment that accomplishes the well-being of oneself and others." The following verse, written by the Master Nāgārjuna, and any other prayers of dedication one knows may also be recited:

> Through this virtue may all beings accomplish
> the accumulation of merit and wisdom;
> May they attain the two holy bodies
> which arise from wisdom and merit.

In each interval between sessions, one should remember the excellent qualities of the Three Jewels and the mindful aspiration to follow them through not abandoning their recollection. One should refrain from acting contrary to the precepts of taking refuge. Since it was taught that all those virtues are useless which are acquired by a person who lacks alertness and mindfulness, it is important always to maintain them. As it was said in the *sPyod.'jug, (Bodhicaryāvatāra)*,

> As if they had been snatched away by thieves,
> the merits one has gathered are lost by the
> thief of non-alertness who follows after impaired
> mindfulness, and so one goes to the lower states.

Thus anyone who wishes to maintain the training that has been undertaken should diligently guard one's mind. Again, the *sPyod.'jug (Bodhicaryāvatāra)* advises:

> A person who wishes to guard the discipline
> should guard his mind with great care,
> for if the mind be unprotected,
> he also cannot protect the training.

The Benefit of Taking Refuge

The benefits of taking the refuge are said to be limitless, such as being the cause which gives rise to all the vows, and so on. In a *sūtra* it is taught:

> If this merit of taking refuge and
> praying had a form, even the entire
> space would be too small to hold it.

So, endowed with special joy, one should reflect in the following way: "In brief, in all the worlds of the gods and others, there is no other deity which is a refuge more excellent than that of the Three

Jewels and, starting from today, I have gained them as my protectors. Gaining them is the best of all gains."

The Precepts of Taking Refuge

If worldlings try to behave themselves in order to please their rulers and refrain from infringing upon any number of rules laid down by officials, who merely help them to accomplish worldly aims, how much more so then should one never act against the precepts taught by the Three Jewels, who are the masters that help one to achieve incomparable awakening. One should certainly think in this way.

Precepts which are common to all three of the Jewels consist of injunctions that one should associate with holy persons and the like. The individual precepts for each of the Three Jewels are: Having taken refuge in the Enlightened One, one should not pay homage to worldly deities. Having taken refuge in the teaching, one must give up all acts of harm and mischief toward other living beings. Having taken refuge in the Assembly, one should not associate with heretical friends. Moreover, one should not forsake the Jewels even for the sake of one's life, and certainly not for rewards. No matter what illness or pain may occur, one must not give up the Three Jewels. When rising and retiring, one should prostrate to a shrine of the Three Jewels. When eating, one should do in accordance with the words of the Master Atīsha:

> Divide the food into four shares; offer the
> first part of pure sustenance to the deities
> (Three Jewels); then to the protectors and
> guardians of the teaching offer ceremonial cakes;
> oneself should eat and drink (a share), and
> the remains of that should be given to all spirits.

In this manner, with the portion of food one has reserved for offering, offer a share to each of the Preceptors, patron deities, the Three Jewels, guardians of the teaching, and wealth deities. To uphold the words of the Enlightened One, present some to Hārītī[22] and her children, and to the spirits who have a right to receive offerings. As it was taught in the *sPyod.'jug (Bodhicaryāvatāra)*,

> This human body is only meant for service.

Eating should be moderated by reflecting, "I nourish this body with food that is in harmony with the teachings in order to employ it in virtuous acts." Whatever remainder of food there may be should then be dedicated to the remaining spirits who have a right to receive it. The *sPyod.'jug (Bodhicaryāvatāra)* advises:

> Food should be divided among those who
> are destitute, those who are protectorless,
> and those meditators engaged
> in the practice of austerities.

In this way, one should actually give to the poor, the unprotected, and the practitioners, thinking, "May this virtue become the cause of benefit and happiness for beings now and permanently." Even with such small precepts, one should train oneself in acting accordingly to the instructions on the dedications of merit, prayers for one's own and others' benefit, and the like. In every activity, whether great or small, one should perform it by relying upon the Three Jewels.

Never think, "Even though I have confidence in the Three Jewels, it is not really certain that this work will be accomplished." Instead, one should know that the Enlightened One is surely able to protect those who surrender and act in accord with his words, because the Enlightened One is endowed with the transcendental wisdom which knows all the paths of practice that are in harmony with the intelligence and nature of all living beings, because he has the compassionate desire to establish his disciples on the right path after turning them from wrong ways, and because he has accomplished the two accumulations of merit and transcendental wisdom and has accomplished the resolve to help beings. So even though one has not yet attained liberation from worldly existence, it is one's fault for not having trusted and not having acted in accord with the words of the Three Jewels, not because the Three Jewels have no compassion. Therefore, as the *mNgon.rtogs rgyan (Abhisamaya Alankāra)*[23] says,

> Just as spoiled seeds do not sprout even
> though the king of gods may make rain,
> so the unfortunate may not experience wholesomeness
> although the Enlightened One has come.

And the *sPyod.'jug, (Bodhicaryāvatāra)* also narrates:

> If, from today, I make no effort I shall sink lower and lower;
> though countless Buddhas have passed by who are
> the benefactors of all living beings, I did not come within
> the range of their salvation because of my own flaws.

In brief, those who do not entrust themselves to the Precious Jewels, who are arrogant and who assume they are intelligent have no certainty in accomplishing their schemes. Even if they are accomplished, it is not certain whether those schemes will turn out well in the long run. So it is important to entrust oneself always to the Precious Jewels.

VAJRADHARA AND THE FIVE FOUNDING LAMAS OF SAKYA

Top: Vajradhara *Centre:* Sachen Kunga Nyingpo
Top Left: Sonam Tsemo *Top Right:* Dakpa Gyaltshen
Bottom Left: Sakya Pandita *Bottom Right:* Chogyal Phagpa

THE MAIN TEACHING

To practice meditation upon the main teaching, (there are three parts): (I) the instructions on the impure vision, in order to produce renunciation; (II) the instructions on the vision of experience, in order to produce noble aspirations; and (III) the instructions on the pure vision, in order to produce enthusiasm.

The Instructions on the Impure Vision to Produce Renunciation

These consist of (A) the instructions on the faults of worldly existence, in order to produce renunciation, (B) the instructions on the difficulty of obtaining the prerequisites, in order to evoke diligence, and (C) the instructions on virtuous and nonvirtuous deeds and their results, in order to show what is to be accepted and what is to be rejected.

The Instructions on the Faults of Worldly Existence to Produce Renunciation

It is said in the *Root Treatise of the Vajra Verses* (of Virūpa, *rDo.rje'i tshig.rkang, Vajragāthā*), **For sentient beings with the afflictions is the impure vision.** This means that if one examines the nature of sentient beings, one will know that all sentient beings are not free from suffering. Therefore, those who strive for liberation, which is a complete liberation from worldly existence, must put an end to their attachment to worldly existence. To relinquish that attachment, one needs to recall the faults of worldly existence, and for that, one should rely upon the Preceptor's instructions in order to know that the nature of worldly existence is entirely suffering. As Jetsun Rinpoche (Dagpa Gyaltshen, rJe.bTsun Rin.po.che Grags.pa rGyal.mtshan) taught in his songs,

> Try to abandon attachment to the three worlds;
> to relinquish attachment to the three worlds,
> try to recall the faults of worldly existence.

As it was said in a *sūtra*,

> The world of desire is with faults;
> the world of form is with faults;
> likewise the formless world is with faults;
> it is only Nirvāṇa that can be seen to be faultless.

Maitreyanātha taught that,

> The five realms of existence lack happiness,
> just as there is no fragrance in a dirty object.
> Their sufferings are constant like the suffering
> produced by the touch of fire, weapons, salt
> (on wounds), and the like.

One might well ask, "What sorts of suffering, what kinds of unsatisfactoriness and faults are found in worldly existence?" It is taught in the *mDo.dran.pa nyer.gzhag (Smṛtyupasthāna Sūtra)*,[24] that

> Hell beings are tormented by the fires of hell;
> hungry ghosts are afflicted by hunger and thirst;
> animals by devouring each other;
> humans are afflicted by short spans of life;
> and gods are undone by carelessness.
> There is never happiness on the needlepoint
> of worldly existence.

To reflect upon the sufferings of these states of worldly existence, it is taught that one should (1) evoke sadness through reflection on the suffering of suffering, (2) reject attachments through reflection on the suffering of change, and (3) meditate longingly for liberation through reflection on the suffering of conditioned existence.

The Suffering of Suffering

Regarding the first of these, Jetsun Rinpoche (Dagpa Gyaltshen) wrote in his songs:

> First the suffering of the suffering
> is the misery of the three lower realms.
> If that were well considered,
> one would begin to tremble, for if it befalls one,
> there would be no way for one to bear it.
> Yet, instead of cultivating the virtue
> which abandons (the cause of suffering),
> people again and again cultivate the lower realms.
> I pity them, wherever they are.

And in reply to Pra.sTon's question, it says,

> The suffering of suffering exists in the three lower realms,
> like blisters arising on top of the wounds of leprosy.
> How could one possibly endure such pain if
> one paused to reflect on it? By reflecting on that,
> one must refrain from unwholesome deeds.

To explicate these three lower realms in detail, one must consider the sufferings of the hells, hungry ghosts, and animals.

The Suffering of the Hells

One should reflect upon (1) the suffering of the cold hells, (2) the hot hells, and (3) the neighboring and minor hells.

1. The eight cold hells are: (a) the Blister Hell, (b) the Bursting Blister Hell, (c) the Brrr Hell, (d) the Alasss... Hell, (e) the Chattering Teeth Hell, (f) the Utpala Flower Hell, (g) the Cracked Like a Lotus Hell, and (h) the Greatly Cracked Like a Lotus Hell.

a) The Blister Hell: One is born in a place wholly encircled by ranges of snow peaks. On a vast, frozen plain one is tormented by the sharp blows of unbearable blizzards. Not even the glimmer of a star can be seen, nor has one even a shred of cloth from which to derive warmth or to rest upon. The beings who inhabit this hell have taken birth here as a result of the ripening of their own former deeds. Instantaneously and miraculously, one is born endowed with a full-sized body and in isolation. Due to the coldness, countless clusters of blisters arise on one's body.

b) The Bursting Blister Hell: Here the chill is twenty times greater than before, and it causes blisters to burst open. Blood and watery fluid flow out of these and freeze.

c) The Brrr Hell: Because of the intense cold, one makes the sound of "Brr...."

d) The Alasss...Hell: The cold is greater still, and one pitifully cries "alasss...."

e) The Chattering Teeth Hell: It being colder still, due to its touch one's body becomes stiff and one's teeth chatter.

f) The Utpala Flower Hell: Being more intense than the previous hell, the cold causes the skin of one's body to turn blue and crack.

g) The Cracked Like a Lotus Hell: Now one's skin itself is carried away by a dragging blizzard and one's body turns red like raw meat. Then it, too, begins to crack into bits and pieces.

h) The Greatly Cracked Like a Lotus Hell: After going through the same experience as before, one's body cracks into hundreds and thousands of pieces. Then one's internal organs spill out and they also crack.

Concerning these, Ācārya Chandragomin said,

> Moreover, in these hells, a wind, fierce beyond
> example, stabs to the bone and carries away the
> quivering flesh of one's entire body, and one lies
> there ready to die. Beings spring forth from hundreds
> of bursting blisters to torment oneself with weapons
> as marrow, blood, and water start to flow.

The length of one's lifetime in these places is described in the *Dzod (Abhidharma Kośa)*:

> The length of time exhausted in emptying a barrel of
> sesame by removing a single seed once a century will
> equal the life span in the Blister Hell. It is twenty-
> fold longer progressively in each of the others.

A barrel of sesame is a vessel which contains eighty *khals* of large brabo seed used in the kingdom of Magadha. If one were to empty this vessel of sesame by removing a single seed once every hundred human years, the time required will equal the span of a lifetime in the Blister Hell.

The life spent in each of the seven lower hells is twenty times progressively longer than that of the one just above it. Thus, the Bursting Blister Hell equals twenty barrels; the Brrr Hell equals 400 barrels; the Alasss...Hell, 8,000; the Chattering Teeth Hell, 160,000; the Utpala Flower Hell, 3,200,000; the Cracked Like a Lotus Hell, 64,000,000; and the Greatly Cracked Like a Lotus Hell, 1,280,000,000 barrels. This estimate of the length of their life span is only approximate. If calculated accurately, they would be longer, for one *sūtra* states:

> For example, monks, if someone were to remove a
> single sesame seed once every hundred years from
> a heaping Magadha sesame barrel containing eighty
> *khals*, the length of time required to empty those
> eighty *khals* of sesame would still be relatively
> quick, for I do not say that the life span of beings
> born in the Blister Hell will come to an end so speedily.

Just as the life span in the Bursting Blister Hell is twenty times longer than in the Blister Hell, so it gets progressively greater up to the Greatly Cracked Like a Lotus Hell.

The manner in which to reflect upon the meaning of this teaching is as follows. After reciting the refuge formula and the prayer for the blessing of the Three Jewels, one should sincerely reflect in the following way:

"Throughout countless aeons, alas, right up to the present time, I have been tossed about and distressed by innumerable floods of suffering as a result of my wandering in these places of worldly existence. Having only experienced these many sorrows in the past, it would truly be wonderful if I might no longer be afflicted by them whatsoever. However, until this machine of subject-object dichotomy is destroyed, I shall continue to be led on helplessly into the six realms of existence and shall have to experience those countless feelings of pain. Then what shall I do? Among those sufferings, what if I were to be reborn tomorrow morning in the cold hells where the place, conditions, and life span are such as explained above?"

Now clearly reflect on those conditions of the cold hells just explained: "If now I can hardly bear even slight contact with the kinds of cold that occur in the human realm, even for a single day, how could I possibly endure it if those feelings of agony in the cold hells were to befall me? Further, I have no confidence that such suffering will not befall me, since the cause of those sufferings is anger, which arises many times each day. When there is no way I can bear those agonies if they befall me, then what shall I do? No matter what happens, therefore, I must rightly practice the holy teaching which is the remedy of all sufferings."

Thus think from the depths of one's heart. Furthermore, one should think, "The teaching to be practiced must not be mere artifice, but should be attuned to the teaching of the Conquerors and derived from an uninterrupted lineage of transmission. Especially now, I shall definitely experience the practice of these instructions of 'The Path Including Its Result,' the Precious Words of the Lam Dre. May the Preceptors and Precious Gems see to it that this happens."

If one wishes to practice at length, then offer the three verses of prayers (as given earlier in the refuge section). On all occasions, one should do as it was said in the *Rin.chen phreng.ba, (Ratnāvalī)*:

> Refrain from alcohol, possess a good livelihood,
> practice total nonviolence, offer gifts with
> devotion, show reverence to the excellent ones
> (Buddhas and Bodhisattvas), and be loving toward
> the lowly; this, in brief, is religion.

So one should think that one must dwell within a conduct which is in harmony with the doctrine. Since at this time there are boundless benefits by merely producing just the aspiration to practice the holy doctrine, one should dedicate, as before, the roots of virtue which arise from these meditations to others. By being endowed with alertness and mindfulness in all activities, one should constantly maintain a strong revulsion toward worldly existence and maintain the conduct which accords with the doctrine.

2. The eight hot hells are, as it was said in a scripture:

> The Reviving, the Black Line, the Crushing,
> the Wailing, the Great Wailing, the Hot,

the Greatly Hot, and the Unceasing.
These are the eight (hot hells).

a) The Reviving Hell: This is a place of birth where the ground of burning iron is pervaded by a greatly blazing fire. The hell being, upon whom the result of his own former deeds has befallen, has a miraculously born, large, full-sized body, with a low endurance for heat and fear. Just by being born there, the thought arises through the power of the unhappy mind that, "Alas, I am born into a place like this. It would be well were no others to harm me in this place." As if this thought were the cause, very powerful and fearful attendants of the Lord of Death, carrying various weapons, come from all possible directions. Just as hunters corner and kill a deer, so the hell being is tormented by the hell-attendants by being simultaneously beaten, cut and pierced many times with weapons. Finally, one experiences a short death or unconsciousness. However, due to the power of one's previous deeds of karma, the sound "Revive!" is heard from the sky, and a wind strikes the body which causes one to be restored as before. Once again, one is tortured by the attendants of death. One experiences this uninterruptedly again and again. As it was said in the *sPyod.'jug (Bodhicaryāvatāra)*,

> Having performed many unwholesome deeds,
> they suffer by being tormented through having
> their skin stripped off by the attendants of
> the Lord of Death, by having molten copper
> melted by the flames of the Greatly Hot Hell
> poured onto their bodies, by being pierced by
> fiery swords and spears, by having their
> flesh sliced into a hundred pieces, and by
> falling upon a fiercely blazing iron floor.

b) The Black Line Hell: The experience of this hell is similar to the previous one, but in addition, many black lines are drawn on the body of the hell being who is born there by the attendants of the Lord of Death. Just as carpenters do with wood, so the attendants saw along those lines with sharp, blazing saws. Also, one experiences pain caused by this act and having one's body split by sharp axes. As it was said in *bShes.spring (Suhṛllekha)*,[25]

> Some are cut by saws; likewise,
> others are split by terribly sharp axes.

c) **The Crushing Hell**: Being born upon a ground of burning iron, the hell being is unable to bear the touch of heat. Wishing to flee in any direction, one looks about here and there. Great mountains resembling the faces of yaks, buffaloes, and the like approach and crush one's body in the way that sesame is ground into powder, so that an endless stream of blood flows out. For a while the two mountains open up and, due to the power of one's karma, one's body resumes its previous shape. Then one again experiences the same suffering as before. As it was said in *bShes.spring (Suhṛllekha)*,

> Some are squeezed like sesamum; similarly,
> others are ground like fine powder.

d) **The Wailing Hell**: Apart from being the same as above, one looks about in all directions and spies a house to which one wishes to flee. One goes while experiencing many heat tortures on top of the ground of burning iron. Finally, one arrives inside the house. The doors close themselves behind one, and due to one's being burned by the blazing flames from every side, there is nothing one can do except to wail as if the sobs were being pulled out from one's very heart.

e) **The Great Wailing Hell**: Apart from all else being as above, the hell being enters two houses of burning iron — one house placed within another. Since the pains of burning are twofold greater, one's wailing sobs are even louder than before.

f) **The Hot Hell**: The hell being is caught by the attendants of the Lord of Death, who strongly push up a blazing iron spear through the anus to the crown of the hell being; thus flames issue out through one's mouth and nose.

g) **The Greatly Hot Hell**: One is impaled with a blazing iron trident which is pushed through the anus and two buttocks up to the crown and two shoulders. Having been pierced, blood, fat, and flames emerge from one's mouth and ears. As it was said in the *bShes.spring (Suhṛllekha)*,

Some are completely transfixed
by greatly heated barbed iron spears.

h) The Unceasing Hell: The hell being's body itself burns as flames in a stove of blazing iron which is 20,000 leagues in size, and one is tormented constantly by measureless agonies difficult to bear. As it was said in the *bShes.spring (Suhṛllekha)*,

As surely as freedom from attachment produces
the most excellent happiness among all happiness,
so surely the very dreadful suffering of the
Unceasing Hell (is the worst) among all suffering.

This, indeed, is the extremity among the sufferings of worldly existence.

Concerning the life span of the hot hells, it is stated in the *mDzod (Abhidharmakośa)* that,

Fifty years of human life is a single day of
the lowest gods of the realms of desire,
whereby their life span is five hundred of
their own years; that of the second higher
heaven is successively twofold. The life of
each of the (six) heavenly states of the
realm of desire is correspondingly equivalent
to one day of life in each of the first six
hells, such as "Reviving Hell", and so on.

This means that fifty human years is equivalent to one day of life in the lowest heaven, the heaven of the "Four Great Kings". Thirty of these days is one month, and twelve of these months is one year. A god in the heaven of the "Four Great Kings" lives for 500 of their years, and this is equivalent to one day of life in the "Reviving Hell". Calculating in this manner, Reviving Hell beings live for 500 of their own years. Similarly, 100 human years is equivalent to one day of life in the second heaven, known as "Thirty-Three". Life in this heaven lasts for 1,000 of their own years, and this is equivalent to one day in the "Black Line Hell". Calculating in this way, beings in the Black Line Hell live for 1,000 of their own years. Two hundred human years is equivalent to one day of life in the heaven of "Freedom From Fighting". Life in this heaven lasts for 2,000 of their own years, and this is equivalent to one day in the "Crushing Hell". Calculating in this manner, Crushing Hell beings live for 2,000 of their own years. Four hundred human years is equivalent to one day of life in the heaven of "Joy". Life in this heaven lasts for 4,000 of their own years, and this is equivalent to one day in the "Wailing Hell". Calculating in this way, they live for 4,000 of their own years. Eight hundred human years is equivalent to one day of life in the heaven of "Miraculous Joy". Life in this heaven lasts for 8,000 of their own years, and this is equivalent to one day in the "Great Wailing Hell". Calculating in this manner, they live for 8,000 of their own years. One thousand six hundred human years is equivalent to one day of life in the heaven of "Empowered by the Miracle of Others". Life in this heaven lasts for 16,000 of their own years, and this is equivalent to one day in the "Hot Hell". Calculating in this manner, they live for 16,000 of their own years. Life in the "Greatly Hot Hell" lasts for half an intermediate aeon, and for a complete intermediate aeon in the "Unceasing Hell". To summarize this, 500, 1,000, 2,000, 4,000, 8,000, 16,000, half an intermediate aeon, and an intermediate aeon are gradually applied to the eight hot hells.

The way to reflect on the meaning of this is to do the preliminaries as before. Then one should produce the desire to practice religion and generate the following thought: "Alas, this world of existence is burning, greatly burning, very greatly burning. Within this, the beings of the hot hells possess such a place, such a nature, and such life spans. If now I cannot bear even the feeling of pain caused by the touch of just a tiny weapon or a small flame against my body, how shall I bear it if such agonies of the hot hells befall me?"

3. The neighboring hells and minor hells are as follows: The neighboring hells are the Fire-Trench, the Mud of Putrid Corpses, the Path of Blades, Forest of Swords, Shamali Trees, and the River. As it was said in the *mDzod, (Abhidharmakośa),*

> On each of the four sides (of the Hot Hells) are found
> the Fire Trench Hell, the Mud of Putrid Corpses Hell,
> the Path of Blades Hell and the others, and the River
> Hell. Thus there are sixteen (neighboring hells).

Described as existing around the whole periphery of the eight hot hells are (in each of the four directions) the six neighboring hells, which consists of the four explicitly named ones and the two extra hells — the Forest of Swords Hell and the Shamali Trees Hell — which are indicated in the verse by **and the others**. Even though the karma of experiencing the major hells has been exhausted, still one must experience each of these neighboring hells in the four directions.

The manner in which these hells are experienced is as follows. The hell being, on being released from those main torments, thinks, "I must escape to some other happier region and stay there." Very quickly going off in any direction, say the east, one first encounters a fearful pit filled with embers. One thinks, "Here is a pleasant plain," and without hesitating, one begins to cross it. One's body sinks to the top of the head and all of one's skin and flesh are seared, producing an agony that penetrates to the bones. On being released from there, one spies something that looks like some dirty water. Since one was afflicted by the great heat, one enters it with the hope that it will cool one. One's whole body sinks and the water transforms itself into bad-smelling, dirty, putrid mud. Worms dwelling in that place with yellow bodies and black heads cause agony by piercing one's body here and there and eating through to the marrow.

On emerging from there, one sees something like a green meadow. Going there it transforms itself into a great path filled with razor blades. Wherever one places one's feet they are slashed, so that, unable to bear the touch of that pain, one loses one's balance and falls down. One experiences the pain of one's entire body being cut.

On being released from there, one spies a great mountain thinks, "I should stay there for awhile." On arriving, winds arise which shake the trees fiercely. The leaves snap off (from their branches) and descend. They change into a rain of swords and one experiences the pain of having one's body cut into pieces.

On being released from there, one spies a great mountain where, when one arrives at its foot, one is torn apart by the fearful dogs of hell. Though one utters terrible, great laments, there is no one at all to protect one. Finally the dogs cut and tear one's entire body into pieces so that one experiences the pain of (being reduced) to mere remnants.

At that time one hears at the top of a mountain the sound of some male or female person who had formerly been an object of attachment, calling down to one. While climbing up this mountain, all the flesh of one's body is destroyed by the down-pointed iron thorns of the Shamali trees which cover the slopes of the entire mountain. Reaching the mountain top, one does not see the object of attachment. Instead, the fearful birds of hell cause manifold injuries such as plucking out one's eyes, drinking one's brain, ripping open one's belly, and the like. Once again one hears that object of attachment calling from the foot of the mountain, and one climbs down. The thorns, showing their tips pointed upward, now cut and rend all of one's body as before. As it was said in the *bShes.spring (Suhṛllekha)*,

> Some with hands outstretched toward the sky
> are overpowered by fierce dogs with iron fangs;
> while others, powerless, are torn asunder by ravens
> with terrible sharp claws and sharp iron beaks.

Then one's body is restored as before.

Wishing to escape elsewhere, one flees. One sees the Unfordable River of Hot Ashes as water. Unhesitatingly, one enters it. One is afflicted by the touch of the river's intense heat, but since the other bank is guarded by the wardens of hell carrying various weapons, one is unable to go ashore. One turns back again and, as if one had been confused concerning directions, comes to the actual place (where one left the hot hell before entering the first neighboring hell). Remembering the experience of suffering that intensely afflicted one there, one quickly flees in a southern direction. As before, one is stricken by the suffering of the Fire Trench Hell, and the others. Again, one returns to the center.

In this way, one must also experience the whole cycle of sufferings in the west and north. Thus it is said that since the three (hells) — the Razor Path, the Sword Forest, and the Shamali Trees — involve an identical type of weapon, they constitute a single class. So, with this one class (are added the other three —

the Fire Trench, the Putrid, and the River Hells), and thus these four multiplied by the four directions give a total of sixteen hells. In the *mDo dran.pa nyer.gzhag (Smṛtyupasthāna Sūtra)*, it was said,

> Each of the eight hot hells has sixteen
> different kinds of neighboring hells.

Now reflect upon the suffering of the minor hells. As it was said:

> The hell being is cooked in great vessels,
> eats iron chunks, drinks molten bronze,
> has its tongue ploughed by ploughs,
> is wrapped into sheets, is bound by chains,
> and is roasted in burning iron powder.

One is cooked in boiling molten bronze in the great vessel of hell, and the wardens of hell feed blazing iron chunks into one's mouth which one, being helpless, must eat. So, too, one must drink boiling molten bronze. One's tongue is stretched about one league in length and ploughed by ploughs of burning iron. One is wrapped up in sheets of burning iron, and one's entire body is bound in chains of burning iron. Also one is roasted together with burning iron powder.

Moreover, there are indescribable hells such as ones which are like pillars, like rows of seats, and like brooms, and hells wherein there is pleasure by day but suffering at night, and others wherein nights hold pleasure, but days have suffering. On these occasions, one should narrate, either in the long or short versions depending upon one's time, the stories about Gro.bshin.skyas (Śroṇakoṭī) going to the ocean's shore.

Thus even the very greatest sufferings of the human realm cannot become an example of even the slightest of the agonies of the hells. As it was said in *bShes.spring (Suhṛllekha)*,

> The sufferings which (one sustains) from violent
> thrusts by three hundred spears in one day in
> this world cannot even be compared to a fraction,
> or a small measure, of hell's suffering.

It may be asked, "From what cause do those sufferings arise?" They arise due to the affliction of hatred. Therefore, those who wish well-being for themselves should train in giving up anger. As it was said in the *sPyod.'jug*, (*Bodhicaryāvatāra*),

> If I am unable to bear these minute pains,
> then why do I not reject anger
> which is the cause of hell's suffering?

Contemplate on the meaning of this as follows: "Alas, these painful torments of the hells are extremely unbearable. How can I even look at the great agonies of the hot and cold hells? The realms of the neighboring and minor hells are such, and their life span is such. How could I bear it if such suffering of the neighboring and minor hells should befall me, if even now I cannot bear just the prick of a thorn in my body?" Thinking in this manner, one should produce a mind which desires to practice religion.

The Suffering of the Hungry Ghosts
As it was said in the *bShes.spring* (*Suhṛllekha*),

> Also among hungry ghosts continuous, unallayed
> suffering is produced through lack of desired
> objects. Very terrible (sufferings) created
> by hunger, thirst, cold, heat, weariness, and
> fear will have to be endured.

In general, it was said in the *mDo dran.pa nyer.gzhag* (*Smṛtyupasthāna Sūtra*) that there are about thirty-six types of hungry ghosts, but if categorized there are three: those with (1) external obscurations, (2) internal obscurations, and (3) the obscuration of obscurations.

1. The hungry ghosts with external obscurations: These have collected a similar type of karma which causes them to be born together in a realm that resembles a tawny-colored blend of sand or pebbles utterly devoid of water and the like. As it was said in the *bShes.spring* (*Suhṛllekha*),

> Some, troubled by hunger, are not able to eat
> even a little discarded, coarse, or impure food,
> (for each has) a mouth as big as the eye of a
> needle and a stomach the size of a mountain.
> Some, like the upper reaches of a dried palm
> tree, are naked with bodies of skin and bones.

As it was said, one has a mouth just the size of a needle's eye, a throat as narrow as a horse-tail's hair, limbs as thin as grass stalks, a belly as vast as a mountain, frazzled hair, dried-out skin and flesh molded onto the bones — thus one resembles the upper reaches of a palm tree. One has no opportunity to dwell at leisure due to one's hunger and thirst. One's body emits groaning sounds and creaks like the pulling of an old cart. Moving about, one's joints rub against each other, causing pain as intense as the blaze of a fire. With many such pains of weariness and fatigue, however much one searches, one does not find food and drink. And even if once in a great while one finds a little, it is guarded by a large number of others who are more powerful than oneself. Carrying weapons, they beat, pelt, and mistreat one in various ways. Not being allowed to eat, one experiences sufferings of both body and mind.

2. The hungry ghosts with internal obscurations: As it was said in the *sLob.spring (Śiṣyalekha)*,[26]

> While his mouth is about (the size of) a
> needle's eye, his great belly is pained since it
> is many leagues in size. Even though he drinks
> the great ocean's water, it does not enter into
> the throat's wide cavity, and even a drop of
> water is dried up by the poison of his breath.

On top of those sufferings, one happens to find, through searching with great effort, a trickle of mucus. Still, due to the power of being habituated to miserliness and avarice since beginningless time, one cannot eat properly. When one begins to eat, the food will not go into the mouth. Even if it enters, it does not go past the throat. Even if it passes through, it is of no benefit on reaching the stomach, for the distress of hunger and thirst becomes greater than before. Thus one experiences the suffering of not being benefited by food and drink.

3. The hungry ghosts with the obscuration of obscurations: As it was said in *bShes.spring (Suhṛllekha)*,

> Some, with flames nightly (issuing) from their mouths,
> devour food of burning sand that has fallen into their
> mouths. Striking one another's faces, they eat the pus
> of ripened goiters growing from their throats.

On top of the above sufferings, immediately on devouring a trifling morsel of food, it blazes up into great flames, so that tongues of flame flutter out of one's nose and mouth and one utters a terrible, great noise. One has many sufferings of eating hot sand. One fights the others for food and eats the pus of ripened goiters on one's throat.

For all categories of hungry ghosts, even the light of the summer moon causes heat and that of the winter sun causes cold. Though one approaches a fruit-bearing tree or a great river, these dry up when merely looked upon with wishful thoughts of enjoying them. In this way, one has inexpressible sufferings. As it was said in the *bShes.spring (Suhṛllekha)*,

> For them even the moon is hot in the summer,
> while even the sun is cold in the winter;
> trees become fruitless and rivers dry up
> if merely looked upon by them.

As it was said in the *mDzod (Abhidharmakośa)*, the hungry ghosts live,

> For 500 (years), where a day is equal to one month.

Thus one will live 500 of one's own years, wherein one human month is equal to one day (in the life) of hungry ghosts. If calculated into human years, this would be 15,000 years.

If it is asked from what causes the sufferings of hungry ghosts arise, they arise from acting with miserliness and avarice due to their attachment to outer and inner property. As it was said in the *bShes.spring (Suhṛllekha)*,

> The Enlightened One taught, "Though the sufferings
> experienced by hungry ghosts are various,
> they are of one taste; the cause is the avarice,
> miserliness, and ignobility of people."

The way to contemplate on the meaning of this is to think: "Alas, those born as hungry ghosts possess such a place, such conditions, and such a life span. If now I cannot bear the pains of thirst and hunger even for a single day, how could I bear such sufferings as those, should I be born in that realm of the Lord of Death due to my karma and afflictions? I have no confidence that such sufferings will not befall me, since attachment and miserliness, the cause of those sufferings, arise countless times every day. Having no way to bear those sufferings should they befall me, what shall I do? Therefore, at any cost I must practice the true holy Dharma, which definitely prevents birth in the realm of hungry ghosts."

The Suffering of the Animals
As it was said in the *bShes.spring (Suhṛllekha)*,

> Even in the animal realm, those without the
> virtues which bring peace experience various
> unbearable suffering, such as eating one another,
> killing, binding, beating, and the like.

There are three types of animals: (1) those who dwell in the outer oceans, (2) those who dwell in the darkness between the continents, and (3) those who are scattered in the higher realms.
  1. Those who dwell in the outer oceans: In the outer great oceans there are said to be countless animals dissimilar in name and type. Common to all of them is the suffering of stupidity and delusion, which presses down on them like a great mountain. There is the suffering of many small fish being eaten simultaneously by a large sea creature, and the like. There is the suffering caused by many small ones penetrating the large ones and constantly eating away at them. There is the suffering of some alligators being pierced and killed by conch shells. The nāgas have suffering caused by a shower of hot sands, and by the

garuḍas harming them. Common to all is the suffering of suffocation and bad smell, the suffering of uncertainty of habitat and companions, the suffering of meeting foes and killers, the suffering of cold in the winter and heat in the summer, the suffering of heat by day and cold by night, and so on. The sufferings which abound for them are indescribable.

2. Those who dwell in the darkness between continents: These animals have many sufferings. On top of the sufferings (just described), they cannot even see their own outstretched or bent-in arms and legs. Due to the power of hunger and thirst, they have the suffering of not finding anything to eat except what appears right in front of them.

3. Those who are scattered in the higher realms: (Among those animals) who are scattered about are those that are ownerless and that are slaughtered, either by other (animals) or by humans and nonhumans for the sake of pearls, furs, bones, flesh, skin, and the like. Those who have owners have, on top of the above sufferings, the sufferings of being enslaved, employed, bound, beaten, and finally slaughtered. Thus their sufferings are beyond conception. As it was said in the *bShes.spring (Suhr̥llekha)*,

> Some die for the sake of their pearls, wool,
> bones, flesh, skin; other powerless ones have
> their arms and legs chained and are made to
> serve by being prodded with iron hooks.

As it was said in the *mDzod (Abhidharmakośa)*,

> The longest (life span among the) beasts is one aeon.

While some can live throughout one aeon, the short-lived die in just an instant. Since the cause of animals' suffering is the ignorance of not knowing what is to be accepted and what is to be rejected, one should diligently apply oneself to the light of the teachings, which are the antidote to that (ignorance).

The way to contemplate on the meaning of this is to think, "Alas, the habitat of those beings born in the realm of animals is such, their sufferings are such, their life span is such. If now I cannot bear even such pains as those incurred in having to work for my own livelihood for even a single day, how could I bear such suffering if I should be born into the realm of animals due to my karma and afflictions? I have no confidence that those sufferings will not occur to me. I have accumulated countless deeds motivated by delusions, which is the cause of the arising (of this realm). Having no way to bear them should those sufferings befall me, what shall I do at that time? Therefore, at any cost I must practice the holy Dharma, which is able to prevent birth in the realm of animals."

The Suffering of Change

One might think, "While it is true that one will have suffering if born in these three realms of misery, one will have happiness if born in the three higher realms." However, this is not the case. As it was said in the *mDo rGya.cher rol.pa (Lalitavistara Sūtra)*,[27]

> All objects of desire are impermanent
> and unsteady, inconstant, changing like
> a dream, like a mirage, like a city of
> illusion, and like lightning and bubbles.

Thus, all these defiled pleasures are only apparent happiness, since they are impermanent, unsteady, changing, passing away, and surely deceptive.

To reflect on this, (a) consider the general suffering of change; (b) particularly, consider the suffering of human change; and (c) consider the suffering of the gods' and demigods' changes.

The General Suffering of Change

Though one be born as Śakra, the lord of gods, since this state is impermanent, again one can fall to the Earth. Though one becomes the universal monarch, since this state is uncertain, one can be born again as a servant. Though one be born as the great Brahma, since this state is unreliable, one can be reborn into the Unceasing Hell. Even if one is born as the son of the gods, the sun or the moon, this is of no benefit since again one can enter the darkness in between the continents. Thus it is not right to be confident about whatever happiness of the higher realms one might obtain. As it was said in the *bShes.spring (Suhṛllekha)*,

> Having become Śakra, worthy of the world's worship, once again one falls to earth due to the power of previous deeds; even though one becomes the universal monarch himself, once again one becomes a servant of a servant in the world of existence.
>
> Though one attains the great bliss of desire in the god's realms and the dispassionate bliss of Brahma himself, again one becomes the fuel of Unceasing Hell's fire and has to undergo unceasing torment.
>
> Having illuminated the whole world with the light of one's own body through having attained the (state of being) the sun or moon, again having gone to the murky, black darkness, one does not see even one's own outstretched hand.

Also, as Jetsun Rinpoche (Dagpa Gyaltshen) said in a song,

> When contemplating the suffering of change, there is (seen): Śakra turns into an ordinary being, a universal monarch turns into a slave, and the sun and the moon going to darkness.
> Though belief in this depends upon the word (of the Buddha), as ordinary people do not have the ability to realize it, look by your own sight at the changes of men.

The Suffering of Human Change

In particular, reflect upon the suffering of human change. As it was said in the *bShes.spring (Suhṛllekha)*,

> Be saddened at worldly existence, which is the source of many sufferings, such as destitution of what is desired, death, illness, old age, and the like, and also listen to some of its faults. There are no certainties at all in worldly

existence, since fathers become sons, mothers become wives, and enemies become friends; likewise, it can happen conversely.

Also, from the Songs of Jetsun Rinpoche Dagpa (Gyaltshen),

> Wealthy men become poor, the mighty become
> weak, many people are replaced by one, and
> so on, exceeding the imagination.

If one examines the condition of our own human realm, one sees many people are replaced by one person, the strong grow weak, the wealthy become poor, the foes become friends, kinsmen becomes foes, and so on. If one examines through detailed contemplation one's own kinsmen, neighbors, and countrymen, none are to be found in their former state, because they have not gone beyond the suffering of change. Not only that, but they are constantly afflicted and powerlessly borne away by the four great rivers of (1) birth, (2) old age, (3) disease, and (4) death. Birth is the suffering of the narrow womb, old age is the suffering of the destruction of youth, disease is the suffering of the destruction of health, and death is the suffering of the destruction of life.

1. The suffering of birth: Since birth is the root of all other sufferings as well as the result of the origination of suffering, its own nature does not go beyond suffering. Furthermore, as far as womb birth is concerned, there is suffering of suffocation by bad odors when residing in the womb; the suffering like being pressed down upon when the mother eats food; the suffering like falling into a ravine when she moves about and sits; and the suffering of being affected by heat and cold when she eats and drinks hot and cold food. During birth, there is the suffering like being drawn through a hole, and on being born there is the suffering like falling into a pit of thorns. Therefore, as it was said in the sLob.spring (Śiṣhyalekha),

> Having entered into the hell-like womb, choking
> on an overabundance of very terrible bad smells,
> and residing in the gloomy darkness of a

very narrow place, so the body in the womb
must experience the suffering of being cramped.

2. The suffering of old age: As it was said in the *mDo rGya.cher rol.pa (Lalitavistara Sūtra)* that,

> Old age turns a beautiful form ugly,
> old age vitiates strength and brilliance,
> old age snatches one's radiance,
> old age causes death, and
> old age snatches happiness and produces sorrow.

On the body turning ugly, it says:

> Changing from what one was before,
> one becomes bent and crooked,
> one's hair turns white or
> becomes bald, and so on.

Concerning one's waning strength, it notes:

> Due to the decline of one's body power,
> one cannot do any difficult work at all;
> one must lean on others even in rising and sitting;
> (one's voice) loses its resonance due to the
> vitiation of one's vocal power
> and one' speech is indistinct and falters;
> due to the decline of one's mental powers,
> one has no enthusiasm for any work whatsoever
> and one immediately forgets everything
> that was said or done;
> and one commits mistakes and errors
> in all activities.

Brilliance also disappears:

> Until now, others praised and honored one,
> but having changed,
> one becomes an object of ridicule even by children.
> One's own sons scorn one,

and one's good fortune decreases.
The body does not experience warmth,
and the mouth does not experience delicious taste;
one's speech is not taken to be true;
and one comes to the point of mentally praying for death.

The snatching of one's radiance occurs as follows:

Losing the former luster of one's body
one becomes bluish, whitish, and the like.
The mouth and nose droop and become pale.

The causing of death:

While one is pressed by old age, which is the
chief fatal illness that leads to death, all
other diseases are brought about. One cannot
digest the food that is eaten. Gasping for breath,
one wheezes. Due to the (growing) old of all
conditioned things, one dies even though one has no
other disease. Such is the nature of that long life
which worldlings think represents happiness and
which is made into an object of their prayers.

3. The suffering of disease: Illness is easy to understand, since it is already apparent to everyone who suffers. Still, one should produce revulsion from worldly existence by examining the condition of one's own and others' illness. Common to all illness is the suffering of intolerable pain; of having to bear rough medical treatment; of having to take bitter medicine; of being forbidden to take desired food and drinks; of having to use what is not desired; of not being able to digest whatever is eaten; of not being able to pass the night if one gets through the day; of not being able to pass the day if one survives the night; of apprehension of not recovering; of apprehension of death; of apprehension that one's wealth will be exhausted; of apprehension that one will be forsaken by one's doctor and nurses; and so on. Thus one suffers endlessly. As it was said in the *sLob.spring (Śiṣhyalekha)*,

Distressed by being stricken with many
hundreds of diseases, these living beings
are like human hungry ghosts.

4. The suffering of death: As it was said in the *sPyod.'jug* (*Bodhicaryāvatāra*):

> Not having yet begun this (work), having begun one,
> and only half finishing another, suddenly the Lord
> of Death comes and you think, "Ah, alas, I am destroyed."
> Their eyes reddened and swollen through the power of
> grief and with tears falling from their faces, your
> relatives lose hope, and you look upon the face of
> death's messenger. Afflicted by the remembrance of
> your own sins and full of fear upon hearing the sounds
> of hell, your body is smeared with excrement and you
> become maddened. Then what will you do?

Thus far, one has only been making arrangements to remain a long time in this life and has had no thought in mind that death will come. One is then seized by a fierce fatal illness. Rituals and other preventatives do not benefit, and medicines and treatment do not succeed. One knows one will die, but cannot bear the thought of death. One does not find any beneficial means. Frightened by the messenger of death, one remembers one's own sins; is afflicted or distressed by the pangs of disease; lies on one's last bed, surrounded for the last time by one's kinsmen; speaks one's last words; is fed one's last spoonful of food; sips one's last drop of thirsted-for water; is powerless to stay on in the house one has built; is powerless to carry all the wealth and prosperity one has collected; and is powerless to consort with the kinsmen one has nourished. Not knowing where one will go next, all of one's work is left unfinished; one must go alone to some unknown, empty region. Hence one has these inexpressible sufferings.

There is no one who is not thus afflicted by change and by the four great rivers of birth, old age, disease, and death. As it was said in a *sūtra*,

> Disease approaches, destroying health;
> old age approaches, destroying youth;
> deterioration approaches, destroying good fortune;
> and death approaches, destroying life.

Furthermore, consider the suffering of not being able to guard one's possessions. If one has wealth, in order to guard it one has neither leisure by day nor sleep by night. (Even though) one spends one's money, one has to become the servant of others. One looks upon all others as enemies. Officials and one's relatives are considered the most vicious of all, because they take away (one's wealth), whether by force or clandestinely. One even loses one's life for the sake of wealth. So one suffers endlessly.

Consider also the suffering of not obtaining sought-after wealth by those lacking it. The poor one does not find breakfast in the morning nor dinner at night. The stars are one's hat and the frost one's shoes. One rides the horse of (one's own) calves and is hit by whips. One offers the flesh of one's calves to the dogs and one's face to men. Though one begs and seeks in various manners, by day one finds nothing to eat, even though one searches, and by night finds nothing to wear. Even if one acquires a little through great hardship, one does not get to enjoy it, for one loses it by taxation or by transport service requisitions from officials.

Not only that, but there is the suffering of meeting a hated foe or the apprehension of meeting him. There is the suffering of parting with loved ones and the apprehension of parting from them. There is the suffering of not obtaining the result of one's hopes. The rich suffer mentally and the poor physically. There is the suffering of the difficulty of protecting one's gross mind; the suffering of being discarded by loved ones if one compromises with a foe; and the suffering of hatred from enemies if one is in harmony with a loved one. Thus there are indescribable sufferings.

In brief, all the various types of suffering of the six realms of beings — heat and cold, hunger and thirst, weariness and fatigue, fighting and quarrels, changing, and the like — are established through the experience of this world's suffering.

The Suffering of Gods' and Demigods' Change

Even though born as a demigod, there is no opportunity for happiness. As it was said in the *bShes.spring (Suhṛllekha)*,

> Since the demigods naturally have hatred for the splendors
> of the gods, they have great mental suffering.
> Though endowed with intelligence the truth is
> not seen due to the veil of their afflictions.

Through the power of a demigod's natural jealousy of the gods' splendor, one is constantly wielding weapons and armor only to fight, quarrel, and start a battle with the gods. In this way, one does not have even a moment of mental or physical leisure. Though one acts in this manner, since the power of one's merit is not equal to that of the gods, one is always defeated in battle. One dwells with the suffering of one's body being cleft and ripped, and even one's mind sinks into grief. Finally, having died as a result of such nonvirtuous conduct motivated by hatred and jealousy, one suffers the need of being born in the lower realms.

When the five signs of death and five signs of approaching death appear, the gods of the realm of desire experience mental suffering that is even greater than the physical sufferings of hell beings. As it was said in the *bShes.spring (Suhṛllekha)*,

> Even in the higher realms, the suffering of transmigration
> (experienced by those) endowed with
> great happiness is greater than that (of hells);
> having thought thus, the good should not thirst
> after higher realms, which come to an end.

The five signs of death are described in the *bShes.spring (Suhṛllekha)*:

> The complexion of the body turns ugly, they do not
> like their seats, and their flower garlands grow old,
> their garments become soiled, and on their bodies
> appear a sweat that was not there before. These are
> the five signs which indicate death in higher realms.

The five signs of death's approach are enumerated in the *Drang.srong rygas.pas zhus.pa'i mdo (Ṛṣhivyāsa Paripṛiccha Sūtra)*:[28]

> The body's light grows dim; when they bathe
> particles of water stick to their body;
> garments and ornaments emit unpleasant sounds,
> their eyelashes blink, and they become attached
> to one place even though they are of a moving nature.

If such (signs) arise, one is abandoned by kinsmen and close friends, who merely throw a single flower toward one from a distance and are unable to come near. At that time, knowing that one will soon die, one surveys the three places.[29] Due to having formerly carelessly enjoyed intense attachment to objects of desire, one realizes that one will be reborn in the lower states. So one begins to roll hither and thither — suffering like a fish cast onto hot sand — and then one dies and is reborn in the lower realms. There, too, one must experience various sufferings. As it was said in the *mDo dran.pa nyer.gzhag (Smṛtyupasthāna)*,

> However much suffering occurs
> at the time of a god's death,
> that of beings in Unceasing Hell
> is not even a sixteenth part of that.
>
> "Alas, oh chariot and groves;
> Alas, oh lands and rivers;
> Alas, oh beloved gods!"
> Thus lamenting, downward they fall.

Even though a god of the realm of form or of the formless realm does not manifest such sufferings, just as birds flying in the sky must swiftly alight on the ground, so upon the exhaustion of the thrust of pure virtue one descends lower and lower due to one's mind being deceived by one's wrong views. Having fallen down into lower states and been born there, one must experience terrible sufferings. As it was said in the *bShes.spring (Suhṛllekha)*,

If one has no merits when transmigrating
from the gods' realm, one helplessly
becomes a dweller in any of (the realms)
of animals, hungry ghosts, and hells.

It may be asked, "For what reasons are the gods of these upper realms, who are said to dwell in the peaceful life of meditation, again reborn in the lower states?" The gods of the upper realms think these meditations to be liberation and the path to liberation. Though they dwell there for a long while, at some time the force of that meditation is exhausted and, arising from it, they produce the wrong view that "Though I have single-pointedly performed only meditation for so many years, if still I am not able to pass beyond the three realms, then that which is proclaimed as 'liberation from the world' is a lie." By that thought, one destroys all of one's roots of virtue and is born into the lower realms. As it was said in *Lan mi.lan.par 'dod.pa.*,

Those, blinded by ignorance, who are
against the Doctrine, having gone to
the summit of existence are again immersed
in the sufferings of worldly existence.

Also, as it was said in the *bShes.spring (Suhṛllekha)*,

All the fully ripened results are terrible
even for a person who practices well
if he still (entertains) wrong views.

To reflect on the meaning of this one should think in detail, "Alas, my hope that 'the higher realm is endowed with happiness' is a delusion brought about by not examining and not analyzing. Although it appears to be a minor happiness, it is insubstantial, a bubblelike object changing every moment, definitely not beyond the stage of deception. Having become attached to the temporary appearance of happiness, I am more insane than the insane to practice acceptance and rejection regarding illusions while toiling greatly to obtain that appearance of happiness. The conditions proclaimed to be foremost among all the good fortunes of the higher realms for Brahma, Śakra, the universal monarch, the sun and the moon are such as explained above; for human beings, even those considered to have the greatest wealth are still possessed of the conditions of birth, old age, disease, death, destitution, unexpected meetings, partings, and hopelessness; and for the demigods and the gods of desire, form, and formless realms, there are such conditions. Alas, who that is wise would still be attached to the appearance of worldly happiness? Therefore, the world of the higher realms resembles the island of cannibals. Whoever desires and is attached to it, destroys everyone."

Like a bird in a burning forest or a swan on a frozen lake, reach the decision to diligently leave worldly existence. Then think, "Now at any cost I must practice from my heart the holy religion which surely liberates one from worldly existence."

The Suffering of Conditional Phenomena

Generally, that which is known as "the suffering of conditional phenomena" is the karma-causing feelings of happiness, unhappiness, and neutrality and the five grasping aggregates, which are flung about due to the cause of attachment to existence. From the moment one obtains the five aggregates, one naturally does not go beyond suffering. Still childish sentient beings fail to recognize themselves (i.e., the five aggregates) to be suffering, because they are distracted by other sufferings. Through attachment they are deceived into believing themselves to be really happy. However, the Noble Ones see it (i.e., the five aggregates) as suffering and always renounce it.

As it was said in the *mDzod' grel (Abhidharmakośa Ṭīkā)*,[30]

> If a single hair be placed upon the palm,
> there is no pain or discomfiture;
> but if it be inserted in the eye,
> it engenders discomfort and pain.
> Since fools are like the hand's palm, they
> do not perceive the hair of worldly suffering,
> (while) the Noble Ones, like the eye, always reject it.

To reflect upon this suffering one should consider (a) the suffering that activities are never-ending; (b) the suffering of not being satisfied by desire; and (c) the suffering of not being wearied by birth and death.

The Suffering That Activities Are Never-ending
As it was said in the *bZhi.brgya.pa (Catuḥśataka)*,³¹

> With efforts our work is done
> and effortlessly it perishes;
> even though it is so, still you
> are not devoid of attachment to work.

Even though one works up to the point of old age and death, one has not time to finish one's work. Even though unfinished, one does not have nonattachment to them.

Furthermore, farmers smear the blood of their feet upon stones and the blood of their hands on wood. Traders make their own country as a foreign one, and make foreign countries as their homeland. Even though they do not have the opportunity, even for a second, to associate with their own relatives and loved ones, still they have not gone beyond the need to suffer more. As it was said in the *sPyod.'jug (Bodhicaryāvatāra)*,

> Some wretched desirers are utterly fatigued
> by working the whole day, and having returned
> home their wearied bodies sleep like corpses.

> Some have the troubles of traveling abroad
> and the hardships of living far away; even
> for many years they cannot see their wives
> and children as they wish to.

The faults of attachment to work are described in the *'Phags.pa lhag.pa'i bsam.pa bskul.ba (Ārya adhyāśaya samcodana)*:³²

> Day and night, without other thoughts,
> they think constantly of food and drink
> and do not aspire to virtues — these are

the faults of those who delight in work. Their attachments increase, they desire savory food, and they are not pleased by small favors — these are the faults of those who delight in work. They delight in many followers, they are very miserable if (those followers) decrease, and they roll about (in pain) like asses — these are faults of those who delight in work.

One should diligently practice the methods of departing from attachment to works which are never finished, like ripples of water.

The Suffering of Not Being Satisfied by Desire
As it was said in the *mDo rGya.cher rol.pa (Lalitavistara Sūtra)*,

> Desire is the root of suffering
> and impairs meditation and penance.
> Desire is like a drink of salty water,
> which causes thirst to increase again.

Furthermore, one should think, "Though there is not one object of desire that could be identified as not having been enjoyed by us since our beginningless lifetimes, still not only are we not content but attachment to our desires increases. Thus through the power of careless behavior we perpetually roam about in worldly existence. There is not a single suffering of which it can be said, 'I did not experience this.' Further, having been born from the womb, all the mothers' milk I have drunk, if collected, would be more than the waters of the four oceans." As it was said in the *bShes.spring (Suhṛllekha)*,

> While each has (already) drunk
> more milk than the four oceans,
> still worldlings who follow other ordinary
> people will have to drink even more than that.

Moreover, having been born in the hells, one has eaten iron chunks and drunk molten bronze countless times. Having been born in the hungry ghost realm, one has eaten pus and blood countless times. Having been born in the animal realm, one has eaten the flesh of one's own kind and one's own flesh countless times. As it was said in the *mDo rGya.cher rol.pa (Lalitavistara Sūtra)*,

> Though one person obtains all his desires,
> not content with that, he searches for more.
> If one relies on desire, one's attachment will increase,
> and the servants of desire are chopped into pieces.

The faults of attachment to wealth in particular appear in the *sPyod.'jug (Bodhicaryāvatāra)*:

> Because of the torments of accumulating, guarding,
> and losing it, wealth should be known as boundless
> misery. There is no opportunity for liberation
> from the world's suffering for those who are
> distracted by the attachment to wealth.
>
> Desires have many misfortunes such as these and
> the like, but little relish; just like the tasting
> of some dry grass by cart-pulling beasts.
>
> For the sake of a little relish, which is
> not rare and can even be earned by beasts,
> they destroy this difficult to obtain,
> propitious opportunity with agonizing works.

The faults of attachment to women are outlined in the *mDo dran.pa nyer.gzhag (Smṛtyupasthāna Sūtra)*:

> In every way, women are the destroyers of wealth
> and the root of the lower realms. How could
> happiness be obtained for men who desire women?
> Women are causers of destruction, therefore if
> one desires benefit for oneself in this life
> and the next, one must renounce women.

Therefore, one should abandon all thoughts of attachment to

desire for the objects of desire, which are the root of all misery. As it was said in the *sPyod.'jug (Bodhicaryāvatāra)*,

> Desires produce misery in this life and
> also in others; here one is killed, bound,
> and cut, and for the next life one accumulates
> (the karma for rebirth) in the hells, and the like.

The Suffering of Never Being Wearied of Birth and Death

As it was said in the *sLob.spring (Śiṣyalekha)*,

> There is no region in which I have not
> dwelt, nor any belly of living beings
> in which I have not been conceived.

From measureless aeons ago until the present, due to the power of karma and afflictions, one has continued to roam about in the various types of birth in worldly existence. There is neither a region into which one has not been born nor any sentient being in whose womb one has not been conceived, nor a single one of the many species of the six kinds of beings into which one has not been born. If one could gather together in one place the bones one has accumulated through again and again being born and dying into just a single species of being, they would be higher than the world of Brahma. And if one were to make a pellet of dust like the size of a juniper tree seed for each of one's mothers, still this great earth would not suffice to represent the quantity of those who have been one's mothers. As it was said in the *bShes.spring (Suhṛllekha)*,

> Everyone has had a pile of bones so large as to
> equal or surpass Mount Meru; also the earth will
> not suffice for counting pellets as big as the seeds
> of juniper trees to equal the mothers (one has had).

Also, the Songs of Jetsun Rinpoche (Dagpa Gyaltshen) say that,

When contemplating the suffering of the conditional
nature of all things, there is seen: no end to
actions, suffering to exist among many and among few,
and suffering to exist among the rich and the poor.

All of human life is exhausted in busyness and
everyone dies while being busy. Since busyness
does not even end at the time of death, one
grasps the beginning of the next life's busyness.

Those who are attached to this world of existence,
which is a heap of suffering, are pitiful.

In brief, this worldly existence is like an ill person who never recovers, a prison from which one is never released, and a traveler who never arrives. Whatever one may do, wherever one may dwell, whomever one may associate with, whatever one may enjoy, these are all never anything but suffering by their own nature, never anything but the source of suffering, never beyond the wheel of suffering. Thus it must be known.

Like the vigor needed to put out a fire blazing on one's head or clothes, the wise must diligently practice the methods of attaining liberation from the prison of worldly existence, for there is nothing to be accomplished that is more important than this. As it was said in the *bShes.spring (Suhṛllekha)*,

> The world of existence is such, so
> birth is not good among gods, men,
> denizens of hell, hungry ghosts, and animals.
> Realize that birth is a vessel of many harms.
>
> (As you would) abandon all other activities to put
> out a fire if it suddenly caught hold of your clothes
> or head, so strive to put an end to rebirth —
> for there is no other aim more excellent than this.

Therefore, it is very important to produce a mind wishing to practice the holy Dharma in order to attain liberation from worldly existence. As it was said in the *sPyod.'jug (Bodhicaryāvatāra)*,

> Since formerly and even now I have
> been devoid of the liking for religion,
> such wretchedness as this has happened.
> Who would forsake the liking for religion?

To reflect the meaning of this, one should contemplate (the following) until it is felt upon one's flesh and in one's bones: "Alas, for many lifetimes, due to my thinking that the grasping aggregates were to be cherished, as many conditional activities as I have performed have, like ripples, only created that many sufferings. There is not even a little something about which I can say, 'This is the result of my hard work.' Though I have carelessly utilized various outer and inner objects of desire, not only has my attachment to desire not diminished but this cherishing of desire has become like piling more wood onto a blazing fire. Though I have taken countless births into the six realms of beings, not only have I not even reached the starting point of the path leading to liberation but I am still in a condition of having to continuously roam about in worldly existence. Such a condition was not caused by someone else. I have been deceived by myself. I have been cheated by myself. My own suffering is the result of what I myself have done. I did not believe in the nondeceiving protectors — the Preceptors and Precious Gems. I held the suffering nature of worldly existence to be happiness. I held the impermanent happiness of the higher realms to be permanent. I was distracted by conditional activities, which are like ripples of water. I was attached to the seductions of the demon of desirable objects. (This condition) is caused by not producing remorse for this contraption of the suffering of birth and death. From now on, in this life, I must throw off like spittle all worldly activities, which are without essence. Having directed my mind toward the Preceptor and Precious Gems, I must enter the path to liberation through relying upon the instructions of spiritual friends. I must unfailingly practice from the depth of my heart the holy teachings, which are able to utterly extinguish the fire of suffering."

Thinking thus, with intense faith and devotion, pray, "May the Preceptor and Precious Gems see to it that I practice the holy teaching leading to the path of liberation."

One should meditate until one has such experiences as tears coming to one's eyes, involuntary moans from one's voice, the hairs of one's body stand up, and the like. If such experiences arise, one should, without stopping the experience, merge it with the object of one's meditation and meditate. This produces an uncontrived mind that desires to attain liberation from worldly existence.

In conclusion, dedicate the root of one's virtue. Through being endowed with alertness and mindfulness in all activities, one should conceive of the world of existence as a prison and liberation as a fine mansion. With such a conception, one should diligently work on the method which turns whatever one does — whether listening, contemplating, or meditating — into a remedy for the sufferings of worldly existence.

The benefits of reflecting thus are from the mouth of Jetsun Rinpoche Dagpa (Gyaltshen), that

> If one arrives at the conclusion that no
> happiness exists wherever one may be born
> in the realms of living beings, then all
> of one's actions turn into religious (practice).

The Instructions on the Difficulty of Obtaining the Prerequisites to Evoke Diligence

One can understand that the saying in the *Root Treatise (rDo.rje'i tshig.rkang, Vajra gāthā)*, *For sentient beings* **with the afflictions** *is the impure vision*, indicates that the result of deeds motivated by the afflictions is only the lower realms, rather than the difficult-to-obtain body of the higher realms. Having realized the nature of worldly existence to be suffering, one must practice the holy teaching which is the means of gaining liberation from it. To practice the holy teaching, one must obtain an unimpaired human body endowed with the prerequisites. That body, along with the prerequisites, is not obtained again and again. As it was said in the *sDong.po bKod.pa. (Gaṇḍa vyuha)*,

> It is difficult also to obtain the
> opposite of the eight restless states;
> it is difficult also to obtain human life;
> it is difficult also to obtain the favorable
> conditions of leisure; it is difficult also
> for a Buddha to appear (in the world).

Also, as it was said in the *sPyod.'jug (Bodhicaryāvatāra)*,

> This opportunity (of possessing the eighteen
> prerequisites) is extremely difficult to obtain.
> Having obtained this, one must accomplish the purpose
> of people. If benefit is not accomplished, it will
> be difficult to gain this opportunity in the future.

To elaborate on this, reflect on (1) the difficulty of obtaining this human body endowed with the prerequisites; (2) the great benefit of this body which has been obtained; and (3) the fact that the prerequisites obtained will not last long.

The Difficulty of Obtaining This Human Body Endowed With the Prerequisites

Under this there are reflections on (a) the difficulty of obtaining a human body from the viewpoint of cause; (b) the difficulty of obtaining it from the viewpoint of number; and (c) the difficulty of obtaining it from the viewpoint of nature.

The Difficulty of Obtaining a Human Body from the Viewpoint of Cause

This is mentioned in the *sPyod.'jug (Bodhicaryāvatāra)*:

> Not having performed virtues but having
> accumulated sins, even the sounds (of the
> words) "happy realms," will not be heard
> for a hundred million aeons.

To obtain the human body endowed with the prerequisites needed to practice the holy religion, one must have the cause, which is the performance of pure virtue. If one does not perform virtue but accumulates sins, it would be difficult to hear the words "happy states" for many aeons, let alone to obtain the prerequisites. Therefore, since practitioners of perfectly pure virtue, which is the cause (of the prerequisites), are rare, attainment of the prerequisites, which are the result, is also rare.

One must also guard pure morality, that virtue which is the cause of the prerequisites. One will not be able to gain a body in the higher realms just by a little giving and the like. As it was said in the 'Jug.pa (Madhyamakāvatāra),[33]

> Even though one be endowed with much property
> due to (previous) giving, if one's leg of morality
> be broken, one will fall into the lower realms.

Therefore, since guarding perfectly pure morality is rare, the attainment of a body in a higher world is even rarer.

The Difficulty of Obtaining a Human Body From the Viewpoint of Number

One might wonder, "Since there are many human beings, how is it that the attainment of such prerequisites is so rare?" This thought shows a lack of good examination by precise analysis, for, in general, there are seen to be more beings in the Bardo who fail to obtain bodies than those who obtain bodies in the realms of beings. The proof is that if one keeps an animal's corpse for several days in the summer time, it becomes fully infested by maggots. Likewise, however many dead corpses one keeps — two, three, or whatever — all will become filled with maggots. If there are infinite Bardo beings due to be born only as worms, then what to say of other kinds of beings? The teachings from the flawless *sūtras* which say "they must dwell in the Bardo for a long time" are obviously quite correct. As long as the conditions that produce a body do not coincide, a body is not seen to arise. Even in the obtaining of a body, the bodies of lower realms are many but those of higher realms are few. As it was said in the 'Dul.ba lung (Vinayāgama),[34]

> (Like) the dust of the great earth are those gaining
> (a body) from higher realms to the lower realms;
> (like) the dust on a fingernail are those gaining
> (a body) from the lower realms to the higher realms;
> like the dust on a fingernail are those gaining
> (a body) from the higher realms to the higher realms;
> like the dust of the great earth are those gaining
> (a body) from lower realms to lower realms.
> Thus the hell beings are like the great earth's dust,
> the hungry ghosts are like a snowstorm, and
> the animals are like the dregs of fresh wine.

Hence, in contrast to (the numbers of) other beings, human beings seem to be just barely existing. Even if one considers only the animals that are scattered about in the higher realms, one sees boundless tiny creatures on the slope of a single mountain in the summer season. Among them, even (the members of) a single species, such as ants, are seen to be inconceivable in number. To illustrate this point through an example, it was said in the *sPyod.'jug (Bodhicaryāvatāra)* that,

> The Lord therefore said that it is as
> difficult to obtain a human body as it
> is for a tortoise's neck to enter a hole
> in a yoke floating on the great wide ocean.

It may be asked, "Did the Buddha state this?" In the *dGa.bo rab.tu byung.ba'i mdo (Nanda parivrajyā Sūtra)*, it says that

> Suppose this world were one great ocean in
> which dwells a blind, long-lived tortoise
> who surfaces once every one hundred years.
> Upon that ocean is a yoke with a single opening
> which is driven from east to west by the western
> wind and west to east by the eastern wind, and so
> on. He spoke on at great length. So monks, there
> will come a time when the outstretched neck of
> that blind tortoise enters the hole of that yoke.
> But I tell you, monks, human life is even more
> difficult to obtain than that.

This means that, like the vast expanse of the ocean, birthplaces of other beings are vast and multitudinous. Just as the yoke has only a single opening, human birth is small in extent and few in number. Just as the tortoise rises up only once every hundred years, so it is rare to accumulate the karma that results in human birth. Just as the tortoise is blind, so one's accumulated karma is feeble. Just as the yoke is tossed about in every direction by the wind, so there are many adverse forces obstructing the coincidence of conditions needed for human birth. As it was said in the *bShes.spring (Suhṛllekha)*,

> More difficult that the placing of a tortoise's
> (neck) in the aperture of a wooden yoke in the
> same ocean is the achievement of human birth
> from (the state of) animals. Oh king, make this
> (human life) fruitful by practicing the holy religion.

The Difficulty of Obtaining a Human Body From the Viewpoint of Nature

It may be asked, "What is that body endowed with the prerequisites?" It is a body endowed completely with eighteen factors: the eight states of leisure and the ten obtainments. The eight states of leisure are to be free of the eight states where there is no leisure to practice religion. The eight restless states are: (1) hell beings, (2) hungry ghosts, (3) animals, (4) long-lived gods, (5) barbarians, (6) those with wrong views, (7) where the Buddha does not arise, and (8) fools.

Of these eight, four are included in nonhuman states and four are included in human states. (Of the first type,) the hell beings are affected by intense suffering; the hungry ghosts are mentally inflamed by nature; the animals are utterly ignorant and their nature is shameless and immodest; the state of long-lived gods produces the conditions for wrong views and pride; barbarians practice erroneous acceptance and rejection, such as taking their mother for a bride, and have difficulty in meeting a holy person; holders of wrong views do not believe virtues to be the cause of higher realms and of liberation, and accept the Precious Jewels and the law of cause and effect (doctrine of karma) not to be the truth; men who are born in a world barren of Buddhas do not possess the holy religion which is to be practiced; and fools have defective organs of speech (and are stupid). All of these do not know how to discriminate between what is to be accepted and what is to be rejected, and thus remain outside the pale of holy religious conventions. Hence a body which is the basis of leisure is extremely difficult to obtain for most of the six realms where beings are in restless states.

The ten obtainments consist of five that are acquired by oneself and five that are acquired through others. The first (five self-obtainments) are:

> (1) To be born as a human being, (2) to be born in a central land, (3) to have sound organs, (4) to have faith in the (holy) Dharma, and (5) not to have committed heinous actions.

It has already been explained how rare it is to be born as a human. It is also rare to be born in a central country. According to Ārya Asanga a region where any one of the four assemblies or groups (of monks, nuns, laymen, and laywomen) dwell is a central country, and (a country where) they do not dwell is called a barbaric land. The places where these four groups of people do not exist are similar to the sky; where they do exist is like a cart's wheel only. For all one's organs to be sound is rare as well. As it was said in the *sDong.po bKod.pa (Gaṇḍa vyuha)*,

> It is rare to be free from defects of organ;
> hearing the Buddha's doctrine is also rare.

It is also rare to have faith in the objects of worship, for only one in a hundred is seen to acquire sincere faith in the well-spoken moral conduct teachings of the holy Dharma. It is also rare not to have committed heinous actions, which consist either of committing the five limitless crimes oneself, asking others to do so, or rejoicing in the commission of these five limitless sins by others, which seems to be the most common of the three.

The five obtainments that are acquired through others are:

(1) The advent of a Buddha, (2) he taught
the doctrine, (3) the teaching has remained,
(4) there are followers of the teaching,
and (5) sincere compassion for others.

The advent of a Buddha into the world is extremely rare. As it was said in a *sūtra*,

Seldom does a Buddha appear in the world,
and this human body is extremely hard to obtain;
alas, in such a world, faith and listening
to the doctrine are also extremely rare.

Generally, an aeon in which a Buddha comes is called a light aeon, and one in which he does not come is called a dark aeon. The present aeon is called a good aeon because a thousand Buddhas will come, and this is followed by sixty dark aeons. Following that, a single light aeon called "Establishment of Qualities" will occur. Then after ten thousand dark aeons, a single light aeon called "Greatly Pleasant" will occur. Then after three hundred dark aeons, a light aeon called "Like a Great Star" will occur. Therefore, during the 10,360 dark aeons, only four light aeons will occur. Since it is taught that the Buddhas do not appear in the light aeons during which beings' life span increases, most of that time also passes without Buddhas appearing. As it was said in the *sPyod.'jug (Bodhicaryāvatāra)*,

If the arising of a Tathāgata, faith, a
human body, and the habit of performing
virtue are so rare, when could I find
(such an opportunity again)?

That the Buddha teaches the doctrine is also rare. It is said that the Enlightened Ones do not teach religion if there are no disciples who are (worthy) vessels for the teachings. Also, our own Teacher,[35] having attained enlightenment, spoke thus:

> I have discovered the nectarlike doctrine which is serene,
> free from conceptualization, clear light and uncompounded.
> Though it be taught, none will understand it,
> so without speaking I should dwell in the forest.

Then, it is explained in scripture,

> While dwelling thus disinclined, it was
> necessary for the god Brahma to offer him
> a thousand-spoked wheel of gold and request
> him to turn the wheel of the doctrine.

It is also rare for the teaching to remain. Upon the exhaustion of each preceding Buddha's teaching in this good aeon, there will be no teaching until the next Buddha appears.

It is rare for others to follow the teaching. Most people follow other doctrines or are disinclined toward the teaching of Buddha. Even most who claim to be the followers of the teaching, imagining that the scriptures, tantras, and their unerring commentaries are merely words of conceptualization, do not even seek to listen with their ears. They follow after the works of fools who write whatever comes to mind, being ignorant of the scriptures' true meaning. Many practice this kind of listening, contemplation, and meditation, while others with substanceless claims of knowing the scriptures are seen to chase after such empty teachings, just as the hare ran away after hearing the sound "chal".[36]

It is rare to have sincere compassion for others. Those people who seek profit through giving, which is wrong livelihood, are repaid by many people. Rare is the giving of alms to renounced persons, who dislike crowds and households and who, solely relying on alms, (spend their time in) study and meditation. As it was said in the *sDong.po dKod.pa (Gaṇḍa vyuha)*,

> Right livelihood is also difficult to obtain;
> rare, too, are those who diligently practice
> religion in accord with the teaching.

As the Master of Dharma, Sakya Pandita (Sa.skya Pan.di.ta),[37] also said,

> Most who are diligent in their vows receive little honor,
> those who are honored have little diligence in vows;
> few are the donors who have faith in the doctrine;
> while the faithful offer to inferior recipients, and
> those offerings are acquired from wrong livelihood.
> If practitioners do not accept offerings that have been
> acquired through wrong livelihood, they are honored less.

Therefore, one should know the full attainment of all the eighteen prerequisites based upon a single body is as rare as a star in the daytime.

The Great Benefit of This Body Which Has Been Obtained

One may think, "Though due to many reasons it is difficult to obtain this body endowed with the prerequisites, what is the benefit of obtaining it?" If one obtains this (body) it is even more beneficial than obtaining a wish-fulfilling gem. If one makes requests to a wish-fulfilling gem only prosperity for this life will occur, but through relying upon this body endowed with the prerequisites, if one practices the Dharma, what need to speak of merely good fortune for this life only? One will be able to achieve higher realms in the next life, the liberation of the lesser vehicle, and even the incomparable enlightenment. As it was said in the *sLob.spring (Śiṣhyalekha)*,

> If one obtains (human life), one can reach the
> further shore of the ocean of birth and sow
> virtue, the seed of excellent enlightenment.
> Having obtained human life, which is of greater value
> than the wishing gem, who would make it fruitless?

And, again, as it was said in the *sPyod.'jug (Bodhicaryāvatāra)*,

> Having obtained this, one must
> acomplished the purpose of people.

In the original (Sanskrit), the word 'people' is called 'purusha', which means power or ability. The body endowed with the prerequisites of an inferior person has the ability or power to achieve the realm of gods or men; that of a mediocre person has the ability or power to achieve liberation; and that of a superior person has the ability or power to achieve omniscience.

It may be asked, "But haven't the bodies of other beings also such abilities?" They do not. Generally, the human body has great power and efficacy in performing either virtue or sin, and among them (i.e., humans), those of this world of Jambudvīpa are strongest because they belong to "karmabhūmika."[38] Among them also, those with bodies endowed with the prerequisites are the most powerful. As it was said in the *sLob.spring* (*Śiṣya-lekha*),

> Whatever path that is obtained by strong-minded humans
> who set about leading living beings by relying on
> the Sugata's path is not obtained by gods and nāgas,
> nor by yakshas, gandharvas, vidyādharas, nonhumans,
> and mahoragas (serpentine creatures).

The human body endowed with the prerequisites is especially suited more, than any other body of the six realms of beings, to serve as the basis for practicing the holy Dharma. Therefore, if one does not practice purely the holy Dharma when one has attained it, there is no certainty that the jewel of a human body endowed with the prerequisites, which is hard to gain and of great benefit, will later be gained again and again. As it was said in the *sPyod.'jug* (*Bodhicaryāvatāra*),

> Depending upon the boat of the human body,
> one crosses the great river of suffering;
> this boat is hard to gain later, so fool
> (there is) no time for sleeping.

One may think, "Even though I do not engage in a pure religious practice in this present body, still I shall obtain a human body again by merely refraining from collecting sins, and at that time I shall practice religion." But even if one does not commit great sins now, there is still no certainty that throughout beginningless lifetimes one has not collected karma that will definitely lead to the experience of hells in one's next life. How then can one be confident of being reborn in the higher realms? As it was said in the *sPyod.'jug (Bodhicaryāvatāra)*,

> If one has to dwell in the Unceasing Hell even
> though the sin was committed in a second, so by
> (committing) sins (from) beginningless (time),
> what need to say that one will go to happy states?

One must practice Dharma in accord with the words of the Victorious One — not mere form and vocal religious practice which are directed for the desire of this life. One cannot obtain a human body, let alone a body endowed with the prequisites, by just the pretense of a religious practice. If it is not obtained, one will constantly experience only suffering, because the bodies of other beings (of the other realms of existence) are not able to perform virtuous deeds. As it was said in the *sPyod.'jug (Bodhicaryāvatāra)*,

> Since my character is like this,
> I will not be able to obtain a human body;
> if I fail to obtain a human body,
> only sins and not virtue will ensue.

Also, it was said in another scripture,

> It is hard to obtain the prerequisites again,
> the advent of a Buddha is rare to obtain,
> and the river of the afflictions are difficult
> to abandon; alas, the succession of sufferings.

In brief, having won this difficult-to-obtain human body endowed with the prerequisites and having met the doctrine of the Enlightened One which is hard to meet, if one does not make fruitful these endowments when one has a chance to practice the profound essence of the doctrine, then it is like returning empty-handed from an island of jewels, and there is no greater self-deception than this. As it was said in the *sPyod.'jug* (*Bodhicaryāvatāra*),

> Having obtained endowments like this,
> if I do not become habituated to virtue,
> then there is no greater deception than this
> and there is no greater foolishness than this.

Reflect upon the meaning of this as follows: "Alas, from beginningless time until now, from one birth to another rebirth, I have been distressed by many sufferings against my wish. If even now I am not able to cross over the great ocean of worldly existence, but am tossed about by the four great floods of birth, old age, disease, and death, there will be no final release from the mouth of the sea serpent of the afflictions. Whatever may happen, I must be liberated from this great ocean of suffering of worldly existence. To cross this great ocean of worldly existence, I have heard that one must rely upon the boat of the prerequisites. Through many reasons, such as cause, number, nature, and the like, this body endowed with the prerequisites is difficult to obtain. Further, its obtainment is endowed with inconceivable benefits, like a wish-fulfilling gem. If such a body is acquired, I can easily attain liberation and omniscience. Hence, it is more valuable than the bodies of the other six types of beings. Here at the present time, when I have found such a body which is called "endowed with the prerequisites", I must achieve benefit for the future generations as best I can. I must get as far from the ocean of worldly existence as I can. I must step as far upon the starting point of the path of liberation as I can. If I do not make this body endowed with the prerequisites fruitful during this lifetime, there is no certainty that later I will regain even a human body. Therefore, I must make this endowment fruitful in every way." Thus one should reflect from one's heart and pray that it will happen so.

The Prerequisites Obtained Will Not Last Long

As it was said in a *Sūtra*,

> Monks, one who ponders on impermanence
> worships the Enlightened Ones;
> one who ponders on impermanence is
> prophesied by the Enlightened Ones;
> one who ponders on impermanence
> is blessed by the Enlightened Ones.
> Monks, the footprint of an elephant is
> the best among footprints; the perception of
> impermanence is the best among perceptions.

The Reflection on Impermanence Has Inconceivable Benefits
(Reflection on impermanence is said to have inconceivable benefits because) (1) it checks attachment for things; (2) it is a goad that stimulates vigor; (3) it is an antidote to suffering, and (4) it is a helper in realizing emptiness, the ultimate truth.

1. It checks the attachment for things: By meditating on impermanence, one realizes that one cannot have confidence in any external or internal phenomena and one does not produce intense attachment for anything.

2. It is a goad that stimulates vigor: In the beginning, knowing that the time of death is uncertain causes one to enter religion; in the middle it acts as a condition which encourages one to practice religion; and finally, it assists in impressing upon one's mental continuity the real Dharma.[39] If one does not understand impermanence, even if one dwells in formal religion, one is no different from a townsman who has donned (a monk's) yellow robes. Even though one vocally claims to be practicing religion, one's heart is seized by desire for this life in cherishing gains, praise, food, and wealth. Whatever one performs of listening, contemplation, and meditation, it is directed solely for the purpose of achieving greatness in this life. If one understands impermanence, then like prodding a fine horse that has been mounted, it causes the unreligious to enter the door of religion, inferior religious practitioners to become mediocre, the mediocre to become superior, the superior to become very superior, and the very superior to attain Buddhahood.

3. It is an antidote to suffering: A person who has realized compounded things to be impermanent is not frightened by the agonies of death, so what to say of other trifle sufferings? Therefore reflection on impermanence is the most excellent method for gaining liberation from suffering.

4. It is a helper in realizing emptiness, the ultimate truth: If phenomena were by nature truly existent, they would not be impermanent. However, since they undergo change and transformation due to various deeds (karma) and conditions, their nature does not exist in any way whatsoever. Through thinking in this way, one will gain realization (into the ultimate truth). As it was said by Maitreyanātha,

> The meaning of impermanence is emptiness, and
> it is characterized by origination and decay.

How to Contemplate Impermanence

(To contemplate impermanence one needs to) (1) reflect on the certainty of death and thus relinquish grasping at permanence; (2) reflect on the uncertainty of the time of death and thus shorten the range of one's plans (literally, mental activities); and (3) reflect that nonreligious activities are not beneficial and thus practice the holy Dharma.

1. Reflect on the certainty of death and thus relinquish grasping at permanence: (a) reflect that death is certain because, having been born, one does not have the power to remain; (b) reflect that death is certain because the body is insubstantial; and (c) reflect that death is certain because life is not permanent.

a) Death is certain because, having been born, one does not have the power to remain: One might think that based on this body endowed with the prerequisites, one must purely practice this holy religion, but that one has plenty of time to practice and can do it in a very leisurely manner. (This is wrong), because one has to practice religion very diligently and starting right now. There is neither time for leisure nor time for practicing in a leisurely way because it is certain that one must die. As it was said in the *Mya.ngan bsal (Śoka vinodana)*,[40]

Like this, death dwells in front of all that
is born. Have you ever seen, heard, or had
any doubt that someone — whether born on
earth or in heaven — who did not die?

Who has ever seen or heard any credible report that someone, having been born in the world, is able to always stay on at will without dying? Thus, there is no grounds for doubt about the possibility of not dying, since death is definitely known to dwell in front of all living beings that have been born. Therefore, death will surely come. From the very moment of conception in the mother's womb, one goes on the path leading to death, without being sidetracked even slightly. As it was said in a *sKyes.rabs (Jātaka)*,[41]

> From the night when they entered the womb,
> worldlings advance on (death's) path, without
> detouring, swiftly going to the Lord of Death.

To make us realize that "having been born one must surely die," even the Noble Ones who have discarded birth and death, which arise from karma and afflictions, pretend on having been born, to pass beyond (Parinirvāṇa). Then what to say of us, who are totally bound by karma and afflictions? As it was said in the *Mya.ngan bsal (Śoka vinodana)*,

> If the Bodhisattvas, Pratyekabuddhas,
> Buddhas, and Śrāvakas relinquish their
> body, what to say of ordinary people?

Therefore, having been born, there is no region where one is able to dwell on without perishing, nor is there any place, either beneath the earth, on the earth, or above it, where the Lord of Death does not reach. As it was said in the *Mya.ngan bsal (Śoka vinodana)*,

> Though a great sage may possess the five supernatural
> perceptions and fly far in space, still he is unable
> to reach any place where there is immortality.

Also, as it was said in a *sKyes.rabs (Jātaka)*,

> And wherever one dwells, there is no
> place where death does not penetrate;
> not in the sky, nor in the ocean's
> depth, nor in between mountains.

In brief, one must understand that "from the time one has taken birth due to karma and afflictions, one is not beyond the range of certain death."

b) Death is certain because the body is insubstantial: As it was said in the *Tshoms (Udāna varga)*,[42]

> Alas, compounded things are impermanent;
> they are subject to birth and death;
> having been born, they come to destruction.
> Better, then, is the bliss of peace (i.e., Nirvāṇa).

In general, since compounded things (arise) due to causes and conditions, being nothing more than momentary and perishable, they are not even slightly fit to merit one's trust. Even this hard, firm, and vast world system, with its mountains, continents, and oceans, which is fashioned by the power of the collective karma of all sentient beings which has been accumulated for a long time is, in the end, burnt by a single flame of fire in which not even ashes remain. If even such a final time occurs when space will become empty, then what to say of our own fragile bodies which are created by small and temporary causes and conditions? They do not go beyond the state of certain destruction. As it was said in the *bShes.spring (Suhṛllekha)*,

> Since not even ash will remain as all things —
> the earth, Mount Meru, and the oceans —
> will be burned by the flames of the seven
> suns, what need to speak of very frail men?

If even Vajra bodies of the perfectly enlightened Buddhas, adorned with marks and signs of perfection, which is fashioned from boundless heaps of merit, are also shown to be impermanent, what of our **insubstantial** bodies, which are surely composed of deceitful things? As it was said in the *Mya.ngan bsal.ba (Śoka vinodana)*,

> If even the Vajra bodies, adorned by marks
> and signs of perfection, are impermanent,
> what to say of (these) bubble(like) bodies
> which are like plantain trees, devoid of essence?

Therefore, one should know that one day this insubstantial body which is held dear by us will be nothing more than an object that will be burned by fire to become ashes, thrown into water to be eaten by insects and become filth, dried by the sun's heat, infested by worms until it is destroyed, carried by wind and dispersed, rendered rot and grown putrid beneath the ground, or cut into pieces by living beings. As it was said in the *bShes.spring (Suhṛllekha)*,

> Understand that the insubstantial body at
> the end — becoming ashes, dried, decayed,
> or impure — will be completely destroyed,
> putrified, and subject to dispersion.

c) Death is certain because life is not permanent: In general, if one comprehends all compounded phenomena to be impermanent due to momentariness, it is easy to realize that the life of a person is also impermanent. And among all compounded matter the exhaustion of a person's life is said to be swifter than any other. For example, if someone very skilled in archery were to shoot an arrow in each of the four directions, and if another skilled person were able to catch each arrow before it drops to the ground, that would be considered very swift. Swifter than that are the hungry ghosts who move on the ground; swifter than that are the hungry ghosts who move in the sky, swifter than that are the chariots of the sun and the moon; swifter than that are the gods of great power; and yet even swifter than that is the exhaustion of a person's life. Therefore, if life is being exhausted at this rate every single moment, what to say of its exhaustion by minutes, days, months, and years? From the time of one's own birth until the present, or from last year until this year, or from yesterday until today — whatever be the length of time that has passed by — so by that much has one's life span been decreased. Therefore, since life only decreases and is not increased even slightly, one is not beyond the pale of certain death. As it was said in the *sPyod.'jug (Bodhicaryāvatāra)*,

> Since this life continually decreases
> without standing still day or night,
> and from no other source is it augmented,
> why won't someone such as myself die?

To illustrate this (point), people are like a steep mountainous waterfall; like a prisoner condemned to certain death; like a fish which has entered a net; and like animals that have entered the slaughterhouse.

(Meditate on the example), "like a steep mountainous waterfall". For example, water falling from the top of a cliff flows so quickly that it is as if the latter water were trying to overtake the former falling water. Life also becomes extinguished quickly, as if a latter instance were to overtake a former, and life ends in death. As it was said in the *rGya.cher rol.pa'i mdo, (Lalitavistara Sūtra)*,

> The three worlds are impermanent like autumn clouds;
> the birth and death of beings is like viewing a dance;
> the life of beings is like a flash of lightning in the
> sky, swiftly passing like a mountainous waterfall.

But these are only examples of swiftness, while the exhaustion of a person's life is swifter even than these.

"Like a prisoner condemned to certain death" is to be thought of thus: Being held by the executioners and led toward the place of execution, the life of a prisoner condemned to certain death draws nearer to death with each step. Likewise, one draws nearer to death with the passage of each minute, day, month, and year. As it was said in the *Tshoms (Udāna varga)*,

> For example, with every step he takes,
> a prisoner condemned to certain death
> draws (ever) nearer to death.
> So, too, is the life of humans.

"Like a fish which has entered a net" refers to the fact that however many of a school of fish might have entered a net, when pulled out of the great water by fishermen, they are all killed one by one, until finally there is not a single one remaining. Likewise, one is born in the river of worldly existence. Having entered the net of (re)birth cast by the fishermen of the afflictions, one reaches the mouth of the Lord of Death and is fit for nothing but death. As it was said in the *sPyod.'jug (Bodhicaryāvatāra)*,

> Having entered into the net of rebirth,
> which was cast by the fishermen of afflictions,
> you have gone into the mouth of the Lord of
> Death — even now, do you not know that?

(Also meditate on) "like animals who have entered the slaughterhouse." Having been forced to enter a slaughterhouse with no avenues to escape, the animals to be slaughtered see the butcher slaughter each of them one by one, but those remaining to be killed nevertheless engage in fighting and searching for food without even thinking about what is happening, until finally all, without exception, are killed. Likewise, one has entered the slaughtering pen of birth and, while observing the butcher, the Lord of Death, slaughtering step by step one's beloved friends, kinsmen, and the like, one does not think, "It will happen so to me." However, one looks to see what things they have left behind and performs the various careless acts of eating, drinking, and sleeping. Yet while engaged thus, one is suddenly slain by the Lord of Death, the butcher. As it was said in the *sPyod.'jug (Bodhicaryāvatāra)*,

> Do you not see that the (Lord of Death) is
> slaughtering your own kind step by step?
> But still you cling to slumber, like the
> slaughterer and the water buffalo.
> The avenues (of escape) are completely
> closed, and the Lord of Death is looking on.
> How can you enjoy food, and how can
> you like sleeping in this way?

To reflect on the meaning of this one should think, "Alas, I have not gone beyond being an object of certain death, being powerless to remain long in this world. There is no one in the past who, having been born, did not die. Nor is there anyone living at present who will not die, nor any who is being born now who will not die. That being the case, how then shall I not die? If even the Teacher, the light of the world, who is free from birth and death due to karma and afflictions, still pretended to pass beyond into Nirvāṇa, and if even the Assembly of Noble Ones discarded their karmically ripened bodies as an example for others, what confidence can I have that I, who am totally bound by karma and afflictions, will not perish? There will be a time when even these extremely hard and firm realms, together with their mountains, continents, and oceans, which arise from the inconceivable karma of living beings, will perish so that not even their ashes will remain. Furthermore, if even the Vajra bodies adorned with signs and marks of perfection achieved through the splendor of hundredfold merits are not permanent, how then would this body of mine, which is insubstantial, a collection, artificial, and hollow, be permanent? Hence this impermanent body that I hold to be permanent, this insubstantial body which I hold to have an essence, will be burned and changed into ashes, cast into water where its pieces will be devoured by fish and others, hung on a wall where it will become dried, eaten by worms so that it becomes empty inside, buried underground where it will rot and become putrified, or cast into a charnel ground where it will be eaten by birds and beasts of prey. Such a condition will come. Alas, a time will surely come when it will be apparent to all that this body of mine is not in the least bit permanent."

If one reflects in this manner and this awareness of death and impermanence still does not arise, then one should reflect in the following manner: "At this time I am free of bodily disease and mental suffering. Together with my relatives and beloved ones, I am enjoying food, clothing, housing, making provisions for a long life, and engaging in various discussions. However, I never have the thought that death will come. Certainly there will be a time when all these will be left behind and the light of this life will suddenly be extinguished. Being permanently separated from them, my relatives will not be able to see me, nor I be able to see or hear them. I shall have to go alone in some unknown, empty, and fearful region. Now, in this evening part of my life, having seriously considered death I must practice the pure death dharma so that it is surely impressed upon my mind. May the Preceptors and Triple Gem see to it that it may happen in this way." Thus think from the depths of one's heart and pray.

Also, in the intervals between sessions, reflect on the meaning (of what was expounded) in the *rGyal.po gdams.pa'i mdo, (Rājāvavādaka Sūtra)*:[43]

> At the time when one is engaged in various
> pleasant conversations together with one's
> relatives, associates, and servants, one
> should think, " Now I am dwelling together
> with my relatives and beloved friends, but
> the time will definitely come when I must
> permanently part from them."

So, too, when one is eating food, one should think, "Now I am eating delicious food, but the time will definitely come when I shall not have any appetite at all for food and drink, and at that time of dying no benefit will be derived no matter what food and medicine I take." When putting on fine clothes one should think, "Now I am wearing fine clothes, but the time will surely come when I shall be wrapped in dirty, odorous cloth and cast away." When riding a fine horse one should think, "Now I ride such a fine horse like this, but the time will surely come when ugly corpse bearers will carry me away." When seated on a fine seat, one should think, "Now I sit upon such a fine seat as this, but the time will surely come when I shall be cast into a dark hole in the ground." Meditate in such ways until one has the certain realization that death will befall oneself.

2. Reflect on the uncertainty of the time of death and thus shorten the range of one's plans: (a) reflect that there is no certainty about the time of death because there is no fixed life span; (b) reflect that there is no certainty about the time of death because the causes of death are manifold; and (c) reflect that there is no certainty about the time of death because the causes of life are few.

a) There is no certainty about the time of death because there is no fixed life span: Having thought that one will die due to the many reasons already described, still it is possible that some might think, "Though certainly I will eventually die, for some years I will not." Or one might think, "During my early years I will work for this life, and toward the end I will practice Dharma." One might also think, "This year I will collect provisions and then I will practice Dharma." However, there is no certainty that this will ever come to pass, because one does not know which will be first — the later years of this life or the next life, next year or the next life, next month or the next life, or tomorrow or the next life. Thus it was said in *Tshoms (Udāna Varga)*,

> Since there is no certainty whether
> tomorrow or the next life will come
> first, it is proper to strive for the
> next life rather than striving for tomorrow.

The reasons for this are explained in the *mDZod (Abhidharmakośa)*

> Here (the length of life) is uncertain — the shortest
> being ten years (and the longest being) measureless.

Though the life span of human beings in the other three continents is fixed, there is not the slightest certainty concerning the life span of those in this world of Jambudvīpa. Thus it was taught. Because there is no uniform age limit (to a life), the life of some is finished while still in their mother's womb; likewise, some die while just being born; some while just crawling; some while just able to walk; some during their youth; and some after growing old. As it was said in the *Tshoms (Udāna varga)*,

> Some die while in the womb;
> so, too, some die on just being born;
> so, too, some die while just crawling;
> some, too, while able to run about;
> some old and some young;
> some while in the prime of life.
> Like the fully ripened fruit,
> one by one they go.

Therefore, there is not the least bit of certainty (whereby) one can have confidence that one's life span will not come to its end this very day and one will die this evening. As it was said in the *sPyod.'jug (Bodhicaryāvatāra)*,

> It is not proper to remain in leisure
> while claiming, "I won't die this very
> day"; there is no doubt that the time
> of my inevitable death will come.

b) The time of death is uncertain because the causes of death are manifold: There is no certainty about the time of death because: (1) body and life are easily separated, (2) the Lord of Death has no love, and (3) there are many hostile forces, diseases, and malignant spirits.

(1) Body and life are easily separated: Even though there may be a small remainder of life force, there is no certainty whatsoever that one will be able to live until it is finished. The reason for this is that obstacles that consist of hostile forces contrary to the continuation of life are manifold, and life and body are very easily separated. Life is like an oil lamp in a windy place. Even though the lamp's oil, wick, and the like are unexhausted, due to wind it has no chance to continue even for a little while and is abruptly extinguished. As it was said in the *sLob.spring (Śiṣyalekha)*,

> Like the flame of a butter lamp shaken by
> a strong wind, there is no surety that this
> life will remain even for a single moment.

To reflect on the way in which body and mind are easily separated, think of how the very chance of awakening from sleep or inhaling after exhaling is a rare marvel. As it was said in the *bShes.spring (Suhṛllekha)*,

> This life has many misfortunes like a lamp in the wind
> and is even more impermanent than a bubble of water;
> so, it is wonderful that one has the chance to
> inhale after exhaling, and to awaken from sleep.

(2) The Lord of Death has no love: The Lord of Death has no intention of thinking with compassion, "This lovely one has not yet finished his work in life so I'll let him stay for awhile" or "Since he is not ill, I'll let him stay." On the contrary, like a hunter chasing a deer, he wishes to kill even a moment ahead of time. Apart from that, there is no other slight distraction. As it was said in the *sPyod.'jug (Bodhicaryāvatāra)*,

> There can be no confidence in the Lord of Death
> who does not wait whether one has finished or not.
> Whether sick or healthy, everyone should
> have no confidence in this accidental life.

(3) There are many hostile forces, diseases, and malignant spirits: Death may occur due to the disturbance of external and internal elements; due to the disturbance caused by spirits that lead one astray; or due to the disturbance caused by male gods and the like, and other malignant spirits.

There are many causes of death by the external elements, such as being buried by a land movement, carried away by water, burnt by fire, or tossed by the wind over a precipice. There are many causes of death by the internal elements, such as phlegm diseases of earth, cold disorders of water, fire disorders of fever, or wind diseases like heart air. There are 80,000 kinds of misleading spirits that constantly cause harm, such as stealing breath, complexion, and dignity. There are 360 kinds of male gods and the like, who will help one if pleased but cause harm if displeased. All of these also can cause death. One may die fighting with enemies; one may die being deceived by kinsmen; one may die by eating unsuitable food; one may die by taking unsuitable medicine; one may die by being suffocated by clothing; one may die by a revolt by the servants; one may die by being struck by animals; or one may die through being bitten by wild animals. Though there is none dearer to oneself than one's own self, still one may cause one's own death, as many are seen to commit suicide by piercing themselves with weapons or jumping off cliffs.

In brief, one cannot have the least confidence that such inner and outer things, either animate or inanimate, will not become the cause of one's death. Since these and other similar things become causes of death for other persons, there is no known reason why they will not become causes of death for oneself.

c) There is no certainty about the time of death because the causes of life are extremely few: One might think that there are many causes of life, such as rituals, medicines, food, and the like. Now if any single one, or even two, of these three — life, karma, and merit — are exhausted, then rituals and the like have the possibility of protecting some people from an untimely death. However, they will not be of the least benefit when all three of these are exhausted. Not only that, but there are many chances of even these becoming a cause of death. As it was said in the *Rin.chen phreng.ba (Ratnāvalī)*,

> The causes of death are many,
> while the causes of life are few.
> These latter even become causes of death.
> Hence, constantly practice religion.

One might reason, "Even though it may be so, still I have youth and good health, I have the resources for food, clothing, and the like, and I am free from harm caused by enemies and ghosts, so I shan't die." However, youth cannot defeat death, since newly born children are seen to die before the old and decrepit who have to lean on a staff. Thus it was said in the *Tshoms (Udāna varga)*,

> Many born in the morning are seen,
> but some are not seen in the evening;
> many born in the evening are seen,
> but some are not seen the next morning;
> many men and women die in the prime of youth;
> what confidence can be placed in the life of a
> man (of whom) it is said, "This man is young"?

Death cannot be defeated by healthiness, for healthy men are seen to die suddenly, long before a person who has been ill for many years. It cannot be defeated by the favorable resources of food, clothes, and the like. Rich men, surrounded by servants, food, and wealth are seen to die before beggars who have to search in the morning for their morning meal and in the evening for their evening meal. Death cannot be defeated by freedom from enemies, for people who do not even hear the sound of enemies are seen to die before people who are surrounded by them. Also it cannot be defeated by not having mischief caused by ghosts and malignant spirits, for many persons who dwell with a normal mental balance are seen to die before those whose every deed is harmful for themselves due to their mind being corrupted by malignant spirits. As it was said in the *sPyod.'jug (Bodhicaryāvatāra),*

> Though I (now) have such a day with health,
> food, and am free of persecution, (still) every
> moment of this life is deceitful and this body
> is a reflected image that appears but once.

Therefore, if other persons are not able to defeat death, I do not have any reason whatsoever that would enable me to defeat it. Hence, if I examine it well, there is not the slightest reasonable confidence by which I and all others might happily dwell believing that we will not die tonight.

The way to reflect on the meaning of this is to think: "Alas, since my birth until now I have spent all these years on the path of distraction, and now I have reached (the point of) death. We who dwell in this world of Jambudvīpa have no certain span of life. Though it is possible that I may have a little remnant of life, still an untimely death can occur. The causes of interrupting life are extremely many, and it is easy to separate the body and the mind. The Lord of Death, that interrupter, has no love. There is no place I can flee to that is free from those causes of interruption, and death may occur by any single one of those causes. I have no confidence that I shall not meet with such causes. Therefore, there is no way to know whether I shall die today or tomorrow. If I die today or tomorrow, I have not at all accomplished my previously resolved practice of death dharma. Oh, no! What will happen to me at the time of death? From this moment on, at this end of life where it is uncertain when I shall die, having cast off all essenceless worldly actions, I must practice the holy religion that will surely benefit me at the time of death. May the Preceptors and the Precious Gems see to it that I may continually impress upon my mind the death dharma." Think thus and make prayers.

In the intervals between sessions, one should not fall under the power of such thoughts as, "Today I must do this" and "Tomorrow I must do that." Instead, one must diligently practice with constant strong remembrance of, "If I die today I must be mindful (of the Triple Gem, and the like)" and "If I die tomorrow I must be mindful (of the Triple Gem, and the like)."

3. Reflect that nonreligious activities are not beneficial, and thus practice the holy Dharma: (a) reflect that the holy Dharma should be practiced because food and wealth are useless; (b) reflect that the holy Dharma should be practiced because kinsmen and associates are useless; and (c) reflect that the holy Dharma should be practiced because eloquence and power are useless.

a) The holy Dharma should be practiced because food and wealth are useless: At the time when one must surely die, however much one may possess of this life's prosperity, food, property, and the like, these will not be of even the least benefit. One cannot avoid death by giving them as a bribe to the Lord of Death, nor can one save oneself by giving them as a ransom. They cannot be carried in the beyond; rather, as with the extraction of a hair from butter, only one's self alone must leave, empty-handed and naked. Thus it was said in the *sPyod.'jug (Bodhicaryāvatāra)*,

> Though having gained many acquisitions and enjoyed
> happiness for a long time, (at the time of death)
> I will go naked and empty-handed, (as if my
> belongings) had been snatched away by thieves.

Not only are the wealth and prosperity of this life not helpful but they cause harm to anyone who has produced a mind of strong attachment to them. As it was said in the *sPyod.'jug (Bodhicaryāvatāra)*,

> Therefore, to whatever objects the ignorant
> mind becomes attached, just those very attachments
> will be amassed to cause a thousandfold suffering.
> Hence, the wise should not desire them, for from
> desire arises fear.

b) The holy Dharma should be practiced because kinsmen and associates are useless: However many one may have of loved ones, friends, associates, and servants, they are of no benefit at the time of death. They cannot reverse death by fighting the Lord of Death, nor will one be exempted on the recommendation of any of them. Nor can they share the pains of death or go along at the time of death, for one must go alone. As it was said in the *sPyod.'jug (Bodhicaryāvatāra)*,

> Lying on a bed, though surrounded by my relatives,
> I alone have to experience the agony of death.
> Of what use are kinsmen and friends when the
> messengers of death seize me? Virtue alone
> can save me then, and that I did not rely upon.

Not only do they not benefit one but the sins committed for their sake follow one and help to create more harm. As it was said in the *sPyod.'jug (Bodhicaryāvatāra)*,

> Here in this very life, many loved and unloved
> ones have departed, yet the unbearable sins
> committed for their sake remain before me.

c) The holy Dharma should be practiced because eloquence and power are useless: However much one may possess of eloquence and forceful power, these worldly powers and riches are useless. For example, the lion, the lord of beasts, overcomes the might of elephants and possesses the power to cause a small deer to be unable to breathe merely due to the sound of its roar. But when the Lord of Death appears, all its own strength and pride weaken and it has to die. Thus it was said in a *sKyes.rabs (Jātaka)*,

> Even the lions who subdue the splendors of the
> great elephant with their sharp nails and rip off
> and cut the head with their claws, or frighten the
> minds of others with the sounds of their fierce
> roars, lose their power and arrogance when the
> Lord of Death comes, and they lie down to sleep.

Not only do these not benefit one but the ripened result of attachment for and pride in this life's possessions follow one and help to create more harm. As it was said in the *sPyod.'jug (Bodhicaryāvatāra)*,

> "I have much gain and honor, many
> like me", if one holds such conceit,
> fear will arise after one's death.

In brief, apart from merely being temporary causes to sustain life, none of the following can prevent death when the actual time befalls: it cannot be prevented by substances, mantras, auspicious events, great forces and eloquence, a brave and strong man, a rich man's wealth, the good conduct of a noble man, or the words of a skilled speaker, nor can it be side-stepped by a clever person, run away from by a swift runner, or tricked by a magician. Thus it was said in a *sKyes.rabs (Jātaka)*,

> Though a good person can deceive the eyes
> of people in the midst of many assembled,
> the wonder of the Lord of Death is that his
> eyes are not able to be deceived by them.

Nonreligious activities are not beneficial, so as it was said to King Prasenajit in the *rGyal.po gdams.pa'i mdo (Rājāvavādaka Sūtra)*,

> Oh great king, when the time of death befalls,
> pierced by the spear of the Lord of Death, one
> parts from one's pride, without a protector, without
> a refuge, without a great retinue; afflicted by
> disease, dry-mouthed, one's face is altered; one's
> hand and feet trembling; one's lips are drawn back,
> one's teeth gnashing; unable to rise, emitting a
> whizzing sound, one's body is smeared by urine,
> excrement, and bad odors; one forgets about
> medicine, doctor, and food; one sleeps in one's
> bed for the last time; sinking into the river of
> (the suffering of) transmigration, one is frightened
> by the helpers of the Lord of Death. The continuity

of breathing stops; one's mouth and nostrils open wide; one relinquishes this world; one goes to the next world; one embarks on the great change; one enters the great darkness; one falls into the great abyss; one is tossed by the great ocean; one is carried by the river of karma; one travels in a stationless region; one has (no part) in the sharing of one's wealth. One cries, "Alas, father", "Alas, mother", "Alas, son". Oh great king, at that time, there is no other protector except Dharma. There is no other refuge, there is no other retinue. At that time, Dharma indeed becomes a protector, a refuge, a support, an island, and a great retinue. Therefore, emperor, when the time of certain death comes, one's body is pierced by the death lord's spears. One parts from pride, one is destitute of protectors, refuge, and retinue, is stricken by disease, dry mouthed; one's face changes, one's hands and feet tremble; one's lips are drawn back and teeth gnash; one is unable to rise and emits a whizzing sound; one's body is smeared by urine, excrement, and odors; one forgets about doctors, medicines, and food; one dwells in one's last bed; one sinks in the river of (the suffering of) transmigration; one is frightened by the Lord of Death; one's breathing stops, one's mouth and nostrils open wide; one abandons this world and goes to the next world; one embarks on the great change; one enters the great darkness; one falls into the great abyss; one is tossed by the great ocean; one is carried by the river of karma; one traverses a stationless region; one is unable to share property; and one emits cries of lament. Think what could protect or save one other than Dharma at that time?

Therefore, from this very moment on, one must diligently practice the holy Dharma and imprint the certainty of death in one's heart. If one does not practice Dharma now, when one's organs are perfect and body and mind are able to function, one will not be able to practice Dharma later, when the body is aged, the mind is senile, and one has become a breathing corpse, on the point of death. As Thro phug Lotsawa (Khro.phug Lo.tstsha.wa) said,

If one does not practice diligently now, then even
if one practices when death is encountered, (it is
like) putting on armour after having been wounded in
battle, and beating one's chest, saying, "Alas".

Though one may think, "I will still die even though I practice Dharma", the manner of death is not the same. A superior practitioner dies happily; a mediocre one dies without fear; and an inferior one dies without regret. As it was said in the *mDo.sde rgyan (Sūtrālankāra)*,

Having realized all things to be like illusions and
birth (to be like) going from one garden (to another),
whether in times of wealth or poverty, one is not
frightened by the suffering of afflictions.

And as it was said in the *sPyod.'jug (Bodhicaryāvatāra)*,

Therefore, having mounted the steed of the
enlightenment thought which removes all sadness
and fatigue, one will move on from happiness to
happiness, so who that is thoughtful would be lazy?

When a person who has not practiced Dharma dies, he firstly has remorse for having committed sins and not having practiced Dharma. He is then wracked by pain from his vital organs and finally dies afraid of the Lord of Death. As it was said in the *sPyod.'jug (Bodhicaryāvatāra)*,

One who today is taken to the block to be maimed
of one's limbs becomes alarmed, one's mouth becomes
dry, one's eyes becomes dull, and the like,
so one appears differently than before.
If that is the case, then what to say about a
weak one (like) myself when I am frightfully
stared upon by the messengers of the Lord of Death,
caught by them and seized by the fever of great terror?

To reflect on the meaning of this, think as follows: "Alas, death will come to me, but it is not known when it will come.

Other than Dharma, there is no method for benefiting death. But until now, I have been distracted by unnecessary worldly activities, have been attached to the objectives of this life, and have held the insubstantial to be substantial, so I have not practiced even a little of the Dharma which imprints death upon the mind. Alas, what shall I do in the event of death?" Thus one should think intensively and meditate until a most unbearable revulsion and intense sadness arise.

Further think: "Now I have become more and more attached to worldly aims. If I do not practice the holy Dharma from the bottom of my heart, it would be like returning from a jewel island empty-handed. There is no greater self-deception than this. Therefore, I must practice the holy Dharma on which I can surely rely at the time of death. Also, I must do it now, without coming under the sway of laziness and tardiness, and I must do it quickly. I must start vigorously, like putting out a flame that has caught my head and clothing on fire. Since food, wealth, property, and my beloved, friends, and kinsmen of this life will not benefit me at all at the time of death, I must discard, like spittle, the acquiring and guarding of them. Having directed my mind toward the Preceptor and the Precious Gems, I will see to it that I have nothing else to do but to practice Dharma. May the Preceptor and Precious Gems see to this and help me to fulfill my wishes." Think this from the bottom of the heart, and with intense longing offer prayers and the like.

Even in the intervals between sessions, one should constantly remember the certainty of death, the uncertainty of the time of death, and that nothing other than Dharma will be of benefit at the time of death. If one sees or hears of others' death, and even up to the point where one sees a corpse, skeleton, and the like, one should think: "I, too, have not gone beyond the potential to become such an object; nor have I gone beyond being the nature of death"; thus cut attachment to this life. Whenever worldly thoughts arise, check the mind by mindfulness and settle it in its own place. Do not associate with sinful friends who are attached to this world's activities. One should also be content with whatever one obtains for the sake of temporary sustenance, such as food, clothing, and the like.

Prior to whatever Dharma practice one undertakes, one

should first remember impermanence, and one should produce encouragement in one's own mind. Having goaded with the stick of impermanence whatever hearing, contemplation, and meditation one does, that becomes a real Dharma practice. Furthermore, it has the benefit of accomplishing one's practice quickly. So, those who desire liberation should always hold impermanence in mind.

The Instructions on Virtuous and Nonvirtuous Deeds and Their Results To Clarify What Is To Be Accepted and What Is To Be Rejected

The words in the *Root Treatise (of the Vajra Verses, rDo.rje tshig.rkang, Vajragāthā), For sentient beings with the afflictions is the impure vision,* indicate that within the impure vision all these appearances of happiness and sorrow can be understood to arise from the performance of virtuous and sinful deeds. This impure vision consists of two appearances: the illusory appearance and the karmic appearance. Of these, the illusory appearance, while nonexistent in ultimate reality, is the appearance of subjects and objects (in the relative sphere). The karmic appearance is a particular aspect of the illusory appearance and consists of different appearances of happiness and sorrow, of long and short lives, of much or little wealth, and the like, because these appearances are the individual results of virtuous and sinful deeds.

To establish this one may ask, "If at the time of death, happiness, servants, associates, sorrow, and prosperity of this world do not follow one, will not the performance of virtuous and sinful deeds also not follow one?" This is not so. As it was said in the *rGyal.po gdams.pa'i mdo (Rājāvavādaka Sūtra),*

> With the affliction of the (passing of) time, oh king,
> at that time of death, property, loved ones, kinsmen,
> and friends do not follow. But wherever that person
> goes, his deeds follow him like a shadow.

Also, it was said in the *mDo.sde las brgya.pa (Karma Śataka),*[44]

> (The result of) actions do not ripen upon the soil,
> nor do they ripen upon a stone; (but they ripen) only
> upon the aggregates that are grasped (by oneself).

A deed committed by oneself does not remain behind, nor does it follow some other person, nor does it disappear. Like a shadow that follows a bird flying in the sky, it follows the doer and is not exhausted through the passage of an aeon or even more than an aeon. Thus it was said in the *'Dul.ba lung (Vinayāgama)*,

> The deeds of living beings are not exhausted even
> after a hundred aeons, but the result will only ripen
> at the time of the assemblage of the right conditions.

To reflect on this, (1) produce the desire to discard nonvirtue by reflecting on nonvirtuous deeds and their results; (2) produce the desire to practice virtue by reflecting on virtuous deeds and their results; and (3) transform neutral deeds into virtuous ones by reflecting on them.

Produce the Desire to Discard Nonvirtue by Reflecting on Nonvirtuous Deeds and Their Results

This first category has three parts: (a) reflecting on nonvirtuous deeds, (b) reflecting on their results, and (c) reflecting on discarding them.

Nonvirtuous Deeds

As it was said in the *Rin.chen phreng.ba (Ratnāvalī)*,

> Actions produced by desire, hatred,
> and delusion are nonvirtues.

Just as the leaves, flowers, and fruits arising from a poisonous root are poisonous, so are actions motivated through these three: attachment to one's own side, hatred toward the other side, and ignorance of the deed and its result. All actions motivated through these three are known as nonvirtuous. If these are classified, they are threefold: the three actions of body — killing, taking what is not given, and sexual misconduct; the four actions of voice — lying, calumny, harsh speech, and idle speech; and the three actions of mind — coveting, malice, and wrong views.

Killing is to take the life of any other being with the intention (to kill), whether done by oneself or having ordered others to do it through poison, fire, weapons, and the like.

Stealing is to take the possessions of another for one's own, through force or gentle methods, whether it be a small or large item.

Sexual misconduct is intercourse with a woman who is not one's own wife; with one who, though not claimed (by a husband), is a relative up to the seventh generation; at an improper time; at the time of pregnancy or the time of fasting; in an improper place, like a temple, in the presence of parents, and the like; and by an improper passage, such as anal or oral.

As it was said (in the scriptures),

> Killing is the taking of another's life with intention,
> whether done by oneself or one ordered others (to do it).
> Stealing is to take possession of another's property by
> force or by gentle means.
> Sexual misconduct is intercourse with another's wife,
> or at an improper place, at an improper time, or by
> an improper passage.

Lying is to speak untrue words with the intention of deceiving others.

Calumny is to speak various true and untrue defiled words with the intention of creating separation among others, whether they be in harmony or in disharmony.

Harsh speech is to speak words that profoundly pierce others when they understand their meaning.

Idle speech is the speech of listening to and contemplating wrong scriptures and the defiled speech of flattery, songs, dramas, and tales of dynasties, armies, harlots, and the like.

As it was said (in scripture),

> Lying is to speak untrue words intentionally with the
> thought of deceiving others.
> Calumny is to speak various defiled words in order to

create separation among others.
Harsh speech is to utter unpleasant words that
profoundly hurt others.
Idle speech is to talk of wrong scriptures and other
defiled speech of flattery, songs, dramas, and the like.

Coveting is the desire to make others' property one's own.

Malice is the wish to harm others, produced by a mind of hatred.

Wrong views consist of believing that the Precious Gems and the doctrine of karma and the like are not true.

As it was said (in scripture),

> Coveting is the wish to make others' property one's own.
> Malice is the wish to harm others arising from a hateful mind.
> Wrong views is to hold the Three Gems and the (law of) cause and effect to be nonexistent.

The Results of Nonvirtuous Deeds

As it was said in the *Rin.chen phreng.ba (Ratnāvalī)*,

> From nonvirtues (arise)
> suffering and the lower realms.

Each nonvirtue also has a threefold result: (1) the ripened result; (2) the result similar to its cause; and (3) the result of ownership. All of these deeds produce the ripened result of the suffering of the three lower realms.

1. The ripened result: As it was said in the *Rin.chen phreng.ba (Ratnāvalī)*,

> The first (result) of all (of these
> deeds) is the going to lower realms.

Furthermore, if one performs an action generated through anger, the result is rebirth in hell; through desire, rebirth in the hungry ghost realm; and through delusion, rebirth in the animal realm.

As it was said in the *Rin.chen phreng.ba (Ratnāvalī)*,

> Through anger one is born in hell;
> through desire, one is born in the hungry ghost realm;
> through ignorance, most go to the animal realm.

By nature, if one performs the ten nonvirtues to a great extent, the result is hell. If one performs them to a middling extent, the result is birth as a hungry ghost. If one commits them to a small extent, one is reborn as an animal.

2. The result similar to its cause is twofold: (a) experience similar to its cause, and (b) action similar to its cause.

a) Experience similar to its cause: (Due to nonvirtuous deeds,) one will experience the suffering of the three lower realms in some future lifetime or, having already experienced (that result), one will again be born into higher realms (but will be subject to the following conditions). By killing, one will have a short life and many illnesses, even though one obtains a body in the higher realms. By stealing, one will be destitute of property and will not be able to use it even if one has a little. By sexual misconduct, one will have many enemies and one's wife will not be faithful. By lying, one will be much slandered, spoken harshly to, and easily deceived by others. By calumny, one will have few friends and even if one has some, they will quickly part from one. By harsh speech, one will hear unpleasant speech and whatever one says will become a basis for fighting. By idle speech, others will not consider one's words to be true, even though one utters the truth. By coveting, one will not obtain the object of one's wishes or even if obtained, one will not be content. By malice, one will always be fearful and apprehensive that others will cause one harm. By wrong views, one will encounter bad views and will be endowed with little wisdom, or one's wisdom will become impaired or corrupted. Thus it was said in the *Rin.chen phreng.ba (Ratnāvalī)*,

> By killing, one's life will be short;
> by stealing, one will be destitute of property;
> by sexual misconduct, one will have enemies;

by lying, one will be slandered much;
by calumny, one will part from friends;
by harsh speech, one will hear unpleasantries;
by irrelevant speech, one's word will not be respected;
by coveting, one's hopes will be disappointed;
by malicious thoughts, one will engender fear;
by wrong views, one will produce more wrong views.

b) Action similar to its cause: Having committed nonvirtues, one naturally has enthusiasm for committing nonvirtues in every lifetime because of the force of mental habituation. For example, present delight in killing is an action similar to the cause of having been accustomed to killing in other lifetimes. So, too, should the other nonvirtues be understood.

3. The result of ownership: The result of ownership is said to ripen as the outer aspects of the world in which one is born and dwells. (In the case of nonvirtuous deeds) it was said in the *Rin.chen phreng.ba (Ratnāvalī)*,

> A region of little splendor with many hailstorms,
> dust storms, bad odors, uneven land, salty, and
> the like, and reversal of seasons, small results,
> bitterness, and having nothing in the least.

To apply (the ten nonvirtues) to each one separately:

> Killing (results in) a region of little splendor.
> Stealing (results in) a region with hailstorms and hoarfrost.
> Sexual misconduct (results in) dust storms.
> Lying (results in) dirty and bad odors.
> Calumny (results in) uneven land.
> Harsh speech (results in) arid lands.
> Idle speech (results in) preventing the changes of seasons.
> Coveting (results in) small results.
> Malice (results in) fruits of bitter flavors.
> Wrong view (results in) not even having a little fruit.

Therefore, one should know that such conditions are the result of ownership of nonvirtues. As it was said in the *sPyod.'jug (Bodhicaryāvatāra)*,

> Although the sinner desires happiness,
> because of those sins (previously committed),
> wherever he goes — here and there — he
> is overcome by the weapons of suffering.

Discarding Nonvirtuous Deeds

One should think, "From the commission of nonvirtue arises the suffering of the lower realms, and also all the adverse conditions of the higher realms. From now on, I must not do any sins even at the cost of my life." As it was said in the *sPyod.'jug* (*Bodhicaryāvatāra*),

> "How can I be released from suffering which
> arises from nonvirtues?" It is fitting for
> me to think of this alone day and night.

Having obtained a human body endowed with the prerequisites, collecting sins is even a greater folly than using a golden vessel adorned by various jewels as a ladle for clearing away impure substances and vomit. As it was said in the *bShes.spring*, (*Suhṛllekha*),

> More foolish than one who uses a gold vessel
> adorned with jewels as a vessel for cleaning
> impure substances and vomit is he who commits
> sins after being born as a human being.

If it is asked, "It is true that if one commits very great nonvirtues one will be born in the lower realms, but a small amount of sin will not yield that much of a result, will it?" (The reply is) that it will most definitely yield (that much of a result). Formerly, a nun called her companions bitches and, due to this, she was reborn in 500 consecutive births as a bitch. A king used to make offerings to venerable Pratyekabuddhas, and among them was one whose body was deformed. Being absent one day, one of the king's daughters, in imitating that Pratyekabuddha's body said, "He who is like this is absent". Due to this action, she was reborn for many births as a deformed woman. Moreover, it is said in the *Nges.pa dang ma.nges.pa la'jug.pa'i phyag.rgya'i.mDo* (*Niyata aniyata gati mudrā avatāra sūtra*),[45]

> A greater sin than that of plucking out the eyes
> of all the people of this world of Jambudvīpa and
> plundering all their property is the sin of merely
> staring with disrespect at a Bodhisattva.

It is also said,

> If one produces anger at a Bodhisattva one
> time, one must experience the result of
> suffering in hell for as many aeons as
> the number of seconds one's anger lasted.

As it was said in the *sPyod.'jug (Bodhicaryāvatāra)*,

> The Buddha has declared that if one produces a wicked
> thought against such a donor, a Son of the Enlightened
> One, that person will remain in hell for as many aeons
> as the number of seconds that wicked thought lasted.

Therefore, since one does not know who is a Bodhisattva and where he exists, one should be careful in behaving toward them in the ways (just mentioned). As it was said in the *sPyod.'jug (Bodhicaryāvatāra)*,

> If one must go into Avīci hell for aeons for a
> single sinful deed done in a moment, what need
> to say that one will not go to happy realms if
> one has accumulated sins since beginningless time?

And, as it was said in the *'Dul.ba lung (Vinayāgama)*,

> Do not scorn even small sins thinking,
> "They will not hurt", for even by a
> tiny spark of fire can a heap of grass
> as large as a mountain be burnt.

In brief, from beginningless lifetimes until now, one has gathered sins without resting even a single day, and the retribution of these will not fall even slightly upon anyone other than oneself. Therefore, one should first be diligent in the methods of not being stained by sin. If it occurs, one should confess it with intense remorse, and one should hold a vow not to commit (such a deed) again. As it was said in a *sūtra*,

> Holy persons are of two kinds: one
> who is not stained by vices and one
> who purifies vices when they arise.

If it be asked, "Will sin be purified by confession?" (The answer is), it will. As it was said in the *bShes.spring (Suhṛllekha)*,

> One who has formerly been careless, but later
> becomes careful — like Nanda, Aṅgulimāla,
> Ajātaśatru, and Udayana — will also be
> splendid like the moon free from clouds.

Nanda, the younger stepbrother (of the Buddha), was overcome by the desire for women, and Aṅgulimāla slew many people, but both attained Arhathood by training in the Doctrine. Ajātaśatru slew his righteous father and Udayana killed his own mother, but they were quickly liberated from the result of their sins by relying upon the Tathāgata's teaching.

Produce the Desire to Practice Virtue by Reflecting on Virtuous Deeds and Their Results

(This second category also has three parts:) (a) reflecting on virtuous deeds, (b) reflecting on their results, and (c) reflecting on their performance.

Virtuous Deeds

As it was said in the *Rin.chen phreng.ba (Ratnāvalī)*,

> Actions that are produced free from
> desire, hatred, and delusion are virtues.

All the actions of the three doors (of body, voice, and mind) generated by nonattachment to one's own side, nonaversion toward the other side, and the wisdom which is nondeluded about deeds and their results are called virtues, just as all the leaves, flowers, and fruits that originate from medicinal roots are medicinal. If these are classified, they are threefold: the three abandonments of actions by the body, such as killing, and the like; the four abandonments of actions by the voice, such as lying and the like; and the three abandonments of actions by the mind, such as coveting and the like.

The individual nature of these consist of taking the vow to renounce killing, taking the vow to renounce stealing, and the like, which are motivated by freedom from the three poisons are the opposite of the ten nonvirtues. Thus virtuous actions consist of the mind that promises to renounce the ten nonvirtues.

The Results of Virtuous Deeds
As it was said in the *Rin.chen phreng.ba (Ratnāvalī)*,

> Virtues (bring about) every happy
> realm and happiness in all births.

Each of the ten virtues has a threefold aspect of (1) the ripened result, (2) the result similar to its cause, and (3) the result of ownership.

1. The ripened result: Every ripened result produces the happiness of the higher realms. As it was said in the *Rin.chen phreng.ba (Ratnāvalī)*,

> By these (ten virtuous deeds) one will be liberated
> from the realms of hell, hungry ghosts, and the
> animals, and one will obtain the royal splendor
> of dwelling among humans, gods, and demigods.

Moreover, by performing great virtuous actions, one will be born as a god; by mediocre virtuous actions, as a demigod; and by small ones, as a human. If it is asked, "But at the time of describing the difficult-to-obtain prerequisites, wasn't the human body said to be the best among those of the higher realms?" The answer is that there it was a matter of explaining the good and the bad basis for the performance of Dharma, whereas here it is different because it is the occasion to explain the superior and inferior results of deeds performed in former lifetimes.

2. The result similar to its cause is twofold: (a) experience similar to its cause, and (b) action similar to its cause.

a) Experience similar to its cause: By abandoning killing, one will enjoy a long life; by abandoning stealing, one will own great wealth, and so on; these are the opposites of the results of abovementioned nonvirtues. As it was said in the *Rin.chen phreng.ba (Ratnāvalī)*,

> Just the opposite of whatever was proclaimed
> as the result of the so-called nonvirtues
> will occur as the result of all the virtues.

b) Action similar to its cause: One will not have any interest in killing and the like; thus one's actions will be the inverse of each of the nonvirtues.

3. The result of ownership: One will be born in beautiful regions and the like — (places that are) the opposites of the ten formerly described bad environments. As it was said in the *sPyod.'jug (Bodhicaryāvatāra)*,

> Because of doing virtuous deeds that are
> motivated by aspiration of mind, wherever
> one goes, here and there, one is honored
> by the results of those merits.

Moreover, if one complements these virtuous deeds with the three special methods — the preliminary practice of creation of the enlightenment thought, the main practice of wisdom which realizes emptiness, and the conclusion of full dedication of merits — then they also become the cause of the liberation (of Arhatship) and the omniscience (of perfect Buddhahood).

Performing Virtuous Deeds

One should think, "Since they are endowed with such benefit, without overlooking even small virtues, I must perform them as much as I can." As it was said in the *sPyod.'jug (Bodhicaryāvatāra)*,

> Therefore, one should have interest in virtues
> and should practice them with great devotion;
> starting with the Vajra Dhvaja ritual,
> one should meditate upon self-confidence.

If it be asked, "Isn't it true that a small virtuous deed cannot yield a result?" (The reply) is, it can. As it was said in the *'Dul.ba lung (Vinayāgama)*,

> Do not despise even small virtuous deeds,
> thinking, "They do not benefit", for even
> a great vessel is gradually filled by
> accumulating drops of water.

Then, if it be asked, "But how are large and small virtues and sins determined?" (The answer) is as follows.

1. By constancy: Having promised to practice, one constantly performs virtue or sin or, if one has not promised to do so but constantly performs virtue or sin, then these virtues and sins are more powerful than an occasional or spontaneous performance (of sin or virtue), which is feeble.

2. By intention: Those actions are more powerful which are known as "generated through a mind greatly attached to its object." These actions are performed through the arising of a strong attachment, along with the completion of these three: the preparation, the performance, and the conclusion. The action is less powerful if one is ordered to do it against one's will by kings and the like, or if one is requested to do so by one's relations. The action is stronger if arising from wrong views, such as sacrificing an animal's life for the sake of attaining liberation. It is weaker if arising from an ignorant mind, similar to the play of small children.

3. By antidotes: The deed is more powerful if one maintains nonregret, rejoices for whatever sins or virtues that are done, and conceals them from others. If one acts opposite to this, it is less powerful. Therefore, it is important not to boast to others of the virtues one has done. If sins are committed, it is important to announce them to others, saying, "I have acted thus," along with a guilty mind, and also to confess it with strong remorse. As it was said in the *sPyod.'jug (Bodhicaryāvatāra)*,

Having done hellish deeds,
how can my mind remain at ease?

4. By object: Whatever virtues and sins are collected through performance toward the field of qualities which is the Guru, the Triple Gem, the abbots, Preceptors, and the speakers of religion are more powerful than those directed toward ordinary people. The result is greater if directed toward an important object like parents, elders, and those who have been kind to oneself, while it is of lesser effect if directed towards others.

5. By the field of mercy: The result of deeds is more powerful if one benefits or harms the field of mercy which is the sick, the lordless, the suffering, and those who trust one. It is less for those who are not thus. As it was said in the *bShes.spring (Suhṛllekha)*,

> From the source of these five great factors — consistency, intention, lack of opposition, endowed with qualities, and beneficiaries — virtuous and nonvirtuous deeds arise (in great proportion); therefore strive to do virtuous actions.

Among these five, the field and the intention are the most important. As it was said in the *mDZod (Abhidharma Kośa)*,

> The categories of field and intention
> endow actions with visible results.[46]

If a great deed is committed without the accompaniment of preparation and conclusion, it is performed but sin or virtue is not accumulated. Therefore, the ripened result is not certain to be experienced. Also, even if one does not commit the deed but only its preparation and conclusion, then that is mentally rejoicing in the virtues or sinful deeds of others, so it is unperformed but accumulated and the ripened result is certain to be experienced.

6. By the number of doers: The result is more powerful if many people performed the work in concord, but less if it is done separately or individually. Therefore, know that if many members of the Sangha recite a *sūtra* together at one time, the merit is multiplied by as many monks (as recited it). If one recites it alone, there will be no more benefit than that individual amount of merit. Similarly, if a hundred men, having consulted together, slay a single being, each of the men will bear the sin of killing a being, and so it is more powerful. If one man kills a being without consulting others, there will be the lesser sin of a single man killing a single being.

7. By place: A deed is more powerful if it is done in temples, in front of representations of the Triple Gem, in places where the Preceptors and the Sangha dwell, and the like.

8. By time: Whatever virtue or sin is done, it is more powerful if done on the four auspicious dates of the waxing and waning (lunar cycle), on holy days commemorating events in the life of Buddha, on the important anniversary days of spiritual masters, and the like, while it is less if done at other times and places.

9. By perpetrator: Whatever virtue or sin is done, the result is much more powerful if done by monks, by one who has taken vows to follow the precepts, or by those who have accepted a discipline. It is less powerful if done by a householder or by one who has not taken any vows. It was said in a *sutra*,

> Greater than the merit of offering lamps that fill
> three thousand great world systems to a Stupa of
> Tathāgatas by a householder Bodhisattva would be
> the merit of a monk Bodhisattva having lit some
> wicks dipped in oil, which merely illumine the doorstep
> of a temple in which a Tathāgata's Stupa is installed.

Similarly, there are three groups of four faults that are more likely to occur to one who has renounced the world and that are more powerful (if done by them). These are: (a) the four dharmas that cause one to go to the lower realms like an arrow being shot, (b) the four dharmas that cause one to go quickly to hell, (c) the four dharmas that cause one not to find any time of release after having gone (to the lower realms).

a) The four dharmas that cause one to go to the lower realms: According to the *Byams.pa seng.ge sgra'i mdo (Maitreya Simhanāda sūtra)*,[47] these are

> To summarize, for those with impaired vows to
> use objects that have been faithfully offered;
> to knowingly indulge in transgressions; to
> associate for a day with transgressors; and to
> hate the good fortune of others. These four
> faults are like an arrow being shot into hell.

   b) The four dharmas that cause one to go quickly to hell: According to the meaning found in the *sPyod.'jug (Bodhicary-āvatāra)* and elsewhere, these are to be arrogant due to much gain and honor; to be proud due to much learning; to be proud due to one's performance of moral discipline; and to be proud due to having helpful donors.
   c) The four dharmas that cause one not to find any time of release after having gone to the lower realms: According to the *lTung.ba sde lnga'i lci.yang bstan.pa'i mdo.* and other *sūtras*, these are,

> To be stained by root downfalls, to criticize a
> Bodhisattva, to be malicious toward the holy Dharma,
> and to hold wrong views; these are the four faults
> for which there is no release from hell.

Out of fear of making this book too long by using many scriptural quotations, I will not write more here.
   Deeds arising out of the motivation of hatred are greater in power than any other nonvirtue. As it was said in the *Nye.ba 'khor gyis zhus.pa'i mdo., (Upāli paripṛccha sūtra)*,[48]

> The sin of producing anger against any living
> being one time by a Bodhisattva who has entered
> the great vehicle is greater than his experiencing
> sexual desires for 100,000 aeons.

Similarly, it is also taught that all the roots of virtue collected through hundreds and thousands of aeons are destroyed at once if one produces a thought of anger for a single instant toward a special object (such as a Bodhisattva). As it was said in the *sPyod.'jug (Bodhicaryāvatāra)*,

> All good deeds accumulated through a
> thousand aeons, like giving, making
> offerings to the Sugatas, and the like,
> are destroyed in one fit of anger.

Also, it was said in the *'Jug.pa (Madhyamakāvatāra)*,

> The virtues of giving and morality collected
> in hundreds of aeons are destroyed in one
> single instant; therefore there is no sin
> greater than impatience.

10. By purpose: Virtues and sins done for the sake of others are of greater strength than those done for one's own sake. Therefore, even though one sins for the sake of others, the result befalls only the doer, while others do not share in that result. As it was said in the *bShes.spring (Suhṛllekha)*,

> Do not commit sins for the sake of Brahmans,
> monks, gods, guests, parents, sons, queen
> and attendants, for there will be none to
> share the result of hell.

Also, it was said in the *sPyod.'jug (Bodhicaryāvatāra)*,

> Here in this very life many loved ones have
> passed away, yet the terrible sins committed
> for their sake remain before the doer.

In brief, the motivation is generally more important than the nature of the deed itself in determining virtuous and sinful deeds. An example is the case of the skillful ship captain who slew *Mi.nag mDung thung can*.⁴⁹ Though the deed itself appeared to be nonvirtuous, it is said that because the motivation was extremely noble, the virtue acquired amounted to the collection of merit accumulated during many aeons. As it was said by the Dharma Master Sapan (Sakya Pandita Kunga Gyaltshen),

> With a steady mind for others' welfare, even

if one performs the four defeats[50] which are
a great sin for the Śrāvaka, they become a
great virtue for a Bodhisattva.

A similar case is that of practicing virtue through the three doors (of body, voice, and mind) in order to win the confidence of others in one's own conduct, for the sake of gaining honor and offerings. This has the momentary appearance of being virtuous although it is in fact nonvirtuous, and is known as a distracted notion. This is essentially the same as a hunter killing deer while wearing the yellow robes (of a monk), or dishonestly selling donkey's meat while showing the tail of a deer. As it was said by the Master Sapan,

> If one doesn't show the tail of a deer,
> one will not be able to sell donkey's meat;
> likewise if one doesn't show good conduct, one
> will not be able to deceive through wrong ideas.

Therefore, since virtues and nonvirtues depend on one's mind, which is the root of all sins and virtues, one should always strive in the methods that produce a mind of virtue. As it was said in the *bShes.spring (Suhṛllekha)*,

> O fearless one, the Blessed One said that
> the mind is the root of all activities,
> so tame your mind; this is beneficial and
> useful advice, so what need to say more?

Also, as it was said in the *sPyod.'jug (Bodhicaryāvatāra)*,

> One who wishes to guard the training
> should guard the mind with great care;
> if this mind is not guarded, one will
> not be able to protect the training.

> As untamed elephant does not cause
> such harm here as the unrestrained
> elephant of the mind, which causes
> the harms of Avīci Hell.

> Having thoroughly bound the elephant of the
> mind with the rope of mindfulness, all fears
> vanish and all virtues come into one's hand.

Transform Neutral Deeds Into Virtues by Reflecting on Them

The third category consists of: (a) thinking that neutral deeds are fruitless, so that one should transform them into virtues, (b) reflecting that neutral deeds have no results, and (c) how to transform neutral deeds into virtues.

Neutral Deeds Are Fruitless

Neutral deeds are neither virtue nor sin, being the indifferent actions of moving, walking, sleeping, sitting, and the like. The reason for this is that they are actions of the three doors which are not influenced either by the abovementioned three poisons of afflictions nor by the absence of these three poisons.

Neutral Deeds Have No Results

Reflect further that neutral deeds are unable to produce any happy or unhappy result, precisely because they are neutral. Thus, the Master Sapan (Sakya Pandita Kunga Gyaltshen) said,

> Since the indifferent (actions)
> are neither (virtue nor sin),
> they have no (good or bad) results.

Transforming Neutral Deeds Into Virtues

Neutral actions are good from the point of view of not producing suffering, but by not producing happiness, they are rendered useless. A person skilled in means must transform them into virtue. As it was said by Maitreyanātha,

> When engaged in the activities of a Bodhisattva,
> whatever type of object confronts the sense organs
> should be transformed into benefit for beings
> by (the use) of appropriate words.

Thus, to whatever appears as an object of the sense organs, one should apply appropriate words. So after having first produced a mind desiring to accomplish good for all beings, one should engage in any activity related to that object, together with mindfulness and alertness. One should know the method of applying appropriate words as described in the summary of *sPyod.'yul yongs.su dak.pa'i mdo*,[51] which was written by Ācārya Jñāna Garbha, and in the *rGyal.sras lam bzang*. If one is not able (to practice) to that extent, one should practice as much as described here.

When dwelling in the house, one should wish: "May all living beings attain the city of liberation." When sitting on a seat, "May they attain the Vajrāsana (i.e., the seat of enlightenment)." When lying down to sleep, "May they attain the Dharmakāya of the Buddha." When rising, "May they attain the Nirmāṇakāya." When putting on clothes, "May they wear the cloth of piety and modesty." When bathing, "May they be separated from the dirt of the afflictions." When eating food, "May they gain the food of meditation." When leaving the house, "May they be released from the city of worldly existence." When embarking on a path, "May they obtain the path of the Noble Ones." When performing work, "May they complete the two purposes." When entering the house, "May they enter the city of liberation." Having arrived, "May they reach the stage of Buddhahood," and the like. One should know what appropriate wishes should be applied to whatever situation arises. These wishes are an elaboration of the meaning of the words in the *sDud.pa (Sañcaya gāthā)*,[52]

> Fully endowed with mindfulness in moving,
> walking, lying down, and sitting.

To reflect on the meaning of this: One should think, "Alas! When the time of death befalls me, none of this life's food, wealth, property, dear friends, servants, and the like will follow me. At that time only the virtuous and sinful deeds that I have done myself will follow me."

One should reflect in detail about these deeds: "The

nonvirtuous deeds arising from the three poisons are such, and among them, the three actions of body are such, the four actions of voice are such and the three actions of mind are such, so there is no chance for any result other than that of going just to the three lower realms. Experiences are similar to their cause — that is, though one is born into the higher realms, one will be short-lived, destitute of wealth, and the like. This is also nothing but suffering, so suffering has not been transcended. Actions similar to their cause are also only sources of suffering from lifetime to lifetime. The result of ownership of nonvirtuous actions is that one must be born into unpleasant and faulty regions. Therefore, nonvirtue is another name for the action of inflicting self-harm, but I have failed to understand this. In this life, I can remember having done many nonvirtuous deeds, and there were also an inconceivable number which were done but are not remembered. Inconceivable also are those deeds which I caused others to do or rejoiced in when committed by others. Even more than that, upon the continuity of my consciousness, there are definitely an inconceivable number of impressions of sins committed in other lifetimes. Therefore, it is sure that I have no other destination but the lower realms. Up to now, by not knowing this, I have caused harm to myself like a madman. Alas, is this mind of mine wrapped in darkness, or has it come under the influence of Māra, or am I a mindless object, or what am I? Alas!" Think thus again and again, and then think, "Now if for the sake of this life, I do not perform even a little nonvirtue, then what to say about doing great nonvirtue?"

In brief, "I must never commit sinful deeds. If, due to ignorance, I happen to commit sins, I must train myself to confess them immediately without remaining associated with the faults for even a single day." Thus think from one's heart.

Concerning virtuous deeds one should think, "Likewise, virtuous actions arising in the absence of the three poisons are such, and among them, the virtuous actions of body, voice, and mind are such." One should think upon each one of these individually in detail. "The ripened result is the body of higher realms; the experience similar to its cause is the prosperity of higher realms, such as longevity and the like; the action similar to its cause is performance of virtues, which is the cause of happiness in all lifetimes; the result of ownership of virtuous actions is a physical world endowed with good qualities."

In brief, "*Virtuous deeds* is just a name for the achievement of benefit and happiness for myself. Therefore the virtues formerly done by me, or those I caused others to do, or those done by others in which I rejoiced, were each well undertaken. Moreover, without despising even small virtues, I must perform virtues devotedly. I must proceed without being overpowered by laziness or tardiness. I must accomplish it just now, and I must do it quickly." Thus think from the bottom of one's heart.

(Concerning neutral deed) one should think, "Likewise, since these present actions of mine, such as moving, walking, sleeping, sitting, and the like are neutral actions which are tiresome and fruitless, I must make an effort to transform whatever I can of these into virtuous actions through skillful means."

In brief, these torments of various sufferings arising since inconceivable lifetimes until now are only a result of the incorrect practice of accepting and rejecting sins and virtues: "Now, if in this short life, where the time of death is unknown, I come under the influence of nonvirtuous and neutral deeds, it is like reaching an island of jewels and returning with some poisonous plants, which is an action that destroys myself. Therefore, in every way, I must abandon nonvirtues, perform virtues, and change neutral acts into virtues without ever coming under the influence of Māra. May the Preceptors see to it that it will happen so." Thus think and offer prayers.

In all the intervals between sessions, contemplate as it was said in the *sPyod.'jug (Bodhicaryāvatāra)*:

> The defining characteristic of protecting
> awareness is in brief, only this: again and
> again to examine the state of body and mind.

Having examined one's own behavior again and again, if the three doors (of body, voice, and mind) are attuned to the teaching, then rejoice and know that it arose through the kindness of the Triple Gem. "It should happen like this in all my lifetimes" — think thus, and to whatever extent one can, increase one's good behavior. If the majority of one's actions are either nonvirtuous or neutral, then one should think, "The reason that I can't gain liberation from this world is because of constantly generating faulty conceptions. If I remain with such a behavior, in my next life there is no certainty I shall be able to gain a higher realm, not to mention liberation and omniscience. Even in this life I will become the laughing stock of gods and worldlings." Produce such thoughts as much as one can.

Moreover, if, motivated by the attainment of fame and gain for this life and hoping to look good in the eyes of others, one's behavior appears to be temporarily beautiful and one appears to be diligent in moral conduct, hearing, and contemplation, then one should think, "What is the use of appearing good in the eyes of others when my practice does not counteract the afflictions? When my practice does counteract the afflictions then even if it is not beautiful, what have I got to lose? If my practice, the antidote, is conquered by the afflictions which are to be rejected, and my religious conduct which is to be guarded is lost, then it is like a medicine that could not be digested and became poison. This kind of verbal and artificial religion can deceive other ordinary beings who are not able to see through it. However, I cannot deceive the Buddhas and Bodhisattvas, who see with unobstructed eyes. They will be displeased with me, and my aims and objectives for generations of lives will be rendered meaningless. If this happens, then there is no greater destruction to myself." Thus think, and recollect all of one's faults as much as one can. As it was said in the *sPyod.'jug (Bodhicaryāvatāra)*,

> "I dwell always before all the Buddhas and
> Bodhisattvas who are endowed with unobstructed
> vision that (penetrates) everywhere." Having
> thought thus, (one should) remain possessed
> of shame, respect, and fear. By that, the
> remembrance of the Enlightened One will also
> arise in one again and again.

Furthermore, one should think, "If I have to follow the advice of a doctor to cure an ordinary disease, then there would be no greater fool than I if I didn't act in accordance with the Buddha's — a doctor to whom there were none prior — instructions of acceptance and rejection while I am in conditions such as suffering from the illness of the afflictions and karma, confined to the bed of worldly existence, and rolling about due to the illness of the three sufferings." Thus one should be diligent in acceptance and rejection. As it was said in the *sPyod.'jug (Bodhicaryāvatāra)*,

> If one must obey the doctor's advice when
> caught by an ordinary illness, then how
> much more so when one is always seized by a
> hundred diseases, such as desire and the like?
>
> If all the people inhabiting this world
> can be destroyed by just one of these,
> and if no other medicine to cure them
> can be found in any quarter,
>
> Then the idea of not acting in accordance
> with the Omniscient Doctor's instructions
> that allay every pain is very ignorant and
> an object of blame.

In brief, the happiness and sufferings of this life and the following ones are entirely dependent upon the actions of virtue and nonvirtue. Therefore, the practice of distinguishing the objects to be accepted and rejected is of utmost importance. As it was said in a *sūtra*,

> These beings are those who are produced and
> sustained by karma, who experience a share of
> karma, and who accept karma as their possession.

Those who are produced and sustained by karma refers to the fact that all good and bad births and places are created by karma. **Those who experience a share of karma** refers to the fact that each happiness and suffering is produced by its individual causal virtue and nonvirtue. **Those who accept karma as their possession** refers to the fact that the creator of karma must experience the results of one's own actions. As it was said in the *mDo.sde las brgya.pa (Karma Śataka)*,

> The Sage taught that the suffering and happiness
> of living beings are the (result of) karma.
> From various types of karma are produced the
> various types of sentient beings who perform
> various (activities, such as) entering and
> wandering in this great net of karma.

It may be asked, "If this is so, then how is it that we see some persons who indulge in nonvirtuous action in this life enjoying great happiness?" This enjoyment of happiness is not the result of deeds in this life, but of virtuous actions in their previous lives, which are ripening here. The result of nonvirtuous actions that one has done in this life will be experienced in the following lives. Furthermore, that some person engaged in great sin enjoys more happiness than other people was taught to be a sign that, because of the power of great sin that one has committed here, the results of all the virtuous actions that one has accumulated in one's previous lives, which were to be experienced in one's future lives, are exhausted merely in the enjoyment of this life. Hereafter one will experience only suffering.

An example is the story of the Nyi.og kingdom. According to the story, it was said that the kingdom of Nyi.og was sinful. A rain of rice and precious jewels occured for seven days each, and finally (for another seven days) there was a rain of sand that submerged it. Similarly, if a practitioner of virtue suffers illness and the like, then this is not the result of the virtuous actions performed in this life, but the remainder of ripened results of nonvirtuous actions of previous lives. That some person engaged in great virtue suffers more than others was taught to be a sign that, because of the power of great virtue that one has committed here, the results of all the nonvirtuous actions that one accumulated in one's previous lives, which were to be experienced in one's future lives, are exhausted merely in the suffering of this life. Hereafter one will not have to experience suffering. As it was said in the *rDo.rje gcod.pa (Vajracchedikā)*,[53]

> Subhūti, noble sons and daughters who memorize the words of a *Sūtra* like this, who retain (its meaning), who keep it, who read and understand it, will suffer, will suffer greatly. If it is asked, why is this so? Subhūti, the afflictions accumulated in their previous lives and which potentially could cause them to gain rebirth in lower realms are experienced in this life, and because of this all their nonvirtuous actions will be exhausted, and they will gain the enlightenment of a Buddha.

Therefore, if a genuine practitioner of the Dharma suffers like that, one should not think, "It is not appropriate that this kind of suffering should happen to me, so there is no truth to the law of cause and effect." Instead, it is reasonable to be happy about it. As it was said in the *sPyod.'jug (Bodhicaryāvatāra)*,

> If a man who was to be executed had his hand
> cut off instead and was released, isn't this
> wonderful? If by human suffering one parts
> from hell, isn't this wonderful?

Therefore, if one has great faith in the law of cause and effect and properly practices acceptance and rejection, it is sure that one will not be reborn in the lower realms. As it was stated by Ācārya Āryadeva,

> For one who is endowed with the great perfect
> view of the world, it will be impossible to be
> born in lower realms even for a thousand aeons.

Up to this point, the teaching which is common to the path of the (Bodhisattva and) Śrāvaka has been shown

The Instructions on the Vision of Experience to Produce Noble Aspirations

This vision of experience is indicated in the *Root Treatise*, where it says, **For the meditator with transic absorption is the vision of experience.** There are two subjects that ascertain its meaning: (A) Meditate until the common experience arises in one's mindstream, and then (B) Meditate happiness at this time, thinking, "I will gain an extraordinary experience in the Vajrayāna path."

Meditate Until the Common Experience Arises in One's Mindstream

For the common practitioner with the common transic absorption is the vision of the common experience. The common practitioner is a person who practices the Perfections and the common path. The common transic absorption consists of loving kindness, compassion, and the enlightened thought. The vision of common experience is the practice which generates a pure and uncontrived wish to selflessly undertake the benefit and happiness of sentient beings throughout space. The method to gain such a wish is (1) to meditate on loving kindness, which is the desire to benefit other beings; (2) to meditate on compassion, which is the desire to destroy the suffering of others; and (3) to meditate on the thought of enlightenment, which is the desire to gain Buddhahood for the sake of others.

Loving Kindness, the Desire to Benefit Other Beings

One may ask "Well then, since the nature of worldly existence is suffering, if, having discarded it, one gains the Nirvāṇa of the

Śrāvakas and Pratyekabuddhas whose body is without substratum, which is a state where there is no suffering, like a fire that has exhausted its fuel, then shouldn't we strive to gain such a state?" It is not like that. From beginningless time one has been disregarding all sentient beings who have been one's kind mother by striving to gain the happiness of liberation for oneself alone. This is like a mother being carried away by a river while her son happily remains indifferent on the dry bank, though he has the means to rescue her. Through being ignorant of kindness, one would be ashamed and one would become the laughing stock of others. As it was said in the *sLob.spring (Śiṣhyalekha)*,

> Kinsmen caught in the ocean of worldly
> existence appear like falling into a
> whirlpool, but one fails to recognize
> them because of the change of birth and
> death. Having left them behind, if one
> strives to save oneself, then wouldn't
> this be most shameful? A son or daughter,
> no matter how wicked, here would not enjoy
> discarding their mother sentient beings
> who lovingly breastfed them while being
> helpless on their laps and who reared them
> with great love and many hardships.

Also, as Jetsun (Dakpa Gyaltshen) said in a song,

> There is no benefit in liberating myself alone,
> since beings of the three worlds are my parents.
> Leaving such parents in the midst of suffering and
> desiring happiness only for myself is shameful.

It may then be asked, "Even though that be the case, since love for oneself is greater than that for others, since one's life is short and the hour of death is uncertain, and since the opportunity to obtain a human body endowed with the prerequisites is very rare, wouldn't it be reasonable to strive for the method of self-liberation from this world?" But it is not like that. The enlightenment of Śrāvakas and Pratyekabuddhas is incomplete because it fails to accomplish the perfect qualities of realization and abandonment for the purpose of self, and lacks the vast activities that benefit the purpose of others. It is like bad workmanship that is hard to correct, and ultimately it will take a long time to gain Buddhahood. Therefore, it is not an object for which intelligent persons should strive.

Furthermore, having discarded the opportunity to obtain the excellent essence (of supreme enlightenment) based on the body endowed with the prerequisites, those who strive for inferior liberation would be counted among the great fools. Though one may think that it is difficult to practice the Mahāyāna path, it is just the same with the Hīnayāna. It is not hard to practice the Mahāyāna path, because the vehicle in which one travels and the path are very comfortable and easy. All sentient beings are friends who assist one to practice the path, because sentient beings who are without happiness are friends on whom to practice loving kindness, sentient beings who are suffering are friends on whom to practice compassion, sentient beings who are poor are friends on whom to practice giving, and sentient beings who harm one are friends on whom to practice patience. Therefore, just as the Buddhas are the indicators of the path, so sentient beings are the friends who help in the practice of enlightenment. Hence one should treat sentient beings with great respect, just like one treats the Buddhas. As it was said in the *sPyod.'jug (Bodhicaryāvatāra)*,

> Inasmuch as qualities of Buddhahood are obtained
> from sentient beings and the Conquerors alike,
> so whose system is this that maintains devotion
> to the Buddhas and not toward sentient beings?

For these reasons, one should love sentient beings like a mother loves her children, and one should diligently practice loving-kindness meditation from the bottom of one's heart with the desire that all sentient beings gain happiness.

The benefits of meditating on loving kindness are that one accumulates greater merit by meditating on loving kindness for sentient beings for a moment than by making a daily offering of one trillion Buddha fields filled with offerings to the Buddha. As it was said in the *zla.ba sgron.ma'i mdo. (Candradīpa sūtra)*,

> There is no match in the quantity and percentage
> (of merit gained) between offering inconceivable
> offerings that fill a trillion Buddha fields offered
> daily to the Excellent Beings and a thought of love.

The reason for this is that if one harms or helps a being, one is harming or helping the Buddha; sentient beings are possessed by the Buddha; and sentient beings naturally possess the essence of Buddha. As it was said in the *sPyod.'jug (Bodhicaryāvatāra)*,

> The Sages are joyful by the happiness of those
> (beings), and they are displeased if harm is
> done to beings. Through the happiness of those
> (beings), all of the Sages are gladdened, and
> harm done to them is harm done to the Sages.
>
> Even though throngs of beings may kick my
> head or even kill me, I shall not respond.
> May the Lords of the World rejoice!
>
> The Compassionate Ones have made all these
> beings their own, of this there is no doubt.
> These very ones who are seen in the disguise
> of beings are by their very nature the Lord
> (Buddha). Why then do I not honor them?

The nature of loving kindness is as follows. One's perception is directed toward the object, sentient beings, through the manner of desiring that they be possessed of happiness and the cause of happiness. As it was said by Ācārya Candrakīrti: (in the *Madhyamakāvatāra*),

> One who engages in work for the welfare of
> living beings is called greatly compassionate.

To meditate on loving kindness, one should begin by meditating on loving kindness for one's relatives, because it is easier to produce loving kindness toward them. In the middle, one should meditate on loving kindness for one's enemies, because it is more difficult to generate it toward them. Finally, one should meditate on loving kindness for all sentient beings.

First, one should meditate on (a) loving kindness for one's mother; then one should (b) merge that meditation with other relatives; and finally one should (c) merge that meditation with ordinary beings.

Loving Kindness for One's Mother
To meditate upon one's mother, one should 1. think of one's mother, 2. think of her kindness, and 3. think of the need to repay her kindness.

1. Think of one's mother: Regardless whether this life's mother be alive or dead, one should generate the thought in one's mind about one's mother's appearance, such as her face, complexion, and the like, just as she is (or was), while remembering the manner in which she loved and cherished one. One should intensely think, "This is my kind mother."

2. Think of her kindness: (a) think of her kindness in giving one one's body and life; (b) think of her kindness in giving instructions of acceptance and rejection; and (c) think of her kindness in bearing hardship in order to bring one up.

a) Think of her kindness in giving one one's body and life: (Concerning the gift of one's body), one should think, "This mother held me for nine full months in her womb. She relied upon food and conduct that would be beneficial for me. She avoided food and conduct that could have been harmful to me. Thus she produced this body of mine endowed with the prerequisites. So, this mother is of great kindness to me."

To think of her kindness in giving one life, one should think, "Having been born, my body was incapable of helping myself, my voice was incapable of communicating, my mind was incapable of differentiating between what to reject and accept, so I was helpless like a worm. In such a state, my mother did not let me die, but cherished me with a very loving mind, looked upon me with loving eyes, called me by sweet names, and gathered me up with her five fingers. Food was given from her mouth, she cleaned my dirt with her hands, warmed me with the warmth of her body, fed me with sweet milk, protected me from fire, water, and cliffs, and guarded me from the harms of heat and cold. She could not bear to be separated from me even for a moment and she nursed me with a love as great as that with which she would take care of her heart if it were to fall out."

b) Think of her kindness in giving instructions of acceptance and rejection: One should think, "When I was completely ignorant, she taught me the way to eat and drink, the way to walk and sit, and the way to communicate. She introduced me to all the names and labels of big and small entities. So my mother was very kind in teaching me inconceivable objects of acceptance and rejection."

c) Think of her kindness in bearing hardships in order to bring one up: One should think, "Without regard for her own health and welfare, my mother always worried that I might get sick, die, or not be equal to other children. In regard to this, she did more than one could describe, such as seeking predictions, consulting astrology, calling doctors, performing rituals, and the like. In order to take care of me, she had no leisure time during the day, no sleep at night, and she worked so hard that her hands and feet cracked. Considering the food and wealth she had too dear to be enjoyed by herself, too dear to give to others, to dear to spend on herself in this life, too dear to spend for her next life, she spent for my sake without the slightest regret. Moreover, she considered this a great accomplishment of her wishes. Had she the right to offer me the emperorship of a universal kingdom, she wouldn't have thought it to be very great. She always worried about my well-being; I was the only object of her thought and meditation. She's the kind mother who took greater care of me than of herself. Not only that, but in this world of sentient beings, it is difficult to hear even the name of the Triple Gem. Beyond that, if one practices the holy Dharma, one will have physical happiness in this life, mental happiness in the intermediate state, a pleasant path in the next life, and will go from happiness to happiness in every lifetime. That I have such an opportunity is due only to this mother's kindness."

Also think, "Not only in this life but since beginningless time until now, she has been my mother again and again. Each time, the way she nourished me with this type of kindness is incommensurable. Countless times, she was born in a poor family and nourished me with food and clothing by begging from others. Countless times she was born as a fisherman or hunter and fed me with food obtained sinfully. Countless times she was born as an animal and gave up her life through protecting me from harm. If I were to collect all the milk that I have drunk from her breast, it would equal the outer ocean. Countless times she has also been my father and has provided food, clothing, wealth, and the like. She has also been born as my close and distant relatives and has showed mutual, inseperable, heartfelt love. Were I to collect all the tears she has shed for me, they would equal the outer ocean. Even if I narrated for aeons how she had been kind and helpful, I would not be able to recount it all. Even if I filled the whole world with gold and gave it to her, still it would would not be enough to repay my debt of her kindness." As it was said in a *sūtra*,

> Even the water of the four oceans is not equal
> to the quantity of milk I have drunk from
> someone who has been my mother (countless times).

> Even the gifts of horses and elephants I
> have received from someone who has been
> my father (countless times) would exceed
> (the height) of the world of Brahma. Other
> living beings have also been like that.

3. Think of the need to repay her kindness: One should think, "If I don't repay the kindness of this mother to whom I owe an inconceivable debt of gratitude, then wouldn't I be the most wicked person? I shall try my best to repay her kindness by kindness and her benefit by benefit. What would be most beneficial for her? She would be most benefited if she were endowed with happiness and the cause of happiness, of which right now she is lacking. Therefore, how wonderful it would be if my mother were endowed with happiness and the cause of happiness." Thus generate such a thought, which is associated with a wish.

Further, one should think, "I will make her gain that condition of happiness and the cause of happiness." Thus generate such a thought, which is associated with the enlightenment thought.

Again one should think, "May it happen like that" (i.e., that she be endowed with happiness and the cause of happiness). Thus generate such a thought, which is associated with a prayer. One should meditate upon whichever of these three is more agreeable to one's mind.

Finally, one should think, "I don't have the power to make my mother happy and enable her to have the cause of happiness. Who has such power? Only the Preceptor and the Triple Gem have such power." Just as a crippled mother whose son is being carried away by water yells for help from others, so one should meditate and pray, "May the Preceptor and Triple Gem see to it that my mother has happiness and the cause of happiness." Through practicing in this way, one will be able to generate genuine and natural love for one's mother.

Merge that Meditation with Other Relatives

One should bring to mind, by stages, other relatives who have been most kind to oneself, such as one's father and so on. One should recollect each of their kindnesses, "They have manifested kindness in this life through taking care of me in ways like this and like that. In many lifetimes, they have been my parents and have been helpful in protecting me from harm. Therefore, they were very kind to me." To think of the need to repay their kindness, one should apply the same thoughts as those applied to one's mother and meditate until one gains a love for them that is undifferentiated from the love one has for one's real mother.

Merge that Meditation with Ordinary Beings[54]

Merging the meditation on loving kindness for one's mother and other relatives with the meditation on loving kindness for ordinary beings has three parts: (1) meditating on neighbors and the like, (2) meditating on one's enemies, and (3) meditating on all sentient beings.

1. Meditate on neighbors and the like: One should bring to mind neighbors and others with whom one has a relation of food and wealth, and think, "In this life they have benefited me like this, and indirectly they have been my parents many times in my previous lives." Thus apply (one's thoughts to them), as previously done to one's mother, and meditate.

2. Meditate on one's enemies: The way to extend the meditation on loving kindness to one's enemies is to bring to mind those who have caused one harm — the objects of one's hatred, such as enemies, evil spirits, and the like — and think, "This enemy has been my mother many times in previous lives, and each time she had been of great benefit to me and protected me from harms. Although this enemy has been very kind (in the past), I failed to repay his kindness by kindness and his benefit by benefit. Therefore, I perceive these beings who pressure me to repay the debts of previous lives as enemies and ghosts, just as a debtor perceives his creditors to be abusive when being pressured to repay his debts. Since both our minds are obscured by karma, the afflictions, and the change of birth and death, we don't recognize each other but see each other as the doer of harm and the recipient of harm. Our minds are deluded in this way. Though we are actually very close relatives, we are without free will and harm each other. For this reason, the gap created between us has become wider and wider." As the Lord of Yogīs (Virūpa) said,

> Though these harmers were my beloved mothers and
> benefited me again and again many times in my
> past lives, (now), like one who is mad, without
> free will, (they) perform deeds of nonvirtue by
> which (they will be born) in the Ceaseless Hell.

One should think, "Therefore, not only has this enemy benefited me many times in my past lives but even now he is helping me through destroying my pride and encouraging me to practice the Dharma at this time, when my mind is fully polluted with pride and false assumptions and my behavior wild, unreligious, and the like. He has been very kind in benefiting me in many different ways." Without mere pretense, one should feel this from the bottom of one's heart. One should meditate on the mind that produces the desire to repay kindness and so on, as explained earlier. As it was said in a scripture,

> Whoever perceives objects that produce
> the afflictions — whether they be

friends or enemies — as spiritual friends,
will be happy wherever one may abide.

If, even though one meditates like this, one fails to produce loving kindness but repeatedly produces anger and desire to harm the enemy, then one should recollect the results of the fault of hatred, as already explained in the section on cause and effect. Thus one should think, "If I can't subdue my hatred, then even though I may have subdued the outer enemy once, I will not have the chance to do so again. If I could subdue hatred itself, then all the outer enemies would disappear." As it was said in the *sPyod.'jug (Bodhicaryāvatāra)*,

> I cannot kill all the wicked beings
> who are like the sky, yet if I slay
> only this thought of anger, all those
> forces are destroyed. How can enough
> leather be obtained to cover the surface
> of this land? Yet, by simply covering
> the soles of the shoes with leather,
> all these lands are as if covered.

One should recollect the meaning of verses such as these.

3. Meditate on all sentient beings: To extend loving kindness to all sentient beings, remember that, as it was said in the *bZang.spyod (Bhadracaryā)*,[55]

> As far as the limit of space,
> so is the limit of sentient beings.

Thus think, "Since space has no limit, so sentient beings are limitless. Even among the countless sentient beings, there is not a single sentient being who hasn't once become my mother. They have all been my parents on many occasions, and each time they have been extremely kind by protecting me from harm. Still I cannot recognize that they were my parents because my mind is obscured by karma, the afflictions, and the change of birth and death. Right now my indifference toward them is not good, so I should repay these kind beings' kindness by kindness and their benefit by benefit as much as I can. What would be most beneficial to these mother sentient beings?" One should meditate and apply the same procedure as for one's present mother. If it is difficult to produce (loving kindness to all sentient beings at one time), then one should think first of hell beings and then, by stages, of all the other beings of the six realms. One should think, "My wish would be accomplished were each sentient being to be endowed with happiness and the cause of happiness." Thus meditate along with a wish, the enlightenment thought, and a prayer. Having meditated in this way, should one produce an uncontrived desire to benefit sentient beings who pervade space, then one's meditation of loving kindness has been accomplished. As it was said in the *mDo.sde rgyan (Sūtrālankāra)*,

> Just as (parents) love their only child,
> so Bodhisattvas who greatly love sentient
> beings from the bottom of their hearts
> always desire to benefit them.

To reflect on the meaning of this, bring one's mother to mind and think, "Alas, this is my mother who has been very kind and dear to me. First, she gave me this beloved body, then she gave me dear life, and lastly she gave me her precious wealth without regret. She enlightened me regarding rejection and acceptance when I was completely ignorant. She made me hear what I had not heard. She made me understand what I had not understood. She made me acquire things I did not have. She made me equal to others when I was not. She matched me with others to whom I was not matched." Thus one should recollect all the things that are explained above. Moreover, if anyone has any other kind (of example), then consider it and think, "Thus she is my kind mother."

One should think from the depths of one's heart, in brief, "It is due only to the kindness of this beloved mother that I could ever become a fully enlightened Buddha should I practice. Not only that, but she has been my mother many times in my past lives. Each time, like my present mother, she was very kind by protecting me from harm and benefiting me. If I couldn't repay her kindness with greater kindness, there would be no one more vile than me. I need to repay her kindness by kindness and her benefit by benefit. What would be most beneficial to my mother? Temporarily she would be benefited by a healthy body and mind, and for a long term she would be benefited were she endowed with virtue, the cause of happiness. However, right now, she is without happiness and is moving in the opposite direction of the cause of happiness. How greatly I wish that she might be temporarily healthy and happy and endowed with virtue, the cause of happiness, for the long term." Thus one should meditate on this along with a wish, the enlightenment thought, and a prayer, and merge it with whichever of these three is strongest.

Finally, one should pray as if words of lamentation are being drawn from one's heart: "Although I need to place my mother in the state of happiness and provide her with the cause of happiness, I do not have the power to do so. Therefore, may the Preceptor and Triple Gem see to it that she obtains happiness and the cause of happiness." Until weariness reaches to the bones and flesh, meditate: "Were it that my kind mother be happy, blissful, endowed with an abundance of resources, and engaged in the conduct of virtuous actions." If one gains an experience of practice, then one should not prevent the flow of this experience.

Similarly, bringing to mind the kindness of one's father, one should think, "This is my kind father. Other than not holding me in his stomach and feeding me with his breast, he had been as kind to me as my mother. There wasn't even a slight difference between him and my mother in the way they brought me up. He has been my parent countless times in previous lifetimes. Each of those times he has been kind and helpful by giving me as much happiness and welfare as my present father." Thus one should meditate as explained above.

Likewise, in regard to other relatives and ordinary beings, think, "In this life they have been kind to me in this and that way. Also, indirectly, they have been my parents many times in my previous lives." In this way, recollect the kindness and helpfulness that they gave, and then meditate on loving kindness.

Likewise, in regard to enemies or ghosts, one should think, "Many times in my past lives this enemy or ghost has been my kind parent. Not having repaid his kindness by kindness and his benefit by benefit, I see him as an enemy or ghost who now only wishes to be repaid the debt I owe him. Presently appearing as enemies, they are helping me by criticizing my misconduct that goes contrary to the Dharma. Appearing as ghosts, they are helping me by encouraging my three doors (of body, voice, and mind) to perform virtuous actions. Directly and indirectly, they have been very kind and helpful in many ways." Thus one should meditate as described above.

If it is difficult to generate loving kindness and one gets angrier, then one should think that the meditation on loving kindness is the only means to gain enlightenment for oneself. Through meditating on loving kindness, how much benefit can there be for the enemy? One should think, "Presently, I cannot bear even the slightest suffering of body and mind, yet I continue to accumulate karma by which in my future lives I will certainly fall into the abyss of the lower realms from which there is no escape. So, who would be a greater fool among Mahāyāna practitioners than I? Through harming myself, how can it harm my enemy?" One should thus meditate and feel ashamed of oneself.

In that way, one should classify each of the other six realms and bring them to mind by thinking, " Since beginningless time I have been born again and again in all the higher and lower realms and have heen roaming again and again until there is no place left where I haven't been born. Also, there is no sentient being who hasn't been my mother limitless, countless times. Each of those times, she gave me a body, food, wealth, and benefit, and destroyed what was harmful. Even at the hour of parting, she was kind and dear to me." Thus apply the same meditation, as explained above.

One should meditate and think until one gains uncontrived love for all sentient beings. In between meditation sessions, one should abandon anger toward any sentient being and should look upon them affectionately, as a loving mother looks upon her cherished son. To those who are endangered through fear, one should give fearlessness and help by saving lives and the like. To those who are destitute and without protection, one should give food, shelter, and the like, and converse with them in a gentle and pleasing voice. For those who are in the realm of animals, one should recite into their ears the names of Buddhas and mantras.

In brief, the root of Mahāyāna practice is loving kindness. If one is able to produce loving kindness, then it is easy to generate compassion. Therefore, one should be careful and diligent in the meditation of loving kindness. As it was said in the *mDo.sde rgyan (Sūtrālankāra)*,

> (The water of) compassion (courses
> through) the canal of loving kindness.

Compassion, the Desire to Destroy the Suffering of Others

The benefits of compassion are described in the *Chos yang.dag. par sdud.pa'i mdo (Dharma samgīti sūtra)*:[56]

> Avalokiteśvara said, O Vanquisher, one who
> desires to gain Buddhahood does not need to
> be trained in many teachings, but should be
> trained in one teaching. If asked, "What
> is that?" It is great compassion. It is
> like this, Vanquisher: wherever the precious
> wheel of the universal emperor exists, at that
> place the seven precious articles (of the king)
> exist also. Vanquisher, like that, wherever
> the great compassion of a Bodhisattva exists,
> there exist all the teachings of the Buddha.

Therefore the entire root of the Mahāyāna path is compassion. As it was said in the *mDo.sde rgyan (Sūtrālankāra)*:

> First of all, the root, and then the excellent
> result — this is the great tree of compassion.
> If there is no root, compassion,
> one will not be able to bear asceticism.

Also, it was said (in another part of this same text),

> Great compassion is the source of many good qualities,
> so who would not produce compassion toward sentient
> beings? Even though one suffers for their sake,
> the joy originating from compassion is measureless.

The compassion endowed with such benefits are of three types: (a) compassion in reference to sentient beings, (b) compassion in reference to the Dharma, and (c) compassion in reference to no object.

Compassion in Reference to Sentient Beings

Having directed one's mind to the suffering sentient beings, one wishes that they be separated from suffering. As it was said by Candrakīrti,

> One who completely protects suffering
> sentient beings is called "greatly compassionate".

The manner to meditate upon this is to bring one's mother to mind and recollect her kindness, her being one's mother in many lives, and so on, as explained above. Then think, "For the reason of having worked and worked for me, she has been roaming in this world without free will and has experienced great torment. This is pitiful. I need to repay her kindness by kindness and her benefit by benefit. What would be most beneficial to her? She can be benefited directly by being separated from suffering, and indirectly she can be benefited by being separated from the cause of suffering. However, at the present time, having gone in a completely opposite direction, she is experiencing suffering manifestly in this life, and through enjoying great nonvirtue she is producing the cause of suffering. This is pitiful."

In association with a wish, one should think, "How greatly I wish that she be free from suffering and from the cause of suffering." In association with the enlightenment thought, one should think, "I will make her gain the state (that is free from suffering and from its cause)." In association with a prayer, one should think, "May she part from suffering and from its cause." In conclusion of practicing any of these three, one should pray, "May the Preceptor and Triple Gem see to it that it happens so."

Likewise, one should meditate on compassion for one's relatives, such as one's father and the like, and for other ordinary beings who are manifestly experiencing the torments of various sufferings and are engaged in nonvirtue, the cause of suffering. Thus feel compassion and meditate as explained above.

To meditate on compassion for one's enemies, think that, "These enemies have been my mother many times, and each time they have been very kind by benefiting me and protecting me from harm." Thus apply the same procedure as explained above. Then, one should think, "Though he is harming me, I feel compassion for him, because his mind is now deluded and he has failed to recognize me (as his son)." As it is said in a scripture,

> Though one is harmed as a repayment of kindness,
> even then meditate on great compassion in return;
> the noble beings of this world
> reciprocate harm with great compassion.

Along with compassion, one should think, "Not only that but, not having obtained control over their own minds, their harming of others will cause them the need to experience the suffering of the Unceasing Hell." As it was said by the Lord of Yogīs (Virūpa),

> Meditate on compassion to the kind beings who
> brought you up with love since beginningless
> time; although they benefited you again and
> again, they are, like madmen without free will,
> committing nonvirtuous actions (as a result of
> which) they will suffer in the Unceasing Hell.
> If you understand it like that, you will be
> able to accomplish the meditation on compassion
> for sentient beings.

Likewise, bring to mind the categories of the six realms and their individual sufferings. In the same procedure as above, consider how each of them acted as one's mother and brought one up with kindness, and generate the desire to repay their kindness. One should produce an uncontrived joy in one's mind, as if they were free from suffering and the cause of suffering.

Compassion in Reference to Dharma
Having directed one's thought to the suffering and the ignorance — the cause of suffering — of sentient beings, one meditates in the manner of desiring to free them from suffering and ignorance, the cause of suffering. The reason for this is that until ignorance, the cause of suffering, is discarded, the result of suffering cannot be relinquished. As it was said in the *rNam.'grel (Pramāṇavārttika)*,[57]

> The root of all faults is ignorance,
> and that (ignorance) is the view that
> perishable entities (are truly existent).

Further, it was said in the *sPyod.'jug (Bodhicaryāvatāra)*,

> Although beings have the wish to discard suffering,
> they run for it (unknowingly); even though
> they desire happiness, because of ignorance,
> they destroy their happiness like a foe.

One should think, "Since that suffering also arises from the cause of karma and afflictions, which in turn originate from ignorance, it is pitiful that sentient beings are endowed with ignorance."

Compassion in Reference to No Object
Even though sentient beings do not exist in their own essence, they are tightly bound by self-grasping, the cause of suffering. Having directed one's thought to this, one meditates in the manner of desiring to free them from suffering and self-grasping, the cause of suffering. As it was said in the *sPyod.'jug (Bodhicaryāvatāra)*,

> Beings are like a dream, and if examined,
> they are like a water reed.

Again, it was said in the *sPyod.'jug (Bodhicaryāvatāra)*,

> If it were asked, "If there is no sentient being
> (in ultimate truth), then on whom should one

(meditate) compassion?" For the sake of a result,
one accepts that which is labeled through
ignorance (as the object of meditation).

One should think, "Therefore, even though in their essence all sentient beings do not exist, they fail to understand (their true nature) and are strongly bound by self-grasping. These beings are pitiful." For this reason, as long as one has self-grasping, one is bound to take birth in this world again and again through the power of karma and the afflictions. As it was said in the *'Jug.pa (Madhyamakāvatāra)*,

> As long as one has grasping at the aggregates,
> one will have grasping at a self.
> If one grasps at a self, karma (is produced),
> and by karma, birth (into this world) is produced.

Contemplate the meaning of this by thinking, "Alas! My kind mother has helped me and benefited me at this time in such ways, and she has indirectly been my kind mother since countless aeons. She benefited and protected me from harm each time. Having constantly worked for my welfare, she has been unable to escape from this world of existence and has become worn out by a variety of sufferings. This is pitiful. Right now, this mother is experiencing suffering against her wishes. Since she is not skilled in the methods for discarding suffering, she is engaged in and enjoying the cause of suffering. This is pitiful. How greatly I wish that she be separated from suffering and the cause of suffering." Thus think from the bottom of one's heart. Meditate upon this in association with a wish, the enlightenment thought, or a prayer — whichever of these is more conducive.

One should produce in one's mind the unbearable feeling of one's mother's suffering having fallen upon oneself. One should think, "Though she is now worn out by the sufferings of this world, still she is accumulating karma and the afflictions, which are the cause of suffering. How awful! What a grave mistake it is for her. This is pitiful! Although I need to place her in a state free from suffering and the cause of suffering, no one other than the

Preceptor and Triple Gem has the power to do it. So, may the Preceptor and the Triple Gem see to it that my mother becomes free from suffering and the cause of suffering." Thus one should pray.

Likewise, one should meditate by applying the same procedure to one's father and other relatives. Especially, one should meditate on compassion for one's enemy for a long time. Similarly, one should think, "It is greatly pitiful that these hell beings, who have been my kind mother, are suffering in the hot and cold hells and are worn out by experiencing suffering." Thus produce in one's mind the unbearable feeling that the suffering of the hell beings has fallen upon oneself, and meditate.

Likewise, one should meditate by applying the same procedure to hungry ghosts, and so on. When one has produced an uncontrived desire to free them from suffering, one feels compassion for sentient beings who are endowed with suffering and ignorance, the cause of suffering, because suffering and the cause of suffering originated from karma and the afflictions, and these two themselves arose from ignorance. One should meditate by thinking, "May these beings be freed from suffering and ignorance, the cause of suffering." That ignorance also originated from self-grasping at an "I", so that even though sentient beings do not exist in their own essence, still they fail to understand this and are tightly bound by the grasping mind. This is pitiful. One should meditate by thinking, "May these sentient beings part from suffering and self-grasping at an 'I', the cause of suffering."

Between sessions, one should continually meditate on compassion by focusing the mind, especially upon enemies and the like, for whom it is hard to generate compassion; upon malicious spirits and the like, whose mind are under the power of delusion; upon kings, hunters and the like, who commit great sins; and upon destitute, poor, sick, and protectorless beings, thinking, "May I be helpful in dispelling the suffering of sentient beings. If I cannot dispel their suffering, may I help by sharing their suffering." In this way one should think by what method one could liberate them from suffering. One should train in the methods by which one does not abandon sentient beings.

The Enlightenment Thought, the Desire to Gain Buddhahood for the Sake of Others

It may be asked, "Well then, is it possible to gain full and perfect enlightenment just by abandoning sinful actions and practicing virtues, by meditating on loving kindness which desires to benefit others, and by meditating on compassion which desires to dispel the suffering of others?" Though these practices are needed in assisting one to accomplish the unsurpassable enlightenment, but through them alone one will not be able to obtain enlightenment. For example, if one doesn't cut the root of a plant, no matter how many times one cuts off the leaves and branches, they will grow back again. Likewise, if one doesn't cut off the root of worldly existence, — self-grasping, — one should forget about enlightenment, because the suffering of worldly existence arises from karma, karma arises from the afflictions, and the afflictions arises from self-grasping. As it was said in the *sPyod.'jug (Bodhicaryāvatāra)*,

> Whatever harm exists in this world,
> and however much fear and suffering may exist,
> if all of these originate from self-grasping,
> then of what use is this "great ghost" for me?
> If one does not completely abandon that self-grasping,
> one will not be able to get rid of suffering;
> likewise if one does not eliminate the fire,
> one won't be able to free oneself from burning.

It may be asked, "How do the afflictions arise from self-grasping?" Being under the sway of complete ignorance of one's own nature, just as one mistakes a colored rope for a snake, so one holds a "self" and an "I" where there is no "self" and "I." Therefore, there arises the grasping at the thought, "I", which is imputed upon a baseless object. Due to this, in relation to that "I" there arises the grasping of "others." In this way, one has attachment to self, hatred toward others, and ignorance of one's own nature. So based upon the accumulation of deeds (or karma), which are motivated by the three poisons, one gains this chain of births in the world of existence, and having taken birth here, all faults arise. As it was said in the *rNam.'grel (Pramāṇavārttika)*,

> If there is a "self," then one knows "other";
> from the aspects of a "self" and "other"
> originate attachment and hatred; through the
> complete relation of these two originate all faults.

Therefore, the root of all faults of worldly existence is self-grasping. The intelligent, wise ones who care for their own well-being should look upon self-grasping as an enemy and should diligently meditate on the two enlightenment thoughts in order to subdue it. Through meditating on them, the relative enlightenment thought restrains self-grasping and the ultimate enlightenment thought is able to extract self-grasping from its root. As it was said in the *rNam.'grel (Pramāṇavārttika)*,

> Loving kindness, and the like,
> do not oppose ignorance, so they
> cannot destroy the great faults.

Also, it was said,

> Since (ignorance) contradicts the view of emptiness,
> all faults, the nature of (self-grasping),
> are established in contradiction to the (view of emptiness).

Therefore, meditation on the enlightenment thought has inconceivable benefit. As it was said in the *dpa'.byin gyis zhus.pa'i.mdo (Vīradatta paripṛccha sūtra)*,[58]

> If whatever merit (arising from)
> the enlightenment thought had form, it
> would fill and even surpass all of space.

Further, it was said in the *sPyod.'jug (Bodhicaryāvatāra)*,

> Even a wretch, a prisoner bound by worldly
> existence, becomes acknowledged as a son of
> the Sugata at the moment of his producing the

enlightenment thought, and he becomes worthy
of salutation by the worlds of gods and men.

Thus, if one produces the thought of enlightenment, one's name and purpose are both changed. As it was said in the *sPyod.'jug (Bodhicaryāvatāra)*,

> Like the philosopher's stone, the excellent
> (thought of enlightenment) transforms
> this impure body which one has taken into
> the priceless jewel of a Buddha's body.
> Therefore, firmly take hold of that which
> is known as the thought of enlightenment.

Thus the enlightenment thought is like the philosopher's stone that transforms a wretched body into an excellent form. Further, it was said in the *sPyod.'jug (Bodhicaryāvatāra)*,

> The measureless knowledge of the holy navigator
> of sentient beings has examined well this
> priceless jewel (of the enlightenment thought).
> Those who desire to part from the world should firmly
> take hold of the jewel of the thought of enlightenment.

Thus this thought of enlightenment is difficult to gain, but it is of great benefit, like a wish-fulfilling jewel. As it was said in the *sPyod.'jug (Bodhicaryāvatāra)*,

> All other virtues are similar to the plantain tree,
> having produced the fruit, it perishes.
> The tree of the enlightenment thought perpetually
> produces fruits which increase endlessly.

Thus it is like the wish-fulfilling tree, which produces only excellent fruit. Further, it was said in the *sPyod.'jug (Bodhicaryāvatāra)*,

> Even if one has committed very terrible sins,
> like a frightened person relying upon a brave man,
> one will quickly be liberated by relying upon that

(enlightenment thought). So why don't heedful people rely upon that (enlightenment thought)?

Thus it overcomes sins which are sure (to produce results) just as a brave general (overcomes enemies). As it was said in the sPyod.'jug (Bodhicaryāvatāra),

> Like the fire at the end of an aeon,
> it surely burns away great sins in a moment's time.

Thus the enlightenment thought is like the fire at the end of an aeon which burns all the sins of unsure (results) from their very roots. Since the benefit of it is said to be inconceivable, in the world of gods and humans there is no teaching superior to this thought of enlightenment.

The characteristic of the thought of enlightenment which is endowed with such benefits is "an extraordinary practice of gaining perfect enlightenment." Being uncommon, this (extraordinary practice) excludes both the worldly mind and personal liberation (Nirvāna). Therefore, it is established that the enlightenment thought is the thought of nonresiding Nirvāṇa (of the Mahāyāna):

> Since "extraordinary practice" is the practice
> which is labeled as the goal to be accomplished,
> there is no fault in its referring to the
> enlightenment thought devoid of obscurations.

Thus it was explained by the Sakya Pandita.

In this way, the obtaining of the enlightenment thought through a ritual is called the "Creation of the Enlightenment Thought." If that enlightenment thought is endowed with the intention of constantly discarding its opposite, it becomes the vows of the enlightenment thought. If differentiated from the point of view of object, there are two enlightenment thoughts, the relative and the ultimate; from the point of view of the manner of its creation it is twofold, through words and through realization of the ultimate truth; from the point of view of its nature it is twofold, wishing and entering; from the point of view of its stages[59] it is fourfold, i.e., obtained through an intention, pure aspiration, full ripening, and devoid of obscurations; from the example point of view, it has twenty-two, beginning with the example of "like the earth" until that of "like a cloud"; and from the assistant point of view, it is composed of twenty-two different views, beginning with "endowed with intention" until that of "endowed with the body of reality (Dharmakāya)".[60]

Having understood its general explanation, the actual practice of the enlightenment thought consists of cultivating: (a) the wishing enlightenment thought, which is the desire for the result for the sake of others, (b) the entering enlightenment thought, which is the training on the path for the sake of the result, and (c) the ultimate enlightenment thought, which is the combination of calm abiding and insight wisdom.

The Wishing Enlightenment Thought, the Desire for the Result for the Sake of Others

The essence of the wishing enlightenment thought is the thought which desires perfect enlightenment for the sake of others. It was said by Maitreyanātha,

> The creation of the enlightenment thought
> is the desire for full and perfect
> enlightenment for the sake of others.

To create such a wishing enlightenment thought is of inconceivable benefit. As it was said in the *sPyod.'jug (Bodhicaryāvatāra)*,

> If just the thought, "May the brain diseases of
> sentient beings be dispelled" is of such a beneficial
> intention that one could gain immeasurable merit,
> then what need to say of one who wishes that each
> sentient being dispel immeasurable unhappiness
> and that each of them accomplish boundless qualities?

Therefore, the creation of the wishing enlightenment thought is very rare, but having generated it, one becomes endowed with inconceivable benefits. As it was said in the *sPyod.'jug (Bodhicaryāvatāra)*,

> Has either a father or a mother a thought so
> beneficial like this? Do the gods, hermits or
> even Brahma have this (beneficial thought)?
> If those sentient beings never dreamed before of such
> a (beneficial) thought even for themselves in a dream,
> how could they generate it for the sake of others?

This being the case, it may then be asked, "What is the cause that produces the enlightenment thought?" (The answer is that) it arises from great compassion. As it was said in the *Byang.chub sems.dpa'i sde.snod (Bodhisattva piṭaka)*,[61]

> Great compassion is that which precedes the
> strong desire for enlightenment by the Bodhisattva.

Hence, if one does not have the cause, compassion, then there will not arise the result, the enlightenment thought. Since compassion is rooted in loving kindness, one should produce uncontrived loving kindness and compassion in one's mindstream. So, if one produces the desire that sentient beings, the object of one's meditation, be endowed with happiness and be parted from suffering, then produce the uncontrived thought, "It is my duty to place all these sentient beings in the state of happiness and liberate them from suffering. Although I'd love to do this, right now I don't have the ability to perform such a task. Even those greater than I, such as Brahma, Śakra and other great worldly beings do not have such power. Also, even those included in the ranks of noble ones, such as Śrāvakas, Pratyekabuddhas, and the like, do not have such power. Then who has it? Only the omniscient Buddhas have (such power). The reason for this is that the Buddhas are free from all faults; they are endowed with all noble qualities; they have acquired power over the state of ultimate happiness; and they have the compassion and the power of transcendental activities to liberate all sentient beings from the disadvantages of worldly existence and personal liberation. If they are prayed to, then only the Buddhas, and no other than them, have the ability to fulfill easily all temporary and final aims. At any rate, I must attain such a state. Further, having gained it — like the skillful ship captain who magically created a beautiful city on an island in order to refresh the traders who were wearied by the long journey at sea — so I will temporarily place all sentient beings upon the stage of personal liberation by means of the three vehicles,[62] in accordance with their individual wishes (to belong to any) of the three classes of practitioners. Having refreshed the three classes of practitioners from the sufferings of worldly existence and having gradually purified them, I will finally place all sentient beings who pervade space upon the stage of Buddhahood."

This is the only lineage which practices the wishing enlightenment thought through guided instructions. Thus it was said.

To contemplate the meaning of this, for a long time one should contemplate, "Alas! Although these beings who were my kind parents desire happiness, due to the lack of skill in the methods of obtaining happiness, some of them are actually experiencing suffering and some of them are creating great nonvirtues, the cause of suffering. They are blinded by a cataract-like ignorance and are separated from the supporting staff of liberation. Unsustained by a Preceptor's guidance, which is like an eye for the blind, they are turning away from the path of liberation and of the higher realms, and are roaming on the edge of the abyss of the three lower realms. This is pitiful." Thus meditate on compassion for a long time.

Then think, "However, just saying "how pitiful" will not be of benefit. I must free them from suffering, and place them upon the stage of happiness. But at present I don't have the power to do so. Who has such power? Such a power is possessed only by a Buddha who has accomplished the two purposes.[63] Even a single beam of light that issues forth from a Buddha's body has the power to place inconceivable sentient beings upon the stage of personal liberation, and even a single Dharma discourse given by the Buddha is able to place an inconceivable number of beings upon the stage of personal liberation. In brief, through directly or indirectly seeing, hearing, remembering, or touching the Buddha, countless sentient beings have the ability to easily accomplish happiness. Such power lies only with the Buddha. Therefore, for the sake of my mother sentient beings, how wonderful it would be if I could win that Buddhahood of complete omniscience. So, by whatever means needed, I will obtain that state of perfect Buddhahood." Thus produce such thoughts, like a thirsty person desires water.

Then, one should think from the depth of one's heart, "Having gained Buddhahood, I will temporarily place all sentient beings in the state of personal liberation through the three vehicles, and I will finally place all of them upon the stage of Buddhahood after having gradually purified the three classes of practitioners." Then one should pray very intensely, "May the Preceptor and Triple Gem see to it that it happens so!" Even between sessions, one should constantly wish, "Wouldn't it be wonderful were I to gain that perfect Buddhahood, which is the source of good qualities, a wish-fulfilling gem." It is of great importance that either in the six periods of the day and night, or in the morning and evening, one should recite the "seven-branched prayer", followed by the brief taking of refuge and the creation of the wishing and entering enlightenment thoughts, as found in the *sPyod.'jug (Bodhicaryāvatāra)*. This should be done on a daily basis, without taking a break.

The Entering Enlightenment Thought, the Training on the Path for the Sake of the Result

The entering enlightenment thought is the training on the path for the sake of the result. To gain perfect enlightenment, one enters the path for the sake of others. The difference between the wishing and entering enlightenment thoughts is that they are in a sequential order, as stated in the *sPyod.'jug (Bodhicaryāvatāra)*:

> Just as a distinction is perceived between one who
> wishes to travel and one who actually travels, so
> the wise should recognize a graded distinction between
> these two (the wishing and entering enlightenment
> thoughts).

Therefore, motivated by great compassion which cannot bear the suffering of others, one produces the thought to gain perfect enlightenment for the sake of others. So one needs to diligently strive in the methods to gain that enlightenment, without sitting idle and without being overcome by the least bit of laziness. As it was said by Maitreyanātha,

> To carry the heavy load of sentient beings on one's head in
> a leisurely manner, O Excellent Beings, is not beautiful;
> while others and I are bound by a variety of bonds,
> it is very reasonable to work with a hundredfold diligence.

If it is asked, "Well then, what is the method of accomplishing the unsurpassable enlightenment like?" (The answer is that) the method to accomplish unsurpassable enlightenment is to disregard one's own welfare and to perform the welfare of others. As it was written in the *sPyod.'jug (Bodhicaryāvatāra)*,

> Whatever happiness there is in this world
> arises from the desire of happiness for others.
> Whatever suffering there is in this world
> arises from the desire of happiness for oneself.
> What need is there to say more? Just see the
> difference between these — children (i.e., worldlings)
> work for their own benefit, while the Capable Ones
> (i.e., Buddhas) work for the benefit of others.

In the past, we have failed to escape from worldly existence and have had to experience a variety of sufferings. The reason is that we have neglected the well-being of sentient beings, who have been our kind parents, and have cherished only ourselves, busily working for our own benefit.

Since beginningless time, having held as "I" and "self" that which is not "I" and "self", one has cherished and cared for oneself. Also, to protect oneself one has harmed others, thus accumulating nonvirtues. Hence one has had to experience various sufferings. It was said in the *sPyod.'jug (Bodhicaryāvatāra)*,

> Oh mind, you who desire to act for the sake
> of your own self have passed countless aeons,
> and yet, with even such great hardship as that,
> you have achieved only suffering.

Having viewed this self-cherishing notion as an enemy, one should train the conduct of the three doors (of body, voice, and mind) in whatever methods that work for the benefit of others.

The practice of this is threefold: (1) to meditate on equality between self and others, (2) to meditate on exchanging (self for others), and (3) to train in the conduct of these two.

1. Equality between self and others: Those who cannot meditate on exchanging (self for others) in the beginning should first train the mind in the practice of equality. Having become used to the meditation of equality, through skillful means one gradually leads this practice into exchanging (self for other). It was said in the *sPyod.'jug (Bodhicaryāvatāra)*,

> In the beginning, one should diligently meditate
> on the sameness of oneself and the other;
> one should protect others as one does oneself,
> since both are equal in (wanting) happiness
> and in (not wanting) pain.

Furthermore, the meaning of the equality of oneself and others is the thought, "Just as I desire happiness, so other sentient beings desire only happiness. Therefore, I will help them to obtain happiness. As I desire not to undergo suffering, so other sentient beings do not desire suffering. Therefore, I will help them to dispel their suffering." As it was said in the *sPyod.'jug (Bodhicaryāvatāra)*,

> When both myself and others are alike in
> wanting happiness, what is so special about me?
> Why do I strive for my happiness alone?
> When both myself and others are alike in
> disliking suffering, what is so special about me?
> Why do I protect myself and not others?

One may think, "It is not appropriate for me to protect them, since it is appropriate that the suffering of other sentient beings be cared for by they themselves." If this were so, it would be inappropriate for one's hand to remove a splinter in one's foot, because other than that which experiences the suffering it would be inappropriate for the foot to be cared for by another. As it was stated in the *sPyod.'jug (Bodhicaryāvatāra)*,

> If (it is thought), "Whatever pain may arise in
> whomever should be cared for by (the sufferer)
> himself," then since the foot's pain is not of
> the hand, why should it be cared for by (the hand)?

One may think that the two cases are not similar because the foot belongs to oneself, while sentient beings are different (from oneself). This is not correct. Being under the power of habituation that grasps the foot which originated from the semen and blood of a father and mother as "my foot", so it merely appears to exist in that way. For this reason, if one holds sentient beings also as "my sentient beings", then through the power of habituation they will come to appear in that way. As it was said in the *sPyod.'jug (Bodhicaryāvatāra)*,

> Therefore, in this way, just as you practice
> self-clinging toward (the body arising from)
> the drops of blood and semen of others, so should
> (you) try to habituate the bodies of others (as "I").

Further, it was stated in the same text,

> Just as through habituation the notion of
> an "I" has arisen toward this selfless body,
> so through habituation why shouldn't the notion
> of an "I" toward other living beings also arise?

In brief, if both oneself and other sentient beings are alike in desiring happiness and are also alike in not desiring suffering, one should abandon all vile conduct which obstructs their attainment of desired objects and which helps them in attaining undesired objects (like unhappiness). Then one should produce the pure aspiration to dispel the suffering of other sentient beings, and should be diligent in the methods that accomplish their happiness. As it was said in the *sPyod.'jug (Bodhicaryāvatāra)*,

> Others' pain should be removed by me because it is pain,
> like my own pain; I should benefit others also, because
> they are living beings, like my own body (is a living being).

One may think, "Although I promised to dispel the suffering and to accomplish the happiness of sentient beings, I am unable to accomplish such a task." Though the beginner is unable to actually do this, one should not part from such thoughts, which are expressed from the bottom of one's heart. In accordance with the actual practice, one should work for the well-being of others as much as one can, in pace with one's own capabilities. Gradually one will be able to work for the sake of other beings in a greater way. As the Master Nāgārjuna said,

> Though one has no power to work for the benefit of
> others, one should always have the thought of it;
> whoever has that thought will naturally enter
> into (activities that benefit) others.

To reflect on the meaning of this, having first taken refuge and prayed, think: "For the sake of mother sentient beings who are equal to the bounds of space, I must achieve the precious state of complete Buddhahood. For that purpose, I will practice the profound path." Otherwise, while keeping in mind its meaning, one should recite the following three times:

> To liberate mother living beings from the world
> of existence, I must attain perfect enlightenment;
> for that purpose I will practice the profound yoga,
> the path of all the Buddhas.

One should think, "Alas! Even though I wish and would be glad to gain the unsurpassable enlightenment for the sake of all sentient beings, as long as I am not able to destroy self-grasping and to convert all the activities of the three doors into benefits for sentient beings, for that long I am bound not to gain Buddhahood. Therefore, from now on, I will abandon grasping upon 'self-cherishing', which is the root of all faults. This is the excellent method to convert all activities into the benefit of all sentient beings, and this is the only path traversed by the

Conqueror's Sons, the Bodhisattvas. So, I must rely and reside upon such a path as this."

Furthermore, for a long time one should think, "Just as I desire happiness, so do all sentient beings without exception desire that very happiness. Therefore, starting from today, I will assist all sentient beings to achieve happiness along with its cause. Just as I do not desire to have suffering, so do all sentient beings without exception not desire to have that very suffering. Therefore, starting from today, I will assist all sentient beings to dispel suffering along with its cause." Then with an uncontrived mind, think, "I wish and would be glad were this to happen."

2. Exchanging (self for others): One who desires to quickly gain Buddhahood should diligently meditate upon the enlightenment thought which exchanges self for other. As it was said in the *sPyod.'jug (Bodhicaryāvatāra)*,

> One who desires to quickly rescue oneself and others
> should perform this most excellent secret (practice),
> the act of exchanging oneself for another.

One may ask, "Wouldn't one attain enlightenment by only relying upon the thought of the sameness (of self and other)?" This is not so. As it was said in the *sPyod.'jug (Bodhicaryāvatāra)*,

> If one doesn't perfectly exchange one's
> happiness with the suffering of another,
> one will not be able to gain Buddhahood; and
> even in the world, one will not have happiness.

The reason for this is that all sentient beings have been one's kind mother since beginningless time, and so were very kind in the past. Even now, since the attainment of unsurpassable enlightenment depends upon sentient beings, they are very kind to one in various ways. Therefore, one should have the desire and be glad to take upon oneself the suffering and the cause of suffering of sentient beings, and give one's happiness and virtues to other sentient beings. If one backslides from such activities and thoughts through desiring one's own happiness and placing others in suffering, then one will not be able to be liberated from the cycle of existence, let alone attain Buddhahood, and will experience only suffering. As it was said in the *sPyod.'jug* (*Bodhicaryāvatāra*),

> Desiring one's own exaltation, one will obtain
> evil states, lowliness, and foolishness.
> Transferring that very desire to others, one
> will obtain the honor of the states of happiness.
> If one uses others for the sake of oneself,
> one will experience servanthood and the like;
> if one uses oneself for the sake of others,
> one will experience mastership and the like.

If one does not soon destroy this giant attachment to self-cherishing by intense mindfulness, then one will not be able to accomplish the activities of this life, let alone the states of personal liberation and omniscience. With whomever one may live, whether it be teachers, friends, or relatives, there will be disagreement on the arrangement of seats and food. Not being able to bear even the forms of language used, one will pass the time only in argument. Throughout one's whole life, one will be unable to accomplish one's desires. Moreover, within the condition of having undesirable things fall upon oneself one will suffer by oneself alone; others will not even come to console one. In brief, all faults arise from the grasping of self-cherishing. Therefore, having looked upon it as an enemy, blame all the faults of other beings upon it, and then subdue this giant of self-grasping.

Since all happiness and benefit arise by relying upon sentient beings, therefore one should look upon them as one's relatives. If one has the intention of dedicating all of one's virtues and happiness to one's parent sentient beings, then whatever virtue one accumulates through activities such as guarding one's moral conduct, study, contemplation, and meditation will become the causes for gaining perfect enlightenment. No matter how learned, earnest, and noble one may consider oneself to be and even though one diligently performs virtuous actions, if one's practice fails to counteract self-grasping, one will not transcend this world. Therefore, it is very important for the religious practitioner to know this vital practice.

One might think, "If I take the sufferings of others (upon myself), I will not be able to carry the heavy load of their suffering, so I cannot practice this meditation of exchanging self for others." But it is not like this, because through the power of the beneficial thought that meditates in this way, the varied types of sufferings of others will be allayed. Those sufferings will not ripen upon oneself, and not only will they not ripen upon oneself but through the power of habituation of meditating in that manner, the notion of grasping at self-cherishing will be reversed. When it is certain to bring benefit to others, there will arise the ability to train by stages in the oceanlike conducts of the Bodhisattvas, such as unhesitantly giving up one's head or limbs. Through relying upon such practices, one will obtain perfect Buddhahood. As it was said in the *sPyod.'jug (Bodhicaryāvatāra)*,

> Therefore one should definitely enter wholeheartedly
> into working for the benefit of others and,
> as the words of the Sage are undeceiving,
> one will later see the virtues (of doing so).

Therefore, since the words of the perfectly and completely enlightened Buddha are not endowed with falsehood, one will accomplish one's purpose through that very practice of benefiting others. Therefore, one should think, "I am late in meditating upon this enlightenment thought which exchanges self for others. If I had meditated on this from the very beginning, by now I would already be enlightened and would be enjoying only happiness and not the arising of such suffering which is now troubling me." So one should endeavour to meditate on the exchanging of self for other. As it was said in the *sPyod.'jug (Bodhicaryāvatāra)*,

> If you had done this at an earlier time,
> the perfection of Buddhahood (would be
> yours) and the present unhappy condition
> such as this would not be possible.

At this time, one should explain whatever stories one knows of the previous lives of the Buddha Śākyamuni, such as when he was a cart-puller in hell or other stories of *mdza.'bo'i bu.mo*.[54] So, one should gain unshakable faith.

The manner to practice this: As it was said in the *sPyod.'jug* (*Bodhicaryāvatāra*),

> Therefore, in order to allay one's own pain
> and to allay the sufferings of others,
> one's own self should be given to others,
> and others should be regarded as oneself.

In the beginning, having directed one's meditation to one's mother of this life, one should think, "This, my mother, has dispelled many harms and accomplished much benefit for me. Therefore, I should also prevent any harm to her and accomplish her benefit. What is it that harms this mother of mine? She is being directly harmed by suffering and indirectly by the cause of suffering. Therefore, I will take upon myself these two (i.e., suffering and the cause of suffering)." One should imagine that both the suffering and its cause are transferred to oneself, and be joyful should it happen so. Think that through this the root of grasping self-cherishing is extracted.

Then one should think, "What would be of benefit to my mother? She can be directly benefited by happiness and in the long run by virtue, so I will give her these two." Having transferred all of one's happiness and virtues to one's mother without any regard for one's own desires, one should think that the body and mind of one's mother is presently comforted and that indirectly she becomes endowed with virtue, the cause of happiness. One should be joyful should it happen in this way. Likewise, one should meditate by applying the same procedure to others as one has to one's mother.

The manner to contemplate on the meaning of this is as follows. First of all, one should clearly visualize one's mother of this life and think, "Alas, this is my beloved and dear mother who gave me this special body through which enlightenment can be achieved, who protected me from various harms and fears, and who accomplished unimaginable benefit and happiness for me.

Therefore, she is very kind. Not only in this life but since beginningless time she has been my mother and has shown immeasurable care. She worked in that way again and again for me, yet she herself is still roaming in this world. This is pitiful. From this time on, I will strive to attain the stage of perfect, omniscient Buddhahood for the sake of this mother. The reason I have failed to gain Buddhahood until now is that I have neglected my kind mother and have maintained self-cherishing only. Now, in this short life, I will subdue this giant grasping of self-cherishing and will abandon being its assistant and servant. I will try my best to repay my mother's kindness by practicing the Dharma. What is harming my mother? She is being harmed by suffering and the cause of suffering. So I will take the sufferings and the cause of sufferings of my mother upon myself."

One should say, "May all of my kind mother's sufferings and nonvirtues, the cause of suffering, ripen upon me," Meditate that both her suffering and its cause fall in the form of a black lump into the center of one's heart, just as a hide will fall having been skinned. For a long time one should think, "I wish and would be happy were this to happen." By that meditation, one should think that the giant of grasping the cherishing of one's mindstream which is without any basis is extracted at its root, like the awakening from the misconception that a colored rope to be a snake.

Again, one should think, "What would be of benefit to my mother? Were she endowed with happiness and the cause of happiness, she would be benefited. Therefore I will give her all my happiness and virtues (the cause of happiness)." Then, one should say, "May all my happiness and virtues, the cause of happiness, ripen upon my mother." Meditate that from one's heart one's happiness and virtues issue forth like the rays of a rising sun and fall upon one's mother. Through experiencing it, she presently becomes blissful. Having assembled all the favorable conditions to practice Dharma and having increased her virtue, she gains the potential to achieve Buddhahood. For a long time one should think, "I wish and would be happy were this to happen."

If, through meditating upon these two — giving one's happiness and taking her sufferings — from the depths of one's heart in this way, one's visualization becomes slightly clear, then one should pray, "May the sufferings of all mother sentient beings ripen upon myself; by my virtues may these mothers gain happiness." At the time of reciting the first and second parts of this prayer respectively, one should meditate with an intense and uninterrupted visualization. Finally, one should think from the bottom of one's heart, "May this mother of mine be endowed with happiness and the cause of happiness; may she be free of suffering and the cause of suffering; and may she gain Buddhahood quickly."

Likewise, one should think, "My father (relatives, enemies) and all the other sentient beings each in their own category who are the object of my visualization are each suffering against their wishes. These desperate beings who are in such a condition are pitiful." Furthermore, think, "From now on I will strive to gain the stage of perfect omniscient Buddhahood for the sake of these beings." Thus apply the same procedure as explained above and then meditate upon the visualization of giving and taking as before.

Finally, for a long time, one should think, "Although sentient beings, the object of this exchange meditation of self for other, oneself, the exchanger, and that which is to be exchanged — i.e., bliss, suffering, and self-cherishing — are not existent whatsoever within the essence of the ultimate truth, still by the power of the deluded mind within the relative truth, one has to experience all these nonexistent visions. This is pitiful." Then pray, "For the sake of these beings, may I quickly attain the stage of perfect, omniscient Buddhahood." Then one should dedicate one's virtues.

In all of one's activities, one should be mindful of the enlightenment thought that cherishes other beings more than oneself, and with one's voice one should recite, "May all the suffering of sentient beings ripen upon me; by my virtues may all of them obtain happiness." One should be diligent in the methods that employ the activities of the three doors (of body, voice, and mind) to benefit sentient beings in any form.

If the grasping of self-cherishing arises in one's mind, then by remembering the meaning of the following saying in the *sPyod.'jug (Bodhicaryāvatāra)* one will not be overpowered by the grasping at self-cherishing:

> By this (self-cherishing) you were harmed hundreds of times in this world; now by remembering this enmity toward self-loving, you should destroy this self-serving mind.

If there arises a temporary illness to one's body or a severe, intolerable suffering in one's mind, then to bring it into the path of practice one should think thus: "In this world there are certainly many tormented by diseases or by severe suffering like me. This is pitiful because all of them are harmed by diseases or by severe suffering against their wishes. May all the sufferings of these sentient beings be ripened upon me." Thus pray and meditate through applying the same procedure explained before. Likewise, one should pity the hell beings who are tormented by the unbearable sufferings of cold and heat against their wishes. One should pray, "May all the sufferings of heat and cold of these beings be ripened upon me." Thus meditate through applying the procedure explained above. Likewise, one should apply this practice to each of the six realms of existence, visualize giving to and taking from each of them, and meditate with a very attentive mind.

Further, one should think, "If such physical illness or mental suffering did not occur to me, then I would be distracted only by the busy activities of this life. Having become intoxicated with pride and arrogance, I would never produce sadness for this world and would never be mindful of the acceptance and rejection of virtue and nonvirtue. So this disease or suffering has caused me to be mindful of the objects of refuge and the Dharma. It has evoked within me strong renunciation and sadness (for this world), and many deeds (karma) that would have caused me to experience the hells in future lives are being settled through ripening here (in this life)." If one practices in this manner, one's illness and suffering will be transformed into the path of enlightenment. As it was said in the *sPyod.'jug (Bodhicaryāvatāra)*,

> Moreover, the good qualities of suffering are
> that one dispels pride by sadness, generates
> compassion for worldlings, produces an aversion
> for nonvirtue, and a fondness for virtue.

If one is harmed by an evil spirit, then one should meditate upon the thoughts, "This evil spirit has acted as my mother for many lives, during which she provided benefits and protected me from harm. Even right now, when my body, voice, and mind are distracted to the wrong path and I forget to apply myself to virtue, this evil spirit is assisting me by encouraging these three doors (of body, voice, and mind) to practice virtue. So this evil spirit is really very kind. However, not understanding it in this way, I regard him as a harmdoer. This is not good. Now I must repay his kindness by practicing the holy Dharma. What would be of benefit to him? He would be benefited were he endowed with happiness and the cause of happiness and, were he free from suffering and the cause of suffering. Therefore, may the suffering and the cause of suffering of this evil spirit ripen upon me." By practicing in this manner, the evil spirit himself becomes an assistant in one's gaining enlightenment. As it was said in the *sPyod.'jug (Bodhicaryāvatāra)*,

> Having known oneself to be possessed of faults and
> others to be oceans of virtues, one should meditate
> upon the thorough abandonment of self-clinging,
> and upon the taking of others (as self).

If there arises an unbearable thought of the harm caused by others, such as that of one's enemy and the like, then one should think in the manner described previously for meditating upon loving kindness and compassion: "This harmer has been my mother for many lives, has cared for me with kindness, and even now is helping me to destroy my pride and arrogance. So she is very kind." With the thought of desiring to repay her kindness, meditate on giving and taking. Otherwise, one should think, "Both of these, the enemy and the ghost, were my mothers for many lives. Though they benefited me, protected me from harm, and were very kind, at this time due to the power of a deluded mind, they are harming me. This is pitiful." Then meditate on giving to and taking from them. If one practices in this manner, then the bad conditions themselves will be transformed into the path to enlightenment. As it was said in the *sPyod.'jug (Bodhicaryāvatāra)*,

> Therefore, (my foe) is like a treasure appearing
> in my house without it being earned by (my) efforts.
> Since he is a helper in the conduct of a Bodhisattva,
> I ought to be pleased with this foe also.

3. Training in the conduct of equality and exchanging: This has three parts: (a) training in the general conduct of the Bodhisattvas, (b) training in the six Perfections, in order to ripen oneself, and (c) training in the four practices of gathering, in order to ripen others.

a) Training in the general conduct of the Bodhisattvas: As it was stated in the *sPyod.'jug (Bodhicaryāvatāra)*,

> In order to accomplish the purpose of other sentient
> beings, I give away my body, my wealth, and even all
> my virtues of the three times, without any regret.
>
> By giving up all, one will transcend sorrow
> and one's mind will accomplish Nirvāṇa.
> Since one must abandon all (at the time of death),
> it would be best to give it to all sentient beings (now).

As in the manner of this saying, one should produce the thought of the desire to give all of one's body, wealth, and virtues accumulated during the three times to all one's parent sentient beings. Then one should think, "Through the virtues of such an action of giving, may all sentient beings, according to their individual wishes, obtain inexhaustible wealth right in front of themselves."

Within the limits of one's actual capabilities, one should help all sentient beings to dispel sufferings and to accomplish happiness. Further, one should benefit them with whatever one possesses. For this, one should first of all train in giving only insignificant articles and then gradually one should give dearer and dearer articles. By acting in such a manner, through the power of habituation, one will later be able to give up one's son, wife, and then even one's own body and life. As it was said in the *sPyod.'jug (Bodhicaryāvatāra)*,

> At the start, our Guide enjoins the giving
> of vegetables, and the like. Later, having
> become accustomed to that, one gradually
> (becomes able to) give away even one's own flesh.
> When the realization arises that one's own body
> is similar to (those) vegetables and the like,
> then at that time, what hardship would there be
> in giving up one's flesh and so on?

b) Training in the six Perfections to ripen oneself has three parts: (1) the defining characteristics of the six Perfections, (2) the method for accomplishing them, and (3) their benefits.

(1) The defining characteristics of the six Perfections: The defining characteristic of the Perfection of Giving is the giving away of all of one's possessions to others, which is a means by which one is caused to arrive at the further shore of both worldly existence and personal liberation. Likewise, one should apply this (to the other five Perfections):... Moral Conduct is the abandoning of faults that harm others which is a means...; Patience is an unagitated mind when harmed by others...; Effort is a liking for virtues...; Meditation is the mind being one-pointedly focused upon a virtuous object of meditation...; and the defining characteristic of the Perfection of Wisdom is the thorough analysis of all phenomena, (which is a means by which one is caused to arrive at the further shore of both worldly existence and personal liberation). As it was said in the *Rin.chen phreng.ba (Ratnāvalī)*,

> Generosity is the complete giving away of one's wealth;
> morality is benefiting others;
> patience is the abandonment of anger;
> effort is to uphold virtue;
> meditation is one-pointed (concentration)
> devoid of the afflictions; and
> wisdom is to ascertain the meaning of the truth.

(2) The method for accomplishing the six Perfections is twofold: (a) to practice the four qualities that are in harmony with the six Perfections, and (b) to discard the seven attachments that are in disharmony with them.

(a) The four qualities to be practiced are:

i) One should be free of (the opposing forces of the six Perfections), which are miserliness, immorality, anger, laziness, distraction, and corrupted wisdom, respectively;

ii) Each Perfection is correspondingly endowed with the friendship of nonconceptual transcending wisdom;

iii) The result of each Perfection is the complete fulfillment of the wishes of other sentient beings;

iv) Their activities are to completely ripen all sentient beings through the doors of three vehicles.

As it was said in the *mDo.sde rgyan (Sūtrālankāra)*,

> Destruction of the opposing forces of giving,
> endowment of nonconceptual transcending wisdom,
> complete fulfillment of all the wishes (of sentient
> beings), and the threefold ripening of sentient beings.

One should apply the other five Perfections, such as moral conduct and the like, to this verse also.

(b) The seven attachments to be discarded: These are described in the *mDo.sde rgyan (Sūtrālankāra)*,

> The Bodhisattva's practice of giving is unattached,
> nonattached, devoid of attachment, devoid of attachment
> itself, unattached, nonattached, and devoid of attachment.

Having applied this to each of the six Perfections, the meaning of this verse is that when one discards the seven attachments, one is training in the seven nonattachments. The seven attachments are:

i) Attachment to what is to be discarded — i.e., the opposing forces of the six Perfections, such as miserliness and the like;

ii) Attachment to postponement;

iii) Attachment to grasping at contentment (for insufficient practice);

iv) Attachment to rewards (for this life);
v) Attachment to result (for the next life);
vi) Attachment to the inclination of the opposing forces;
vii) Attachment to distraction.

Also concerning this, the great Sakya Pandita said,

> Discarded by the wise are these seven:
> attachment to what is to be abandoned,
> postponement, being satisfied (with
> insufficient practice), reward, result,
> inclination, and distraction.

(3) The benefits of the six Perfections: These are set forth in the *Rin.chen Phreng.ba (Ratnāvalī)*:

> Through giving (one gains) wealth,
> through moral conduct, bliss,
> through patience, radiance,
> through effort, splendor,
> through meditation, peace,
> through wisdom, liberation, and
> through a loving heart one
> accomplishes the purpose of all (others).

c) Training in the four practices of gathering to ripen others: As it was said in the *sKyes.rabs (Jātakamālā)*,

> Having summoned with the signal of generosity,
> one speaks in a pleasing tone. Carefully establish
> (sentient beings) through purposeful conduct and
> have discussions on the subject of harmonious purposes.

(1) Giving: In accordance with the *Drang.srong rgyas.pas zhus.pa'i mdo (Ṛṣhivyāsa pariprcchā sūtra)*, one should discard the thirty-two types of impure giving, such as giving with impure motivation — for example, giving for the sake of gaining a high rank in this life and with hopes of rewards and results, and so on; giving to impure recipients, such as the rich, kings, prostitutes, and the like, but excluding the destitute; and giving impure objects like meat, intoxicants, and animals for slaughtering. So

one should gather disciples for religious purposes through pure giving.

(2) Speaking pleasantly: Having pleased others through a gift of pleasing speech, in order to ripen them one teaches the holy Dharma in accordance with their individual capabilities.

(3) Purposeful conduct: Through special skillful means one causes others to take up the practice of the meaning of the teachings which, though they had previously heard them, they had had no inclination to practice.

(4) Acting with a harmonious purpose: To make others enter into practice of virtue, as an example oneself enters into virtuous activities with great diligence. As it was said in the mDo.sde rgyan (Sūtrālankāra),

> Through giving, (suitable) teaching, causing to
> take up, and oneself entering into the practice,
> one desires to speak pleasantly, act purposefully,
> and (act) with a harmonious purpose.

The manner to contemplate on the meaning of this is to think, "Alas! Up until now, I could not repay the kindness of mother sentient beings in accordance with the Dharma. Due to the power of grasping at the cherishing of my own self, I have engaged in various shameless activities motivated by jealousy of those superior to myself, contempt for inferiors, and competition with equals, and so I have been roaming in this endless world of existence while being tormented by numerous sufferings. Now I will give up all thoughts directed toward my own purposes and I will completely give, without any regret, all the virtues accumulated in the three times by my body, voice, and mind for the sake of the bliss and happiness of my parent sentient beings. Through giving in this way, may those sentient beings who desire food obtain food, those who desire clothes obtain clothes, those who desire shelter obtain shelter, and those who desire servants obtain servants; may the sick obtain medicine, a doctor, and a nurse; may the poor obtain an inexhaustible treasure; may the protectorless gain a protector and the refugeless a refuge; may travelers obtain guides, and those wishing to cross a river obtain a boat, raft, bridge, or the like. In brief, may whatever objects of wealth they desire be inexhaustibly obtained right in front of each of them." Then one should produce the thought, "How glad I would be were this to happen so."

Furthermore, one should think, "Since I have already given away my body and all my wealth to sentient beings, I do not continue to have the right of ownership over these things. Therefore since my body belongs to sentient beings, they may inflict whatever harm they wish upon me, such as killing me, cursing me, beating me, dirtying me, disturbing me, ridiculing me, and so on. I am completely subservient to their wishes."

Again, one should think, "In the same way as the Buddhas and their Sons resolved to practice the oceanlike conduct of the Bodhisattvas, such as the six Perfections, the four practices of gathering, and the like, through the power of wishing to accomplish the great purposes of self and others, so I also will conduct myself in the great training of the Perfections, from giving to wisdom. Also, I will give gifts that are devoid of faults, and having gathered disciples who are vessels of the holy Dharma, I will teach them the holy Dharma in accordance with their capacities. I will make them take up the practice of the correct meaning of those teachings, and to cause others to enter the path I also will practice the holy Dharma, which is profound and vast. This is my joy and desire." Then think, "How glad I would be were this to happen so."

If one wishes, during or in between meditation sessions, one may recite the verses such as this one found in the *sPyod.'jug (Bodhicaryāvatāra)*:

> By whatever virtue I have accumulated
> through acting in all these ways,
> may all the sufferings of all
> sentient beings be dispelled.

The Ultimate Enlightenment Thought, the Combination of Calm Abiding and Insight Wisdom

Though in most texts there are differences in the manner of meditating upon the ultimate enlightenment thought, there are none with regard to the subject matter. As it was stated in some of the old texts: "I think that the meaning of 'Then the ultimate enlightenment thought...' is selflessness, which is free from all substantiality, free from subject and object." To meditate upon the meaning of this, there are (1) the explanation of the nature of the ultimate enlightenment thought, (2) the teaching of the actual methods for producing it upon the mind, and (3) the showing of the manner in which to practice those methods.

1) (The nature of the ultimate enlightenment thought): Beliefs that are held to be the truth, such as the self or soul ascribed by the Hindus, the aggregates and sense-spheres ascribed by the two schools of the Śrāvakas (of the Hīnayāna tradition), the self-knowing mind ascribed by the Cittamātra (of the Mahāyāna tradition), and the like are mere imputation (of the name "ultimate enlightenment thought") upon an understanding which grasps at a conceptual extreme, but they are not the ultimate enlightenment thought. Instead, the root of all phenomena of both Saṃsāra (i.e., worldly existence) and Nirvāṇa (i.e., personal liberation) is the nature of the primordial mind, which from the very beginning has always remained free from all conceptual extremes. This is the ultimate enlightenment thought, as was stated by the Master Nāgārjuna:

> The enlightenment thought of the Buddhas which is not
> obscured by conceptualizations of self, of aggregates,
> and of self-knowing consciousness is explained to have
> the defining characteristic of emptiness always.

This is the root of happiness and suffering of worldly existence and personal liberation, because if one realizes its essence (i.e., its thatness), one will simultaneously realize the essence of all phenomena also. As it was said by Ācārya Āryadeva,

> The essence of one entity is the essence of all entities,
> and the essence of all entities is the essence of one entity;
> whoever realizes the essence of one entity
> will realize the essence of all entities.

2) The methods for producing the ultimate enlightenment thought upon the mind: This has the two aspects of calm abiding and insight wisdom.

a) Calm abiding: Having relied upon the method which holds the mind, all discriminating thoughts are pacified and the mind is placed upon and remains in its own radiance.

b) Insight wisdom: Having dispelled the obscuring veil of subject and object, one penetrates into the true nature of all phenomena individually without confusing them and sees the face of the primordial mind itself.

As it was said in the *dKon.mchog sprin (Ratna megha)*,[65]

> What is calm abiding?
> It is one-pointedness of mind.
> What is insight wisdom?
> It is the perfect realization
> of each and every phenomena.

Also, it was said in the *mDo.sde rgyan (Sūtrālankāra)*,

> Having settled (the mind) in the right way,
> to rest the mind upon the mind and to
> thoroughly penetrate all phenomena is
> called calm abiding and insight wisdom.

3) The manner in which to practice whichever method has been taught: This is to (a) meditate on calm abiding, (b) meditate on insight wisdom, and (c) meditate on the merging of these two.

a) Calm abiding: As it was said in the *sPyod.'jug (Bodhicaryāvatāra)*,

> Having known that the afflictions are thoroughly
> destroyed by insight wisdom which is thoroughly
> endowed with calm abiding, one should first of all
> strive for calm abiding. That, too, is achieved by
> being without attachment to worldly pleasures.

Therefore, insight wisdom is necessary to extract the affliction of self-grasping from its root, and calm abiding is necessary to produce that insight wisdom. Since calm abiding depends upon isolation of the body and mind to arise, one should first abandon all worldly activities like farming and trading, and all mental relations to outer and inner sense-desire objects like attachment to other living beings. If one does not abandon these, one will not be able to produce the real meditative state of one-pointedness of mind. Furthermore, there will be the fault of attachment to worldly activities. As is was said in the *Lhag.pa'i bsam.pa bskul.ba'i mdo (Adhyāśaya samcodana sūtra)*,

> If advised by the teacher, one's mind isn't
> pleased by the order, and if instructed to follow,
> one doesn't follow it accordingly: the moral conduct
> of such a person is quickly spoiled. These faults
> are caused by fondness for worldly activities.
>
> If one is a layman, since one's mind is always
> (attached) to the activities of one's residence,
> that person will always suffer, will not meditate,
> and will not practice abandonment (of faults and the like).
> These faults are caused by fondness for worldly activities.

Concerning the fault of attachment to sense-desire objects, it was said in the *sPyod.'jug (Bodhicaryāvatāra)*,

> Desires produce harmful results in this
> world and in the next; here one is killed,
> bound, and cut, and in the next will obtain
> (the suffering of) the hells and the like.

And also, (one should recollect the verse from the *sPyod.'jug (Bodhicaryāvatāra)* quoted above:

> Because of the torments of accumulating, guarding,
> and losing it, wealth should be known as
> boundless misery. There is no opportunity for
> liberation from the world's suffering for those
> who are distracted by the attachment to wealth.

Concerning the fault of attachment to sentient beings, it was stated in the *sPyod.'jug (Bodhicaryāvatāra)*,

> If one has attachment to sentient beings,
> (the view of) reality becomes completely obscured;

even the mind of sadness is destroyed, and,
finally, one becomes afflicted by grief.

Through thinking only of them,
this life uselessly passes away.
Even the perfect Dharma will be destroyed
by these impermanent friends and relatives.

If one equally participates in the behavior of
childish people, one will definitely go to the
lower realms. If it leads to unfortunate conditions
what is the use of associating with the childish?

In one moment they become friends,
and then instantly they turn into enemies.
Since they are angered in joyful situations,
worldly people are hard to please.

Though one speaks beneficially, they are
angered and also turn one away from benefit.
If one does not heed their counsel, then due
to their anger they go to the lower realms.

They are jealous toward superiors, competitive toward
equals, condescending toward inferiors, conceited when
praised, and become angry when spoken to unpleasantly.
When is benefit ever derived from the childish?

If one associates with the childish, there
will definitely arise nonvirtue, such as
praising oneself, belittling others, discussions
of the delight of worldly existence, and so on.

Also, it was said by Jetsun Rinpoche Dakpa (Gyaltshen),

Having resided in an isolated place,
there one should meditate upon concentration,
since if one associates with the childish,
one will not obtain isolation.
Therefore one should meditate
renunciation from living beings.

Through this one will obtain isolation
and will abandon wrong livelihood.

Likewise, one should also abandon a hateful mind toward enemies. As the *sPyod.'jug (Bodhicaryāvatāra)* said,

If the pain of hatred is held in the heart,
the mind does not experience peace. Not
obtaining joy and happiness, sleep will
not come, and one will become undependable.

Though they depend upon him through whose
kindness (they receive) wealth and respect,
still servants wish to kill
the master who possesses hatred.

By (anger) one's friends and relatives become
revulsed; though gathered by one's generosity,
they do not support one. In brief, there is
no one who can dwell happily with anger.

Besides these (verses), one should also recollect other excerpts stated on the occasion of the discussion of cause and effect (in the same text).

In this way, one should abandon all attachments toward the objects of hatred and desire, and taking up residence alone in such places as in a hermitage, in the mountains, on the edge of a forest, and the like, one should meditate on transic absorption. As it was said in the *sPyod.'jug (Bodhicaryāvatāra)*,

Therefore, I myself should dwell alone in
very pleasant and beautiful forests (while
remaining) happy, blissful, with little
difficulties, and pacifying all distractions.

Also, in the same text it was said,

Having contemplated the virtues of solitude
in these and other ways, one should completely
still conceptualizing thoughts and then
meditate on the enlightenment thought.

(1) The five faults and the eight antidotes (or corrective measures): Having resided in a solitary place, one should meditate on calm abiding through first recognizing the five faults to be rejected, then relying upon the eight corrective measures of those faults. Finally one should seek calm abiding through the nine methods of placing the mind.

The five faults are:

i) Laziness which does not apply the mind to virtuous action;

ii) Even though applied to virtue, one forgets the instructions for meditating upon transic absorptions;

iii) Even though not forgotten, the mind is clouded and unclear, or due to sluggishness and unruliness one's thoughts do not settle;

iv) Even though one knows that one's mind has fallen into a sluggish or unruly state, one is inactive and does not look for its antidotes;

v) Due to overapplication of the antidotes, one's mind becomes overactivated and cannot remain settled.

As it was said in the DBu.mtha' (Madhyānta Vibhanga),[66]

> Laziness, forgetting of the instructions,
> a sluggish and unruly (mind), inactivity
> and overactivation — these are believed
> to be the five faults.

From among the eight corrective measures that relinquish the faults, four are the antidotes for laziness, the first (fault) to be abandoned. These are earnestness, diligence, faith, and purity. Earnestness is the abode of the states of transic absorption. Diligence is to remain in that abode. Faith is the cause of earnestness. Purity is the result of diligence.

Among these four, diligence is the principal one. Since effort is the meaning of diligence, it is very important to abandon laziness and to arouse effort. As it was said in the *sPyod.'jug* (*Bodhicaryāvatāra*),

> Through being patient in this way, one should
> arouse effort, for enlightenment exists only for

those who have effort. Just as there is no motion without air, so merit does not arise without effort. What is effort? It is fondness for virtue.

The opposing forces of effort are described in the same text,

> Its opposing forces are explained to be laziness, attachment to vices, tardiness, and self-despising. Through experiencing the pleasures of idleness and craving for sleep, one will not feel sadness for the sufferings of worldly existence and laziness will be strongly produced.

Therefore, one should discard all these causes of laziness and should diligently meditate upon the transic absorptions by recollecting the faults of worldly existence, the difficulty of obtaining the prerequisites, and the impermanence of life.

The antidotes for "forgetting the instructions" are mindfulness and alertness. Whatever subjects of instructions for meditating upon the transic absorptions are given, they should be brought to mind through mindfulness and should be held there without forgetting through alertness. As it was said in the sPyod.'jug (Bodhicaryāvatāra),

> The hearing, contemplation, and meditation of those possessing the fault of nonalertness will not be retained within their memory, like the water in a leaky vase.

The antidote for failing to recognize the sluggish and unruly states is to see whether one has come under the influence of sluggishness or unruliness. Since sluggishness and unruliness are the principal opposing forces to the transic absorptions, if one fails to recognize them, one will not be able to rely upon the antidotes. Even though recognized, one does not (necessarily) activate the methods for dispelling sluggishness and unruliness, so the antidote itself is activitation. The reason for this is that even though one recognizes what is to be abandoned, if the antidote is not relied upon, the qualities of meditation will not be produced upon one's mind.

The antidote for the unsettled mind that has become very agitated through strong overapplication is to rely upon the mental activity of equanimity. If the mind is maintained through balance, as gold is carefully weighed or a wise man is careful in his speech, then one will easily and happily gain the aims for which one wishes. Concerning these also, it was said in the *DBu.mtha'* *(Madhyānta Vibhanga)*,

> Abode, abiding in it, cause, result,
> not forgetting (the instruction of)
> meditation, knowing the sluggish and
> unruly states, the mental activity to
> manifestly discard them, and to place
> (the mind) in meditation when it is calmed.

(2) The nine placements of the mind: The actual method of resting the mind (in tranquillity) is said to have nine stages,

> The nine stages of placement are: (i) placement,
> (ii) continual placement, (iii) repair and placement,
> (iv) perfect placement, (v) subdued, (vi) calmness,
> (vii) perfect calmness, (viii) one-pointedness, and
> (ix) placement in equanimity.

i) Placement of the mind: This requires four endowments: (a) an unmoving object of meditation, (b) an unmoving body, (c) unblinking eyes, and (d) a clear object of meditation.

(a) An unmoving object of meditation: In a very isolated and delightful place one should arrange a beautiful and pleasing object of meditation, such as an image or painting of the Buddha, and the like. As it was said in the *Ting.nge.'dzin rgyal.po mdo* *(Samādhi rāja sūtra)*,[67]

> A Bodhisattva who places his mind upon an object of
> meditation like a very beautiful image of the Lord
> of the World (i.e., Buddha), whose body is similar
> to the color of gold, is said to be in meditation.

Otherwise, one can place any suitable object, such as a blue flower, blue silken cloth, and the like, directly in front of oneself, neither too far nor too near, and unmoving.

(b) An unmoving body: One should practice this by following the teaching found in the meditation manual *'bsGom. rim (Bhāvanākrama)*, written by Kamalaśīla. There it is stated that one should neither open one's eyes too widely nor should they be closed, but they should be directed to the tip of one's nose. One should sit erect and in balance, with mindfulness directed inward. One's shoulders should be held level, with the head held neither too high nor too low. One should not be leaning to any side, but the tip of one's nose should be straight in line with the navel. The lips and teeth should be held naturally, and the tongue should be kept near the teeth. The inhalation and exhalation of breath should be natural, without making any sounds, hyperventilation or heavy breathing. At any cost one's breathing should be gentle, inhaling leisurely and spontaneously, and exhalation should proceed in the same manner. Therefore, one should sit on a soft cushion with a straight and unmoving body, complete with all the parts of the meditation posture.

(c) Unblinking eyes: The eyeballs should be only half covered by the upper eyelids. With partially opened eyes and without blinking, one should gaze at the object of meditation. If tears and so on arise, they should not be wiped away by the hand, but allowed to fall freely. If pain arises, one should not direct one's mind to the pain, but should remain in meditation and keep one's mind strongly upon the object itself.

(d) A clear object of meditation: The object of one's meditation is not to be judged as good or bad and the like, but whatever the object of one's meditation, that object should be held clearly and vividly by one's consciousness, devoid of any conceptualization.

ii) Continual placement: It is not possible for a beginner to meditate for a long time in such a manner. Therefore, one should place the mind upon the object for short periods of time and repeat such placement continually.

iii) Repair and placement: If one's mind is distracted from the object of meditation, one should recognize the distraction and redirect the mind back to the object of meditation.

iv) Perfect placement: In order not to let the mind wander, through mindfulness one gathers the mind upon the object of meditation.

v) Subdued: Through fondness for the good qualities of transic absorption, if sluggishness or unruliness arise, one should subdue the mind by the antidotes.

vi) Calmness: If one's mind becomes unhappy due to the cause of distraction and the like, then make the mind calm by directing it to the object of meditation.

vii) Perfect calmness: If the opposing forces of meditation, such as covetousness and the like, arise, then for that also the mind should be made to calm down by relying upon the object of meditation.

viii) One-pointedness: Though one has applied the methods that discard sluggishness and unruliness, if one's mind does not proceed into one-pointedness then place the mind upon that (nonproceeding) itself.

ix) Placement in equanimity: By the power of habituation, one will be able to enter into a state of transic absorption without the need of effort. From this point up to the point where the bliss of accomplishment is produced is the calm abiding of the one-pointedness of the mind of the realm of desire. Having produced that bliss of accomplishment, that one-pointed meditation is the real defining characteristic of calm abiding which places it within the "concentration states" (of the realm of form).

Concerning these, it was said in the *mDo.sde rgyan* (*Sūtrālankāra*),

> Having directed one's mind toward the object of
> meditation, (the mind) should not be distracted
> from continually (remaining) there; having quickly
> realized that it is distracted, it should be
> repaired by placing it again upon the object.
>
> The wise gather the mind inward to higher
> and higher (states), then having seen the
> good qualities (of meditation), one
> subdues the mind for transic absorption.
>
> Having seen the faults of distractions one
> is displeased with them and calms (the mind);

the arising of covetousness, unhappiness,
and the like should likewise be pacified.

Then (the meditator), enriched with vows,
together with applying the mind (in one-
pointedness) obtains the state of mind
resting within itself.

Through habituation to that, (the mind)
does not need to be applied; then having
obtained the great accomplishment of body and
mind from that (meditation), this is known as
"activation of mind" (i.e., transic absorption).

To make these nine stages efficacious, at each stage one needs to dispel the five faults through relying upon the help of the eight antidotes, as explained above. Also from among these one should recognize that the two main faults to be abandoned are sluggishness and unruliness. If sluggishness arises, one should reduce the amount of food prior to meditation and sit at a higher elevation. One's clothes and cushion should be thin, and one should recite the refuge, complimentary prayers, and so on, in a clear and loud voice. Arouse the body and mind into alertness and meditate. If unruliness arises, prevent it by relying upon the methods opposite to those (used to prevent sluggishness). When sluggishness and unruliness are pacified, relax (the mind) and meditate.

(3) The five experiences of meditation: By meditating in this way, a continuous stream of thoughts will arise, one after another, which cannot be measured by the gross mind. Actually these thoughts were previously there, but since one never placed the mind in meditation they were never noticed. Now having become aware of them, there will arise such ideas as, "my thoughts have become more than before," or "I have failed to produce meditation". However, this is the first experience (of meditation), the experience of recognizing thoughts, which is known as "like a steep mountain waterfall".

Through meditating in such a way, one will see one thought following after another. After a while, one's thoughts will cease, but immediately one will see the flow of thoughts arising again. In this way, one's thoughts will flow (and cease) alternately. This is the second experience (of meditation), the experience of the resting of thoughts, which is known as "like the water in a deep, narrow gorge".

Again, through meditating with great diligence upon continually placing (the mind), at some point the flow of thoughts will reverse, like at the time of sneezing,[68] and thoughts will cease. Through meditating upon this (ceasing) with greater sharpness, one's clarity of consciousness is occasionally interrupted by a sudden stream of thoughts. This third experience is the experience of tired thoughts, which is known as "like the pool of three converging streams".

Again, through meditating in this continuous manner, most of the flow of thoughts will be allayed, and the mind will remain by resting in the state of one-pointed concentration. In that state, only one or two consecutive thoughts will arise, but then instantly they will die down again. This fourth experience is the experience of waves, which is known as "like an ocean with waves".

Again, through meditating upon the continuity of that previous meditation itself, all outward and inward projection of thoughts completely disappear. The abiding of the one-pointedness of mind along with mind's clarity has arisen. This fifth experience is the experience of pacification of thoughts, which is known as "like an ocean devoid of waves". Even though at this time the mind remains in clear one-pointed concentration, free from the activity of thoughts, if one fails to gain the sparkling clarity of consciousness, then it is the calm abiding of the unclear elements of mind.

Therefore, to keep the mind in one-pointedness, one should meditate until the sparkling clarity of consciousness arises, which is like the flame of a lamp unagitated by air. By meditating in this way, if the clear aspect of the object arises, then without looking at the object of one's meditation, one should place one's mind on the clear aspect of one's own consciousness itself by turning the mind inward. If sluggishness and unruliness arise, dispel them by the (above) methods. Without any effort and at ease, remain within the state of the sparkling clarity of mind. By meditating in this refined way, if one's meditation is not good in the beginning of the session but improves toward the end of session, then one needs diligence; therefore one should meditate upon one-pointedness diligently. After applying diligence, if one's mind projects outward, does not like to remain in one-pointed concentration, and one becomes mentally and physically uncomfortable, this arises because of the application of too much diligence. So, one should meditate in a relaxed state. One should eat moderately and eat whatever is suitable for one's health. One should restore one's health by sleeping properly, not reversing day and night for sleep. When one has restored one's health, then meditate diligently.

To contemplate on the meaning of this, one should reside in an isolated place, seated upon a comfortable cushion in Lord Vairocana's posture, and precede the session by reciting the refuge, the complimentary prayer,[69] and the creation of the enlightenment thought. Then one should think, "Alas! From beginningless Saṃsāra until now, my mind has been blown around by the wind of conceptualization, and has been doing whatever it desired. It has not been able to abide even the time of the snap of the fingers in one-pointed concentration on a virtuous object. Therefore I have still not crossed the ocean of worldly existence and have not obtained the power to liberate others. This is not good. So now, having relied upon the instruction of a spiritual friend, I must accomplish the special joy of complete purification of body and mind. Having placed my mind in the absorption of one-pointedness, I must obtain the great enlightenment."

To accomplish this, having abandoned hyperventilation, unruly and noisy breathing, count one's inhalation and exhalation of breath twenty-one times without making a mistake in the count. In this way, bring both the body and the voice into balance. Examine the flow of thoughts in one's mind to see which thoughts are gross: if thoughts of attachment to sense-desire objects arise, then they should be pacified through meditation on the impurities of the body, and the like. Likewise, for hatred, meditate on loving kindness; for ignorance, think about the twelve links of interdependent origination; for jealousy, meditate on the equality of self and other; for pride, meditate on the exchange of self and other or on the distinctions of the parts of the body.

Again, one should examine to see whether the flow of gross afflictions are there or not. If there are such thoughts, then apply the antidote for whichever affliction has arisen. Do not allow one's mind to fall under the power of the afflictions and thoughts of this life. When the outwardly projected and the inwardly stimulated afflictions and so on cease, one should remember the above-described instructions on directing one's mind. Then, first, forcefully place the mind on the object of meditation without coming under the power of sluggishness and unruliness. If it is forced too strongly, then it will become unruly. So, in the middle, one should relax the mind and not be parted from mindfulness and alertness. If it is too relaxed, it will lead to sluggishness. Finally, keeping the mind in its own naturalness (i.e., the nonduality of clarity and emptiness), gently place the mind — without being rough on it — within the state of the clarity of the object. The first two stages are the application of the antidotes for sluggishness and unruliness, while the last is the manner of showing the application of equanimity when sluggishness and unruliness are pacified. Therefore, for whatever transic absorption one may meditate upon, these three essential points are very important.

Through meditating in this way, when the functioning of thoughts disappear, then place the mind for a long time on the sparkling clarity of consciousness. When one's meditation upon that sparkling clarity of consciousness becomes steady, one should not look on the meditation object but strongly look at the clear appearance of the radiance of mind itself. If one experiences this in the manner of singular clarity, then relax the mind upon that experience. Do not reflect on the past, do not think about the future, do not keep an account of one's present activities, but completely cut any conceptualizations, regardless of being good or bad, as they arise one after another. Remain in the manner of being inwardly at ease but outwardly attentive. When arising from the meditation session, part from meditation on good terms with it, and dedicate its virtues for the sake of sentient beings. Then refresh oneself. Even in between meditation sessions, do not break the continuity of isolation. Discard all the causes of distraction and outwardly directed activities of the mind, and quickly enter into another meditation session. In the beginning, make meditation sessions short, but repeat them many times. Having become habituated, prolong the sessions. Eventually, one should practice until one can pass a day and night, and so on, in one continuous meditation session.

b) Insight wisdom: The Bodhisattva, who has attained the joy of one-pointed concentration of mind through meditating on calm abiding in this way, should then strive to master the ways which produce the discriminative understanding of insight wisdom. The reason for this is that the true purport of all the Sage's discourses is just that (i.e., wisdom). As it was said in the *sPyod.'jug (Bodhicaryāvatāra)*,

> It was for wisdom's sake that
> the Sage taught all these parts;
> therefore, wisdom must be produced
> by those wishing to end suffering.

If one lacks the mind which thoroughly discriminates all entities (i.e., dharmas), then no matter how diligently one meditates on emptiness or engages in the practice of the methods of giving and the like, still one will be unable to eradicate the afflictions and self-grasping from their root. As it was said in the *sDus.pa (Sañcayagāthā)*,

> How could even ten million blind men who are
> ignorant of the way ever reach the city without
> a guide? So, also, if wisdom is lacking, these
> five eyeless transcendent perfections cannot draw
> near to enlightenment because they have no guide.

Also, it was stated in the *mDZod (Abhidharmakośa)*,

> Without analytical (wisdom) to discriminate entities,
> there is no method to extinguish the afflictions;
> lacking in that (method) also, one roams here in
> this ocean of worldly existence. Hence, for that
> reason, the Teacher taught this (analytical wisdom).

It is thus quite possible that, even though one meditates on the view of emptiness unaccompanied by the practice of the extensive method, one would attain nothing higher than the enlightenment of Disciples (Śrāvakas) and Solitary Buddhas (Pratyekabuddhas). Thus it was said in the *sDus.pa (Sañcayagāthā)*,

> One who lacks method and wisdom
> falls to the stage of Disciples.

And also, it was said in the *'Jam.dpal rnam.par 'phrul.pa'i mdo (Mañjuśrī vikurvāṇa sūtra)*,[70]

> It is a deed of Māra if one comprehends the
> emptiness of each and every (entity), yet
> abandons beings; it is also a deed of Māra
> if, although one analyzes this through wisdom,
> one still clings to the object of great compassion.

Also, it was said by Ācārya Saraha,

> By emptiness alone where compassion has been
> discarded, one will not gain the supreme path;
> yet is there any liberation from this world
> of existence if compassion be meditated alone?

So one will not be able to transcend worldly existence because the root of viewing self-existence cannot be cut off by the mere meditation on emptiness devoid of the realization of the two types of selflessness, nor by mental concentration devoid of discriminative insight wisdom. As it was said in the *Ting.nge.'dzin rgyal.po mdo (Samādhi rāja sūtra)*,

> Even though worldlings meditate on emptiness,
> by that (meditation) the grasping at entities
> (as real) cannot be cut off; instead, by it even
> more of the afflictions will be generated later,
> just as when Udraka meditated in transic absorption.

Although Udraka meditated in transic absorption for twelve years, he was eventually reborn as a rodent. Also, it was said in the *sPyod.'jug (Bodhicaryāvatāra)*,

Though (conceptualization) may be cut (for a while),
since the mind lacks (the realization of) emptiness,
they will emerge again, as in the case of the meditation of
nonperception. Therefore, one must meditate upon emptiness.

The attainment of enlightenment requires these three factors to be present: wisdom, which is like an arrow; compassion, which is like a bow; and a person well-versed in the right methods, who is like a skilled archer. As it was said in the *rGyud bla.ma (Uttara tantra)*,[71]

> Having dispelled, through wisdom, all the craving for
> self, the loving one does not attain Nirvāṇa because
> of attachment to living beings. Thus the noble one,
> employing the methods of attaining enlightenment,
> neither remains in Saṃsāra nor crosses beyond into Peace.

Also, it was stated in the *bsLab.bTus (Śikṣā samuccaya)*,

> Through developing (a realization of) emptiness which
> has as its essence compassion, one's merit becomes pure.

For this reason, intelligent persons endowed with understanding who wish to benefit themselves should strive to master the ways of producing the wisdom that realizes selflessness, the remedy for suffering and its cause, and that, too, without being separate from the methods of great compassion. As it was said in the *sPyod.'jug (Bodhicaryāvatāra)*,

> The cause of suffering, egotism, increases
> through delusion about the self. Were it argued,
> "There is no means to discard it (the delusion
> about the self)," (it is said) that the meditation
> of selflessness is the excellent remedy for it.

To ascertain this realization of selflessness, one has to (1) recognize the nature of appearances, (2) keep the mind in the state free from conceptual extremes, and (3) develop the unshakable understanding that the nature of mind is inexpressible.

(1) Recognize the nature of appearances: One should understand that the appearance of outer and inner phenomena, which are mere appearance and without (true, independent) existence, arise entirely through the power of the deluded mind of the viewer. In ultimate reality, there is not the smallest entity that exists.

One may object by saying that "It is not true that they are nonexistent, because the existence of a self as the agent who creates happiness and suffering is accepted by non-Buddhists, and the existence of 'I' and 'mine' and the like are easily established without disagreement even by the innate knowledge of ordinary folk." But this is not so. If there were a self, which is the object that is grasped in the manner of "I," then one must inquire whether it happens to be (a person's) name, one's body, or one's mind.

It is not the first of these three, since name is a mere conventional label and not anything that can be established as real. As it was stated in a *sūtra*,

> The name is emptied (by the fact of
> just being a) name, names (themselves
> naturally) are devoid of a name; all
> phenomena (i.e., dharmas) are devoid
> of name, yet by names are they denoted.

Nor is the body the self, for if one were to examine it analytically, the body itself would not be found. As it was said in the *sPyod.'jug (Bodhicaryāvatāra)*,

> The "body" is not the feet, nor calves,
> nor is it thighs, nor hips. The stomach
> and the back are also not the body, also
> the chest and shoulders are not the body.
>
> The ribs and hands also are not the body,
> the armpits and shoulders are also not the body,
> and the inner organs are also not it.
>
> If the head and neck are also not
> the body, then among all these
> (parts), which one is the "body"?

> If this body dwells equally among all its
> parts, then (it is true that the body)
> resides in each of these parts, but where
> does that body itself (without parts) reside?
>
> If the body as a whole resides in the
> hand and other (parts), then there
> will be as many "bodies" as there are
> (parts, such as) the hand and the like.
>
> If the body does not exist either outside or
> inside, how is the body (to be found) in the
> hand and so on? Since it is not perceived
> separate from the hand and so on, how does it exist?
>
> Therefore, through delusion, there is the notion
> of a body in the hand and other (parts) which
> are actually devoid of any "body", just as there
> arises the notion of a "man" upon an effigy,
> due to the particular arrangement of its shape.

Therefore, if the body itself does not exist, how could it rightly be accepted as the "self"? As it was said in the same text,

> The "self" is not the nails, hair and
> teeth, nor are blood and bones the "self".

Mind, too, is not the "self", for if subjected to examination, the mind itself is not found. As it was said in the *sPyod.'jug (Bodhicaryāvatāra)*,

> Mind does not dwell in the organs of sense,
> nor in forms and the rest, nor in between;
> mind is to be found neither in nor out
> (of the body), nor in any other place.

Hence, since the mind itself is nonexistent, how could it be acknowledged as a "self"? As it was said in the *sPyod.'jug (Bodhicaryāvatāra)*,

> The six consciousnesses are also not self.

And, again in the same text, it was stated,

> Past and future minds are not the self,
> for they do not exist. And, supposing
> the present mind to be the self, again
> no self exists when it ceases.

Further, it was said in the *rGyal.po 'char.byed.la gdams.pa'i mdo*,

> Name is not the "self", for it is a mere imputation;
> body is not the "self", for the flesh and bones are
> a collection of elements like an outer wall; mind
> is also not the "self", for it is not an entity.

If one investigates and meditates upon them thus, one will understand that these three — name, body, and mind — are not "self". In this way, the delusive notion of grasping them to be the "self" will be reversed.

Again, it may be asked, "If there is no self, then what is the object that is grasped in the manner of 'I' even by the innate knowledge of ordinary people?" Through the power of habitually holding "I" upon the five aggregates, like misapprehending a rope for a snake, one grasps "I" with no fundamental reasons. Therefore, the object that is grasped in the manner of "I" or "self" does not exist.

Therefore, since there is no self, so also "my" does not exist. It is an error, therefore, to grasp these notions of "I" and "mine," which are the roots of all misfortunes. Having firmly understood this by the analytic mind, one needs to practice diligently the method of reversing the belief in the self. As Ācārya Candrakīrti said (in his *Madhyamakāvatāra*),

> Having understood through (analytical wisdom)
> that all the faults of the afflictions arise
> from the view of (holding) the impermanent
> aggregates (to be truly existent), and having
> realized, too, that the "self" is the object of
> that (view), so the meditator rejects the self.

So, too, one needs to gain an unshakable understanding

through relying on scripture, reasoning, and the instructions of Preceptors that, just as no "personal self" (pudgalātma) exists, neither does there exist any external entity that is the objective aspect of the notion of the "self of entities" (dharmātma), as commonly imputed by the two schools of Disciples (i.e., the Vaibhāshika and Sautrāntika).

The manner of establishing this through scriptures is as was said in the *'Phags.pa sa.bcu.pa'i mdo (Ārya daśabhūmi sūtra)*:

> O Sons of the Victorious One, all
> these three realms are only mind.

Furthermore, it was said in the *Lang.kar gshegs.pa (Lankāvatāra Sūtra)*,[72]

> Since the mind has been agitated by mental impressions,
> external appearances arise. Outer appearances (by their
> own nature) do not exist, but are only of mind itself.
> So, the perception of external phenomena is incorrect.

Also, it was said in the *Byang.chub sems.'grel (Bodhicitta vivaraṇa)*,[73]

> Consciousness appears in the manner of
> subject and object; apart from consciousness,
> not the least outer object exists.

Further, it was stated in the *Rigs.pa drug.cu.pa (Yuktiśaṣhtikā)*,[74]

> The elements and so on that are explained
> (in treatises) are part of consciousness.
> By realizing thus, these (external objects) disappear.
> Therefore, are these not false imputation?

The manner of establishing (the validity of this insight) through reasoning is to consider that these external appearances are not true because it happens that an existent thing appears not to exist, a nonexistent thing appears to exist, a single thing appears to be many, and many things appear to be one. The first two points can be established (by citing an example). A patient afflicted by a severe bilious disorder does not perceive the conventionally existent white conch, but instead perceives a nonexistent yellow conch to exist.

That a single thing appears to be manifold is established by the consideration that a single entity that is known to appear to humans as water appears to beings of the hot hells as a floor of molten iron, while to beings in the cold hells it seems to be a mass of snow. Hungry ghosts see it as blood and pus; for certain animals it appears to be a drink, while still others see it as their home. The demigods perceive it to be a shield and weapon, the gods of the realm of desire know it as ambrosia, and the gods of the meditative sphere apprehend it as a transic absorption. To the gods of the sphere of space, it appears as space; to the gods of the sphere of consciousness, it is consciousness; to the gods of the sphere of nothing whatsoever, it appears to be nothing at all; and for the gods who meditate that all things are neither existent nor nonexistent, it appears to be neither existent nor nonexistent. As it was stated by Ārya Asaṅga,

> Since a single object is seen differently in
> accordance with whatever class (one belongs to),
> such as hungry ghost, animal, man, or god, it
> cannot be accepted to be ultimately existent.

Also, it was said in the *sPyod.'jug (Bodhicaryāvatāra)*,

> Who forged those floors of molten iron?
> Where did those assemblies of women spring from?
> All of these arose from the sinful mind,
> so the Sage has taught.

Further, it was stated in the same text,

> The actual existence of form and the like are
> popularly acclaimed (to exist), but (they are
> not established) through valid knowledge;
> they are false, like impurity and the like being
> acclaimed (by worldlings) to be purity and so on.

That many appear as one is also established, since a heap of many atoms assembled together appears to be a single mass. It may be asserted, "Though the mass does not exist, nondivisible atoms do exist", but these are nonexistent. If one were to examine through analysis these nondivisible atoms by placing an atom in the center and surrounding it by atoms on each of its six sides, one would not find a nondivisible atom. Hence, it was stated in the *Nyi.shu.pa (Vimśaka)*,[75]

> If conjoined by six atoms at one time, the
> most minute atom (in the center) has six
> parts; and even if all six exist in a single
> place, they become just a molecule or mass.
> If an atom cannot be joined (to other atoms due to
> nondivisibility), then what is that collection (of atoms)?

This insight is also established by instructions. On the authority of all the profound instructions of the meditators and scholars of India and Tibet, which have been passed down in an unbroken lineage, it is only taught that all outer appearances, though they appear, do not exist.

This can also be established through experience, as follows. A great meditator of the "Path Including Its Result" teaching experienced thirst due to the activation of "veins" and "airs" in his body. He went out to drink water from a jug, a spring, and a river, but found no water in any of them. Doubt arose within his mind, and he returned to his seat after having left one of his robes on the other side of the river. When his sensations of thirst passed the next day, he saw that there was water in each of the places he had looked the previous day, and he had to cross the river in a boat to retrieve his robe. So it was recounted.

If one asks, "Well then, how do these various appearances come about?" The answer is that these appearances arise from the full development of mental impressions of the deluded mind itself, just as, for example, the appearances in a dream. Thus it was said in the *Ting.nge.'dzin rgyal.po mdo (Samādhi rāja sūtra)*,

> Just like people who, in their homes, dream that
> they experience the joys of sense-desire objects,
> but upon awakening do not experience the desire caused
> by them since they know that it was only a dream,

likewise, all these things which are seen, heard, touched, and cognized are unreal and like dreams.

One may say, "No matter how strong mental impressions might be, still it is impossible for them to be solid and remain so long (as appearances do)." But this is possible, as it was said in the *'Jam.dpal rnam.par 'phrul.pa'i mdo (Mañjuśrī vikurvāṇa sūtra)*:

> Mañjuśrī was asked by Devaputra Padma Vikrīḍita, "Mañjuśrī, how should one regard these outer appearances? Mañjuśrī replied, "One should regard them as having arisen by the power of full development of mental impressions of a conceptualizing mind." Devaputra then asked, "How is it possible that mental impressions, no matter how strong they may become, could appear to be so hard and solid (as external entities are)?" Mañjuśrī said, "They do appear like that (hard and solid), just as, for example, in the case of a certain Brahman in the city of Vārāṇasī who meditated his body to be a tiger. As a result, the townsmen also saw him as a tiger and fled, so that the town became empty."

Also, it was stated in the *Tshad.ma rigs.pa'i gter* (of Sakya Pandita),

> That which appears as an external object is mind itself; appearance itself has no external existence. Discriminating (phenomena) as true and false depends upon the firmness and weakness of mental impressions.

If one thinks, "If external objects are unreal, is the mind which causes them to appear real, just as the Sakaravadin school maintains?" No, it is not. As Ācārya Vasubandhu explained,

> Because the object does not exist, there is no subject.

Also, it was stated by Dharmakīrti,

Neither consciousness devoid of an object,
nor an object devoid of consciousness
is verified through experience;
therefore, they do not differ.

Further, it was taught in the 'Jug.pa (Madhyamakāvatāra),

In brief, understand this point that just as objects
do not exist, so likewise mind does not exists.

Since no apprehensible object exists, so the mind, the cognizer, is also devoid of existence. The reason for this is that subject and object are established only through mutual dependence. Further, the meaning of the establishment of their mutual dependence is the very reason for their ultimate nonexistence. Thus it was said in the 'Jug.pa (Madhyamakāvatāra),

It is taught by the holy that whatever
is established as existing through mutual
dependence is not truly existent.

Therefore, one needs to understand and think that since beginningless time, though both subject and object are nonexistent, still they are mere appearance, which arises due to the power of one's being habituated to dual appearance. In this way, the consciousness that is empty of subject and object is self-cognizing and self-illuminating, like a translucent crystal. This was explained by the Great Yogī (Virūpa) as the clarity of mind, which is the defining characteristic of mind. This is also referred as "sphere of reality" (Dharmadhātu) in the Buddha's final turning of the wheel of the Dharma, as well as in its commentaries. As it was said in the *Chos mngon.pa'i mdo (Abhidharma sūtra)*,

That sphere since beginningless time has been
the substratum of all phenomena; due to its
existence, all beings and Nirvāṇa arise.

Further, it was stated in the *mDo.sde rgyan (Sūtrālankāra),*

Having realized that nothing else but mind
exists, know then that mind also does not exist.
The wise know that both (subject and object)
are nonexistent and dwell in the sphere of reality
which is endowed with neither.

(In the Sanskrit language) that "sphere of reality" is known as Dharmadhātu. "Dhātu" may convey the meaning of "cause", "sphere", or "element": in this case it indicates "cause", for that cognizing, clear aspect of consciousness which is the cause of all the phenomena of worldly existence (Samsāra) and liberation (Nirvāna) is the "all-base consciousness" (Ālaya Vijñāna). As it was said in the *rDo.rje gur (Vajrapañjara)*,[76]

This sphere of reality is peace supreme
and hailed as the jewel of the mind;
the dispenser of every fruit desired,
naturally pure is the true state of mind.

This sphere of reality is also said to be the clear light of the nature of the mind. As it was said in the *brGyad.stong.pa (Aṣṭasāhaśrikā Prajñāpāramitā Sūtra)*,[77]

As for the mind, no mind exists, but
the nature of the mind is clear light.

If one knows the nature of that mind, one will know the nature of all phenomena of Samsāra and Nirvāṇa. Thus it is said in the *rNam.snang mngon.byang (Vairocana abhisambodhi)*,[78]

The conquerors explained that "the transic
absorption of all the Enlightened Ones is
emptiness." That emptiness is obtained through
the full understanding of mind and in no other way.

Also, it was stated in the *dKon.mchog sprin (Ratna megha sūtra)*,

Mind indeed is the precursor of all phenomena.
If mind is thoroughly known, all phenomena
will be known thoroughly.

Again, it was mentioned in the *Doha mdzod (Doha kośa)*,

> Mind alone is the seed of everything, and
> upon this Samsāra and Nirvāṇa issue forth.
> I salute the mind which is like a wish-fulfilling
> jewel that bestows every desired fruit.

Therefore, one should know that the root of all happiness and suffering of Samsāra and Nirvāṇa is one's own mind, which is self-cognizing and self-illuminating. So, one should constantly maintain certainty that all the various appearances of subject and object that arise due to the power of the deluded mind itself possess no real nature of their own. In that state of meditation one should look directly, without any obscuration, at the self-radiance of the appearance of the clear mind. If a stream of thoughts arise, then having cut off whatever has arisen, be more attentive to produce sharper clarity of mind in meditation. Having meditated in that way, one will experience in one's meditation the distinct clarity of mind. Also, subsequent to that meditation, a very sharp memory will be produced in oneself.

Up to this point, all these stages of the method to meditate upon the ultimate truth are in common with the Yogācārya school. As it was said in the *Ye.she snying.po kun.las.btus (Jñānasāra Samuccaya)*,[79]

> The oceanlike Mahāyāna treatises of the Yogācārya
> school proclaim that there is a consciousness in
> Ultimate Truth which is free from object and subject.

(2) Keep the mind in the state free from conceptual extremes: It may be asked, "Well then, is there a truly existent consciousness which is free from subject and object, as one of the branches of the Yogācārya School believes?" There is not. Since what is to be refuted, the subject and object, are not existent, there cannot be a truly existent consciousness that is devoid of both subject and object which have already been denied. If it does exist, then how is its existence known? One might think, "Its existence can be established through experiencing it at the time of its existence," but it is impossible for consciousness to simul-

taneously function as two aspects of what is to be known and the knower, just as the blade of a sword cannot cut itself and the flame of a lamp cannot illuminate itself. As it was said in the *sPyod.'jug (Bodhicaryāvatāra)*,

> Just as a sword blade cannot cut itself,
> so, too, mind (cannot perceive itself).

Further, in the same text it was said,

> The lamp is not illuminable because
> it is not obscured by darkness.

Likewise, it was stated in the *'Jug.pa (Madhyamakāvatāra)*,

> If there is an entity, the dependent mind (paritantra),
> which is emptied by the freedom from object and subject,
> then how will one know its existence?
> It is incorrect to establish as existent something
> which cannot be grasped. (Its existence) cannot be
> established through it experiencing itself.

Hence, the past mind, having become extinct, is not existent, and it is not correct to consider that which is extinct to be an entity. The future mind, not yet having been born, does not exist, and it is contradictory to consider that which has not been born to be an entity. The present mind has no form, no color, and it does not abide inside the body nor outside the body. However much one may search for it, one will not find it. Therefore, it is devoid of existence.

The reason that the mind has no color and no form was taught in the *rNam.snang mngon.byang (Vairocana abhisambodhi)*:

> Guhyapati, the mind was not seen by the Buddhas,
> it is not seen, and it will not be seen. The
> mind is not blue, not yellow, not red, not white,
> not orange, and it is not of the color of glass
> (i.e., transparent). The mind is neither short,
> nor long, nor round, nor square. It is neither

light nor dark. The mind is neither masculine,
nor feminine, nor of neuter gender. Guhyapati,
the mind is not of the nature of the realm of
desire, it is not of the nature of the realm of
form, nor is it of the nature of the formless realm.

The reason that the mind abides neither outside the body nor inside the body was stated in the 'Od.srung kyi zhus.pa'i mdo (Kāśyapa parivarta sūtra),[80]

> Kāśyapa! The mind is neither inside
> the body, nor outside the body, nor in
> between the two. The mind is nonperceptible
> (because of its nonexistence).

The reason that however much one may search for it, one will not find the mind was stated in the same discourse:

> Kāśyapa! If that mind is thoroughly searched for,
> it will not be found. Whatever (entity) cannot be
> found is nonperceptible (due to its nonexistence).
> Whatever (entity) is nonperceptible exists neither
> in the past, nor in the future, nor in the present.
> Whatever (entity) exists neither in the past, nor
> in the future, nor in the present has completely
> gone beyond the three times.

Also, it was said in the 'Phags.pa gzung.kyi rgyal.po zhes.bya.ba'i mdo (Ārya dhāraṇī rāja nāma sūtra),

> Devaputra! All phenomena are merely mind, and
> that mind cannot be shown. It is without barriers,
> without form, and it cannot be discerned. Even
> though the mind be thoroughly searched for by the
> true nature of the mind, it cannot be found. That
> very mind which is in the process of searching for
> itself is nonperceptible. Since it is nonperceptible,
> one should view all phenomena also as nonperceptible.

It may be asked, "What is the reason for failing to obtain the mind when it is thoroughly searched for?" It is answered that the reason for this is that the mind was never born. If mind originates, then where does it originate from? Is it born from its extinct cause or from a nonextinct one? It is incorrect to think that mind originates from its extinct cause, because something extinct is insubstantial. Therefore, it is impossible for an entity to arise from an insubstantial entity. Nor can mind originate from a nonextinct cause, because if a result originates from a nonextinct cause, then cause and result will exist simultaneously. Thus there is no cause that produced the mind in the beginning. Without its origination, there can be no essence of its abiding in the middle. Without its abiding, there is no result of its cessation in the end. In this way, the mind is like space, being free from birth, cessation, and abiding. As Jetsun Rinpoche (Dagpa Gyaltshen) said in a song,

> In the beginning, mind was never born, so how is
> it possible (for that mind) to abide and to cease?
> Since the very thought of nonorigination and
> noncessation is a conceptualization, it should be
> discarded. That very act of discarding should
> also be discarded. Discarding itself is just a
> conceptualization.

It may be asked, "Well then, is that nonexistence of mind the ultimate truth?" It is answered that since the existence of mind could not be established, the nonexistence of that mind whose existence has been refuted cannot exist. As it was said in the *sPyod.'jug (Bodhicaryāvatāra)*'

> When it is said that "some entity does not exist" and
> that entity which is under examination is not apprehended,
> then at that time, how will that insubstantial entity
> which is devoid of a support remain before the mind?

In this way, since existence and nonexistence are contradictory, the mind cannot be both existent and nonexistent. Since mind is not both (existent and nonexistent together), so the mind is also not neither existent nor nonexistent, both of which have already been refuted. Therefore, the mind is free from the four conceptual extremes. As it was said in the *Ye.shes snying.po kun.btus (Jñānasāra Samuccaya)*,

> The learned do not accept consciousness to exist
> in the Ultimate Truth, because it is devoid of the
> nature of singularity and plurality, like a sky
> flower. (The mind) is not existent, not nonexistent,
> not both existent and nonexistent, and not neither
> existent nor nonexistent. (The true nature of mind)
> is free from the four conceptual extremes. Thus the
> followers of the Mādhyamaka School understand.

Therefore, the mind is empty of the four conceptual extremes. That emptiness is not a mere mental conception but is free from the four conceptual extremes, and this is from the beginning, the nature of its own being.

Through not being parted from the wisdom which is understood to be free from the four conceptual extremes, relax the mind for a while in the state in which even the discriminating wisdom itself does not appear — the state which is devoid of perception, which is the clear light, free from conceptual extremes, and in which it (i.e., the mind) does not exist in any form whatsoever. This is the instruction for cutting the conceptual activity of grasping the characteristic of entities. As it was said in the *sPyod.'jug (Bodhicaryāvatāra)*,

> When neither an entity nor a nonentity
> remains before the mind, at that time,
> since it lacks any other aspects, the
> unsupported (mind) achieves quiescence.

Through meditating in that way for a long time without interference from sluggishness and unruliness, one's meditation (will experience a state) devoid of appearances, like space. Subsequent to that meditation, there will arise the experience of understanding all phenomena to be nondual appearance and emptiness, like magical illusions.

(3) Develop the unshakable understanding that the nature of mind is inexpressible: It may be asked, "Should one accept the nature of mind which is free from the four conceptual extremes to

be the ultimate truth itself?" This is also not the case. Since each of the four conceptual extremes that are to be refuted do not exist, there cannot be (something) known as "devoid of the conceptual extremes" — which is the refutation of the four extremes as truly existent (in the ultimate sense). Therefore, that which is known as "the middle path free from the conceptual extremes" is also inexpressible. The ultimate truth completely transcends all objects of speech and conception. As it was said in the *Ting.nge. 'dzin rgyal.po mdo (Samādhi rāja sūtra)*,

> What are known as "existence" and "nonexistence"
> are conceptual extremes, and what are called
> "pure" and "impure" are also conceptual extremes.
> Therefore, having discarded any two conceptual extremes,
> the wise should not even abide in the middle.

Further, it was taught by Jetsun Rinpoche (Dagpa Gyaltshen) in a song,

> The term "free from conceptual extremes"
> transcends the object of expressibility.
> Such words as "Middle Path" (Mādhyamaka),
> "Mind Only" (Cittamātra), and the like are
> activities of expression, and all thoughts
> arising within the mind are conceptualizations.

Again, (Jetsun Rinpoche Dagpa Gyaltshen) said,

> Having failed to understand the true nature
> of self-arising wisdom and having failed to
> become accustomed to the special instruction
> of nongrasping, whatever one thinks still
> falls within the sphere of grasping. Further,
> if one thinks of nongrasping, this also falls
> within (the sphere of) grasping. So, understand
> that the merging together of the emptiness and the
> nonceasing clarity (of mind) is the Ultimate Truth.

In this way, one should first thoroughly cut through all doubts and false assumptions by means of study and contemplation. At the time of the practice of meditation, place the mind within the state of nonceasing clarity. The nature of that very mind cannot be expressed as free from conceptual extremes, nor expressed as not free from conceptual extremes, nor is there anything to be refuted by refutations, nor is there anything to be accomplished through practice, nor is there anything to be discarded through abandonment, nor is there any antidotes to be relied upon, nor is there any worldly existence (Saṃsāra) to be abandoned, nor is there any liberation (Nirvāṇa) to be obtained, nor is there any hope of Buddhahood. Without any doubt, all these conceptualizations — such as acceptance and rejection, ascertainment and refutation, hope and doubt, existence and nonexistence, emptiness and nonemptiness, and so on — are mere names, mere signs, mere convention, mere expression, collections, hollow things, meaningless, essenceless, pure from the beginning, empty from the beginning, and free from the beginning. So, through not being parted from the unshakable understanding that mind transcends all objects of speech, thought, and expressibility, keep the mind, without distractions, in the manner of being free from meditator and subject of meditation. As both the Master Maitreya and the Noble Nāgārjuna said,

> There is nothing whatsoever to be dispelled
> (in Ultimate Truth), and there is not the
> least to be established (in Ultimate Truth).
> One should perfectly perceive the right view. If
> one sees rightly, one will be completely liberated.

Further, as Sakya Pandita said,

> The true nature of entities is devoid of existence,
> nonexistence, and the like. There is no process of
> meditation consisting of a meditation, a subject of
> meditation, and so on. Since the mind is devoid of
> essence, there is no description of mind (to be of
> certain qualities). Since it transcends the object
> of words, there is nothing whatsoever to be described.

All of this can be confirmed by the precious discourses (of

the Buddha). As it was said in the *Yab sras mjal.ba'i mdo (Pitāputra samāgama sūtra)*,[81]

> Since there is no phenomenon that can be perceived
> in Ultimate Truth, so there is nothing whatsoever
> that can be ascribed. In other words, these are
> mere names, mere signs, mere convention, mere expression,
> and mere ascription. Other than that (relative truth),
> all phenomena are nonperceptible in the Ultimate Truth.

Also, it was said in the *Byang.chub sems.dpa'i sde snod (Bodhisattva piṭaka sūtra)*,

> When one does not accept or reject all phenomena,
> one will not abide in all phenomena. When one does
> not abide in all phenomena, one neither originates
> nor ceases. When one does not originate and cease,
> one will be completely liberated from birth, old
> age, disease, death, sorrow, lamenting, suffering,
> unhappiness of mind, and agitation of mind.

Moreover, in the *sūtras* of the *Prajñāpāramitā*, it is said,

> By conceptualizing, one will be involved
> in the realm of desire, the realm of form,
> and the formless realm. By the lack of
> conceptualizing, one will be involved nowhere.

Again, it was stated in the same text,

> Since enlightenment is imperceptible, so the term
> "enlightenment" is merely a name. Since Buddha is
> imperceptible, so the term "Buddha" is merely a name.
> The omniscient Buddha has no essence, and whatever
> is devoid of its own nature is inexpressible.

It may be asked, "Well then, how can one work for sentient beings?" (The answer is that) when there are no sentient beings in ultimate truth, there is no need to talk about work to be performed for the sake of sentient beings or about the one who works. As it was said in the *Gang.pos zhu.pa'i mdo (Pūrṇa paripṛcchā sūtra)*,[82]

> While I was dwelling under the Bodhi tree,
> I gained the complete Buddhahood of the
> unsurpassable, full and perfect enlightenment.
> At that time I did not perceive sentient beings
> and I did not even perceive the name, "sentient beings".

Again, it was said in the *sūtras* of *Prajñāpāramitā*,

> Subhuti! I do not perceive any sentient being.
> However, sentient beings who lack substantiality
> are perceived as substantial (by sentient beings).
> Therefore, working for their welfare is the mere
> conventional imputation of worldlings. However,
> this does not exist in the Ultimate Truth.

If one realizes in this way, than grasping the mere state of the inexpressible (as the ultimate truth) will cease. As it was said in the *sPyod.'jug (Bodhicaryāvatāra)*,

> Through the habituation of the mental impression of
> emptiness, one will get rid of the mental impression
> of existing entities. Through the habituation that
> "nothing whatsoever exists", finally one will discard
> that (notion of emptiness).

Having understood thus, if one meditates one will experience the nongrasping of clarity and emptiness during one's meditation session. Subsequent to that meditation session, spontaneous compassion for worldlings will arise in one's grasping mind.

For these reasons, those who wish to uproot the two obscurations along with their residual mental impressions and to obtain quickly the stage of omniscience should diligently meditate upon wisdom, the true meaning of emptiness. As it was said in the *sPyod.'jug (Bodhicaryāvatāra)*,

> Emptiness is the antidote to the darkness of the obscurations of afflictions and knowable objects. Why should one who desires to quickly attain omniscience not meditate on emptiness?

To realize emptiness, one should train in the collection of the vast accumulation of merit. Otherwise, it is difficult to realize emptiness, and even if it is realized, one will fall into states such as the cessation of the Śrāvakas and the like. As it was said in the *mdo sdud.pa (Sañcaya gāthā sūtra)*,

> As long as the root of virtue is not completely accumulated, the realization of sacred emptiness will not be accomplished.

Also, the Master Sakya Pandita said,

> Emptiness is also meditated upon by Śrāvakas, but its result is gaining cessation.[83]

Therefore, to practice wisdom and method inseparably is the essence of the Mahāyāna Path.

The manner to practice the meaning of this is as follows. Abiding in an isolated place, one should strongly recite the refuge and other prayers to the Preceptor and Triple Gem. Motivated by great compassion, meditate on the enlightenment thought for a long time. Having relied upon the meditation object of calm abiding, if a slight amount of abiding is produced upon the mind, then think in the following way.

"Alas! The nature of my primordial mind is clear light. From the beginning, it has been free from all conceptual extremes. Further, it has been abiding in the state of clarity and emptiness without discriminating between, or siding with, either clarity or emptiness. Due to not realizing it in this way, 'I' has been held as the object of a self, and so I have roamed in endless worldly existence. Furthermore, through the power of holding these collections, hollow things, essenceless phenomena, nonexisting appearances that arise from the habituation of the mental impressions of the delusion of subject and object to be truly existent, like a madman I have engaged in delusions only, and so I have constantly been tormented by various sufferings. Now, by relying upon the holy Preceptor's instructions, I shall understand the unsurpassable secret of the profound mind which is the essence of all the teachings, the eighty-four thousand articles of the Dharma spoken by the Buddhas of three times. Further, I shall never allow myself to be overpowered by the ghostlike grasping of substantiality."

Again, one should think, "I shall bind the body and mind by moral conduct and think that, in accordance with the excerpt, "the unexamined alone is pleasing",[84] the grasping of 'I' and 'my' as directed upon the grasping aggregates is a delusion."

Then one should repeatedly think in the following way: "The reason for this is that if there were something known as 'self', then it would have to be either the name, the body, or the mind. The name is not the self because it is merely a conditional label. The body is not the self because it is merely imputed upon an aggregation of many parts, such as flesh, blood, and so on, and from the top of the head to the soles of the feet the self exists neither inside nor outside of the body. The mind is not the self because the past mind has already ceased, the future mind has not yet been born, and the present mind ceases instantly. For these reasons, that which is known as the self is only a delusion which is imputed upon a baseless subject."

In the same way, the appearance of the various outer phenomena, such as mountains, houses, and the like, are neither created by accident, by God, or by the four elements, or are they made out of atoms or by any other creator. The appearance of phenomena that by nature do not exist is entirely due to the delusion of one's own mind, which is based upon the mental impressions of worldly existence. For example, these appearances are similar to the appearances of such things as a city, horse, elephant, and the like, in a dream. One should think of this for a long time and produce a strong, unshakable understanding.

Thus one should think, "For these reasons, since appearances which are grasped to be objects are similar to the appearances in a dream, the consciousness which grasps those appearances resembles the mind during the state of dreaming. Therefore, in the ultimate truth, there is nothing whatsoever that truly exists. So all phenomena consist of the appearance of subject and object, which are delusions, falsehoods, and deceptions."

Now turn the mind inward, and for a long time look upon the naked self-radiance of consciousness, which at this very moment is free from the veil of subject and object. When one experiences consciousness in a clear and distinct manner, one should then examine the clarity of consciousness (in the following manner): First of all, when one looks for the source of its origination, one fails to find a cause for its origination in the beginning. Therefore, this is the stainless emptiness of nonorigination. In the middle stage, when the place of residence of the nature of consciousness is sought, it is found to reside neither inside the body, nor outside the body, nor in between the two. It has neither color nor form. No matter how one may search, one will fail to find its existence. Therefore, consciousness is stainlessly nonabiding. In the end, when one looks for where it ceases, one finds that the resultant consciousness does not cease anywhere. Therefore, consciousness is utter blissful noncessation. In this way, the distinguishable naked appearance of mind in the state of emptiness is free from cause, result, and essence, and is devoid of existing in its own nature.

The self-radiance of the clarity of mind of the meditator who experiences emptiness does not cease anywhere whatsoever, and this is the experience of the lustrous clarity of mind. While within the state of clarity, nothing whatsoever exists. While within the state of emptiness, the clarity of mind does not cease. (Therefore, this is the combination of) clarity and emptiness devoid of grasping. It is devoid of the conceptual extremes, devoid of classifications, devoid of expressibility, and transcends the intellect.

Within this state, keep the mind nakedly, starkly, and distinctly; keep the mind free even from the concept of mere inexpressibility. If a thought arises, do not let it develop into a stream of thoughts, but completely cut this thought and again place the mind in the state of nongrasping. In the beginning, place the mind with force; in the middle, place the mind in a relaxed state; and finally, keep the mind free of hope and doubt.

In brief, never let the mind be distracted from the state of the merging of the nonduality of clarity and emptiness devoid of grasping. Effortlessly keep the mind in the state which is devoid of anything to be meditated upon. In this way, practice intensely, but for short periods, again and again. One should not lose interest in one's meditation, but should meditate and then part from the meditation on good terms with it.

At the end of the meditation session, before one discontinues the posture of meditation, one should think, "Although all phenomena are naturally free from conceptual extremes, devoid of classifications, devoid of expressibility, transcending intellect, without any basis, devoid of any roots, and like space, these mother sentient beings fail to understand it in this way and bind themselves with the tight bindings of the grasping of a subjective 'I' and of objects. Thus they are involved in illusory appearances only, and I feel pity for them. At any cost, for the sake of these sentient beings, I must gain the stage of complete, omniscient Buddhahood, which is the realization of mind free from the great conceptual extremes." Then one should dedicate the virtues (of this practice to all sentient beings).

In between meditation sessions, one should recite such verses as "The magicians create magical forms ..."[85] and the like. One should understand all appearances whatsoever to be the nonduality of appearance and emptiness, like magical illusions. Within this state of understanding, one should strive for the sake of sentient beings.

c) **The merging of calm abiding and insight wisdom:** Mixing together the stilling of all thoughts, in which there is no mental activity whatsoever at the time of calm abiding, and the destruction of all imputations by perfect wisdom, in which no objects of mental activity whatsoever are found at the time of insight wisdom, into the one taste of the practice of meditating nothing whatsoever is the practice of the merging of calm abiding and insight wisdom. As it was said in the *mDo.sde rgyan* (*Sūtrālankāra*),

> This path of merging together
> should be understood to be a vow.

Most of the methods to practice this are the same as those described above. However, here (one may proceed as follows).

Without being parted from the wisdom which understands that all these three — the object to be meditated upon, the method of meditation, and the meditator — do not exist in their own nature, clearly and distinctly settle oneself in the manner of the nondifferentiation of the essence of these two: (1) the calm abiding which effortlessly remains one-pointedly upon the aspect of the appearance of the clarity and noncessation of consciousness, and (2) the insight wisdom which superbly realizes the nonorigination of mere appearances. If that placement is very stable, then sharpen the wisdom of discrimination. If the mind does not remain stable due to excessive searching, then relax the mind.

Through placing the mind in this way in many short periods with short intervals in between, one will accomplish this merging meditation and will be free from deviating from the path. If one fails to understand these essential points, then no matter how firm one's calm-abiding practice may be, it will still be within one of the four worldly meditative states,[86] and no matter how good one's realization of insight wisdom may be, it will deviate into one of the four formless realms. Therefore, it is very important to cut off all deviant transic absorptions and practice correctly.

Even between meditative sessions, one should not let the consciousness of the sense organs be widely diffused into their respective objects, and one should understand that all appearances are not beyond the sphere of reality (i.e., Dharmadhātu) and so are merely projections of mind. Within that state of mind, one should work for the welfare of sentient beings as much as one is able.

Up to this point, the instructions that are common to the path of the Bodhisattvas have been explained.

Meditate With Unshakable Understanding That an Extraordinary Experience in the Vajrayāna Path Will Arise

The extraordinary path is applied to the *Root Treatise* in the following manner: "For the extraordinary practitioner with the extraordinary transic absorption is the vision of the extraordinary experience." The extraordinary practitioner is the practitioner of the Vajrayāna path, which will be discussed later (in *The Beautiful Ornament of the Three Tantras*). The extraordinary transic absorption is the Vajrayāna path of the ripening empowerment and the liberating special instructions, along with its accompanying teachings, which will be discussed later. The vision of extraordinary experience will then arise through relying upon these (two — i.e., empowerment and special instructions).

Though to describe this in detail is inconceivable, in brief there are three paths: the path of dispelling (obstacles) to enter into (the path), the path of destroying attachment; and the path of great enlightenment. There are also three experiences — the experience of body, the experience of mind, and the experience of dream; three "heat" realizations — the "heat" realization that is preceded by conceptualization, the "heat" realization that gathers the nine elements, and the "heat" realization that burns the seed element; three interdependent arisings — the interdependent arising of the reversal of vital airs, the interdependent arising of visionary appearances, and the interdependent arising of dreams; and three transic absorptions — the transic absorption of various characteristics, the transic absorption of being empty of own nature, and the transic absorption of the co-mergence of essence. Furthermore, these fifteen may be subsumed into one transic absorption alone.

The manner of meditating unshakable understanding for this is described by Jetsun Rinpoche (Dagpa Gyaltshen):

> Between the sessions of meditating upon
> the two enlightenment thoughts, one should
> be diligent in reciting *sūtras* and making
> offerings to the Triple Gem.

As this verse states, if one has purified one's mindstream by the common path and gains a slight experience of the two aspects of the enlightenment thought and the like, then leading the mind by great compassion one should think, "Even if it takes three incalculable aeons to gain complete Buddhahood for the sake of sentient beings, this is really not very long. Moreover, it is possible that the Tathāgata who is skilled in means and endowed with great compassion might have also taught some other method by which one can gain complete enlightenment quickly."

If one has repeatedly read, understood, contemplated, and looked up points in the precious collection of *sūtras*, one will have seen the *sūtra* known as *mdo.sde gdams.ngag 'bogs.pa'i gyal.po.*, sometimes called *gsang.wa lung ston.pa'i mdo*, where it states,

> Although it is certain that all the three vehicles
> which lead (beings to liberation) were taught by
> the Lord (Buddha), why didn't you teach a sure path
> that practices the cause and the result spontaneously
> and does not search for the Buddha elsewhere? (The
> Buddha) answered this question, "Having turned the wheel
> of the cause Dharma for anyone who desires that cause,
> in the future the short path of the Vajrayāna will arise".

Also, one will see the place in the *Lang.kar gshegs.pa (Lankāvatāra Sūtra)* where it states,

> The holder of the mantra who wishes to
> propitiate the mantra should not eat
> any meat, since it obstructs accomplishing
> the mantra and the obtainment of liberation.

When one sees the words of these and other *sūtras*, one understands that there is a path known as the collection of discourses of the holders of the mantra, or Vajrayāna. This is also called the "result vehicle" and is more extraordinary than the common "perfection vehicle" or "cause vehicle" (the Mahāyāna path).

Having understood this, one produces the desire to search for and practice the Vajrayāna path. Thus one should think, "Since I have achieved understanding and experience of the enlightenment thought just by practicing the path of the perfections, having met this path of the Vajrayāna which experiences the cause and result spontaneously, should I practice it I would certainly gain inconceivable transic absorptions and experiences of the path. At that time I should recognize whatever good or bad experiences that arise and, with neither hope and doubt nor acceptance and rejection, I should be indifferent to all those experiences. So, I should think of them in this way."

Here, at the time of the preliminary stage, the need to meditate on unshakable understanding for the experience that will arise (in the Vajrayāna path) is as follows. When one later practices the path of the Vajrayāna, agreeable experiences will arise, such as visions of the Buddhas and the like, and disagreeable experiences will also arise, such as receiving a beating from demons and cannibals and the like. Some beginners fail to understand these visions as experiences of meditation and consider the Buddhas, demons, cannibals, and the like to be real. Through producing thoughts of hope and doubt and through having failed to understand that these visions are to be brought into the path, the gaining of good qualities is obstructed. To prevent such misunderstanding, one should cut off all doubts and false assumptions of one's experience before they arise.

Although the previously mentioned *gsang.wa.lung ston.pa'i mdo.* was not actually translated into Tibetan (from Sanskrit), some excerpts, such as "Having turned the wheel of the cause Dharma for (anyone) who desires that cause ...," are quoted in Jñāna Śrī's *mTha'.gnyis sel.ba*,[87] *(Dispelling the Two Extremes)* and in the Great Translator's[88] *sNgags.log sun.'byin (The Refutation of Wrongly Practiced Mantrayāna).* Although some scholars say that *mdo.sde gdams.ngag 'bogs.pa'i gyal.po* and *gsang.wa lung ston.pa'i mdo* are two different texts, it is said that the title of the Sanskrit text known as *Awabād Byākarana* was translated into two different titles (in Tibetan), although it is only one *sūtra.*

To contemplate upon the meaning of this, one should think, "When I enter into the profound path of the Vajrayāna, I will gain inconceivable visions of experience of the path. However, I should be neither happy when I experience agreeable visions nor unhappy when I experience disagreeable ones, because all the various experiences of worldly existence (Samsāra) and liberation (Nirvāṇa) that arise are simply due to the power of the mind interdependently related to one's veins, vein letters, element nectars, and essence of transcendental wisdom airs. Thus it is like this. If all these experiences are summarized, they are subsumed into five threefold experiences, whose total is therefore fifteen, and which are in turn subsumed into three transic absorptions. When those arise within me, I shall recognize them individually as, 'this is the experience of body,' 'this is the experience of mind,' and so on, and remain indifferent to them."

In brief, one should think, "I shall enter into the path of the Vajrayāna, the only path traversed by all the Buddhas. Having entered that path, I shall also practice until each experience arises upon my mindstream. Having practiced, I shall treat whatever experiences arise in accordance with the teaching."

The Instructions on the Pure Vision in Order to Produce Enthusiasm

It may be asked, "Well then, what is the need to diligently enter into the path of the Mantrayāna and treat each experience individually?" (The answer is) to gain the result of Buddhahood, as stated in the *Root Treatise of the Vajra Verses*, *(rDo.rje'i tshig.rkang, Vajragāthā)*,

> For the ornamental wheel of the Sugata's inexhaustible enlightened body, voice, and mind is the pure vision.

Moreover, **Sugata** (i.e., the Buddha) means having thoroughly gone through the path of the two accumulations (of merit and transcendent wisdom) to the result of the four enlightened bodies. The special qualities of the Sugata are: (A) the ornamental wheel of the inexhaustible enlightened body, (B) the ornamental wheel of the inexhaustible enlightened voice, and (C) the ornamental wheel of the inexhaustible enlightened mind.

The Ornamental Wheel of the Inexhaustible Enlightened Body

The **enlightened body** has two aspects: the inconceivable secret of the enlightened body, and manifesting all forms. The inconceivable secret of the enlightened body means that the body of a Buddha is not able to be measured by anyone. For example, as it was said in the *dKon.mchog btsegs.pa (Ratna Kūṭa)*,[89]

> The Bodhisattva Vegadhārin wished to perceive the end of the Buddha's uṣhṇīṣha (knot on the top of

the head). Having gone (by stages) to the top of Mount Sumeru, the heavenly realm of Trayastrimśa, the world of Brahma, and likewise having gone to the world of Padmavatī where the Tathāgata Padma Shrī Sāra Rāja resides, which is one billion world systems beyond the upper limit of this world, still he was unable to see the end of the uṣhṇīṣha.

Manifesting all forms means that, whatever form is required to discipline those to be trained, the Buddha accordingly takes that form, such as any form from that of the excellent emanation (of the Nirmāṇakāya) to that of a rabbit, tiger, lion, boat, raft, bridge, and the like. Having taken that form, he works for their benefit.

The Ornamental Wheel of the Inexhaustible Enlightened Voice

The **enlightened voice** also has two aspects: the inconceivable secret of the enlightened voice, and manifesting all voices. The inconceivable secret of the enlightened voice means that though one hears the Buddha's speech from a short (or long) distance, such as a mile, seven miles, and so forth, the volume is not less. For example, Maudgalyāyana went to the world system of Prabhāvatī, where the Tathāgata Prabhāvat resides along with his retinue and which is one billion world systems beyond the realm of Sukhavatī. When he listened (to the speech of the Buddha), its volume was no smaller than before. Manifesting all voices means that the Buddha is able to teach the Dharma in the language of each of the realms of living beings individually, such as from that of the pure language of the gods to that of serpent-spirits, demons, cannibals, and the like.

The Ornamental Wheel of the Inexhaustible Enlightened Mind

The **enlightened mind** also has two aspects: the inconceivable secret of the enlightened mind, and manifesting all minds. The inconceivable secret of the enlightened mind means that no one knows all knowable objects as (the Buddha) does. For example, though the noble Arhat Maudgalyāyana, who was endowed with miraculous powers, did not know where his mother was reborn, the Buddha knew. Since none of the Arhats knew that the householder dPal-skyes was endowed with the seed of the liberation, they would not ordain him. However, the Buddha knew that during his seventh previous lifetime, dPal-skyes had been born as a dog. At that time, being chased by a pig, he circumambulated a stupa and thus created a seed of virtue. Because of that, the Buddha ordained him. Manifesting all minds means that the Buddha possesses the transcendental wisdom which completely knows the nature and characteristics of all phenomena. Knowing the nature of all phenomena means knowledge and mastery over the uncontrived ultimate nature of all entities. Knowing the characteristics (of all the phenomena) means knowledge of the conditional relation of the cause and result of all phenomena, such as the reason for the sharpness of a thorn, the roundness of a pea, the squareness of pha.wang stones,[90] the colorfulness of peacocks, and so on, without confusedly mixing them up.

With regard to the ornamental wheel, **ornamental** means beautified. It is beautiful because the purpose of both self and others spontaneously and effortlessly arises.

Wheel means the wheel of transcendental activities. Having achieved full and perfect enlightenment, the Tathāgatas turned the wheel of Dharma and 100 billion sentient beings gained enlightenment. Also, each one of them taught the Dharma and caused an equal number of sentient beings to gain enlightenment. Further, each one of them taught the Dharma and caused more sentient beings to gain enlightenment, and so forth. In brief, until the world of existence is emptied, the wheel of activities for the sake of others will continue without a break.

With regard to the instructions on the pure vision, **pure vision** means that at that time (of Buddhahood), through realizing that all the phenomena of the world of existence (Samsāra) and of liberation (Nirvāna) are the display of one's own undefiled transcendental wisdom alone, there is neither an unpleasant world to be discarded here nor a good state of liberation to be attained elsewhere. Rather, both worldly existence and liberation are seen to be of one taste (i.e., nondual). Previously one was a sentient being, but through the power of practicing the path, one has become a Buddha; hence the mindstream of a sentient being and that of a Buddha are one. Previously there was the practitioner on the path, but through that path dissolving into the result, both the path and the result are of one taste. Previously all conceptualizations were to be discarded, but through the power of habituation to discarding them, all conceptualizations are dissolved into the ultimate truth, so the conceptualizations to be discarded and their antidotes are of one taste. Moreover, one is endowed with inconceivable qualities, such as the nonduality of rejection and acceptance, the nonduality of abandonment and obtainment, the one taste of worldly existence and the state of liberation, the one state, the appearance of one mindstream, and so on.

To contemplate the meaning of this, one should think, "Having entered into this path of the Vajrayāna and through relying upon the treatment of all experiences of the path in accordance with the teachings, I shall gain such a state of Buddhahood, which is endowed with inconceivable qualities, such as the ornamental wheel of a Sugata's inexhaustible enlightened body, voice, and mind, and the like. Thus I shall become an unceasing wheel of transcendental activities which spontaneously and effortlessly works for the welfare of sentient beings." Therefore, from this moment on, one should meditate with enthusiasm (that one will gain such a result).

★   ★   ★

It is best to meditate four times in one day on the meditation subjects (described in this text); three times a day is mediocre, and two sessions a day is inferior. If one fails to gain experience on one meditation subject, then one should not move onto the next meditation subject. In every session one should take refuge, recite the other prayers, perform the main practice of meditating upon the meditation subject at which one has currently arrived, conclude with the dedication of virtues, and maintain a continuity of the meditation subject in the periods between sessions by mindfulness and alertness.

In this way the greatly compassionate teacher, through being especially skilled in means, will teach the impure vision and so will cause the beginner's mind to renounce this world. Then through the vision of the common experience, the desire to gain complete enlightenment for the sake of others will be produced in the practitioner's mind; through the vision of the extraordinary experience, the enthusiasm to enter the path of the Vajrayāna will be produced; and through the pure vision, the enthusiasm for the result of Buddhahood will be produced.

Without any exclusions, all the levels of instructions to establish a genuine receptacle for obtaining the tantric empowerment that ripens the disciple, the first stage of the path of the profound Vajrayāna, are concluded.

Colophon

Having compiled the preliminary teaching of the Three Visions, the profound meaning of the three baskets of the scriptures in their entirety, this method of establishing those imbued with faith as a receptacle is the fundamental function of the Three Visions.

"What is the basis for the arising of the visions? What is the cause of these visions? And what is the essence of these visions?" Having included the Three (Visions endowed with) these three (basis, cause, and essence) into the foundation, the path, and the result, the manner of explaining the Three Visions is unique.

If one understands the differentiations of these, the meaning of many teachings will be illuminated in one's mind, such as the manner of practicing separately or the merging together of the seven common teachings of worldly existence and liberation, and the like.

I composed this, *The Beautiful Ornament of the Three Visions*, by briefly indicating the sections of the teachings in summarized introductory phrases, by extensively explaining the teachings with quotations from scriptures, and by joining a summarized meditation of that section's teaching.

I confess whatever faults have arisen to the Root Guru, Buddhas and Bodhisattvas. Through this excellent virtue, may all mother sentient beings reach the island of the bliss of co-merging.

This exposition of the preliminary practices of the path, explained in accordance with the *Root Treatise* known as *The Beautiful Ornament of the Three Visions*, was ordered by the unequaled lord of knowledge, the king of Dharma, Kunga Samdrup Tashi Pal Zangpo (Kun.dga' bsam.'grub bkra.shis dpal bzang.po), who is a descendent of the precious lineage (of Khon), among whom there were many sons and nephews who were emanations (of enlightened beings) and who are renowned as the Venerable Sakyapas, the owners of the Buddhist teachings of this world. Having been born into this (Sakya) tradition and having been fortunate to enjoy the nectar of the teachings of, and be watched with the eye of compassion by, the kind and holy teachers who practiced in accordance with the Dharma, such as the excellent leader, the king of Dharma, Ratna Wardha, who was not different from Vajradhara himself, the lord of limitless compassion Muchen Sangye Rinchen (Mus.chen sang.rgyas rin.chen), the lord of knowledge Jamyang Kunga Sonam Dragpa Gyaltshen Pal Zangpo ('Jam.dbyangs Kun.dga' bSod.nams Grags.pa rGyal. mtshan dPal bZang.po), and the like, I, the Śakya monk Konchog Lhundrub (dKon.mchog Lhun.grub), composed this book in accordance with the teachings of the foremost masters (of the Sakya tradition), who were second Vajradharas. Having extracted the excellent parts of the explanatory teachings of the great beings who were the later holders of their lineage, and having adorned it especially with the teachings of my three holy, venerable Gurus, this text was completed in the year of the water female rat in the 'mdzes.byed' cycle (A.D. 1543), on the sixteenth day of the eight lunar month, a Friday on which the stars were in a very auspicious alignment. This text was written out by the great scholar Gonpo Rinchen Pal Zangpo (mGon.po Rin.chen dPal bZang.po) with great respect.

The explanation of *The Beautiful Ornament of the Three Tantras*, the main practice of the path, should be understood from texts other than this.

With all the sections included, it is the extensive teaching. If the scriptural quotations are deleted, it is the medium teaching. If both the scriptural quotations and the supplementary explanations are deleted, it is the brief teaching. One should utilize either the extensive, medium, or brief teaching in accordance with conditions and one's understanding.

Notes to the Preface

1. The five founding lamas of the Sakyapa tradition, known in Tibetan as the Jetsun Gongma Nga (rJe.btsun Gong.ma lnga — literally, "the Five Foremost Ones") are: Sachen Kunga Nyingpo (Sa.chen Kun.dga' sNying.po), 1092-1158; Sonam Tsemo (bSod. nams rTse.mo), 1142-1182; Jetsun Dagpa Gyaltshen (rJe.btsun Grags.pa rGyal.mtshan), 1147-1216; Sakya Pandita Kunga Gyaltshen (Sa.skya Pan.di.ta Kun.dga rGyal.mtshan), 1182-1251; and Chogyal phagpa (Chos.rgyal 'Phags.pa), 1235-1280.

2. The full title of the "Path Including Its Result" commonly known as the Lam Dre (Lam 'Bras), is "The Instructions on the Path Including Its Result," (Lam 'Bras.bu Dang bcas.pa'i gDams.ngag).

3. The full title of the *Root Treatise of the Vajra Verses* of Virūpa is *gSung.ngag Rin.po.che Lam 'Bras.bu Dang bcas.pa'i gZhung rDo.rje'i Tshig rKang Zhes Bya.ba bZhugs.so*. It is more commonly known as *Lam 'Bras rDo.rje'i Tshig rKang, Mārgaphala Vajragāthā*.

4. Because receiving the tantric empowerment or initiation is a prerequisite for entering upon the Vajrayāna path, the present translators have deemed it appropriate not to translate the teaching on the "three tantras" for general publication. We feel it would be contrary to the norms set within the Vajrayāna teachings as well as against our own vows as Vajrayāna practitioners.

5. The English titles of these six texts are: *The Beautiful Ornament of the Three Visions, The Beautiful Ornament of the Three Tantras, The Beautiful Ornament of the Tree, The Classification of the Three Methods, Adorning the Intention of the Foremost Teachers' Good Explanations,* and *The Immaculate Mantra of Counterarguments.*

Notes to the Text

1. Lord of Yogīs refers to Virūpa.

2. The fearless Shrī Dharmapāla refers to Virūpa, who was known by this name when he was abbot of Nalanda University.

3. In Buddhist terminology, Māra refers to those negative forces which hinder living beings, and especially those on the path to enlightenment. The four basic categories of Māra are: (i) death, (ii) the afflictions of desire, hatred, ignorance, and so forth, (iii) the grasping aggregates of form, perceptions, feelings, mental predispositions and consciousness, and (iv) the son of god (similar to the Greek concept of Cupid).

4. The Tripiṭaka consists of the three "baskets" or categories of the Buddha's word — namely, moral discipline teachings (vinaya), discourses on meditative techniques and on the virtuous life (sūtra), and teachings on wisdom (abhidharma).

5. See the information in the introduction concerning this text.

6. *Lam 'Bras Khog Phub* is a text basically describing the history of the 'Path Including Its Result' teaching written by Jamyang Khyentse Wangchug ('Jam.dbyangs mKhyen.btse dBang.phyug).

7. The Great Sakyapa, Sachen Kunga Nyingpo (Sa.chen. Kun. dga' sNying.po), 1092-1158, was one of the five foremost founding lamas of the Sakya tradition and is the third patriarch of the sect. Having received the "Path Including Its Result" teaching from Zhangton Chobar (Zhang.sTon Chos.'bar) as well as from

Virūpa himself (which occurred during a visionary experience), Sachen late wrote eleven commentaries on it, such as the *Lam 'bras Don bsDus Ma (The Compiled Meaning of the Path Including Its Result)*.

8. Jetsun Dagpa Gyaltshen (rJe.btsun Grags.pa rGyal.mtshan), 1147-1216, the third son of Sachen and the fifth Patriarch of the Sakya tradition, also wrote many texts concerning the "Path Including Its Result", as well as on other aspects of the Vajrayāna teachings.

9. The three visions are the impure vision, the vision of experience, and the pure vision.

10. The three "tantras" or "lines" refers to the teaching of *The Beautiful Ornament of the Three Tantras* written by the same author where the path of the Vajrayāna teaching of the "Path Including Its Result" is taught. The three tantras are "the tantra of the cause, the all-base mind (ālaya vijñāna)", "the tantra of the path, the body-method", and "the tantra of the result, the Great Seal (mahāmudra)".

11. *Chos.bcu.pa'i mDo: 'Phags.pa Chos.bcu.pa zhes.bya.ba theg. pa chen.po'i mdo*, or *Ārya daśadharmaka nāma mahāyāna sūtra*.

12. *Chos mngon.pa'i mdzod kyi tshig le'ur byas.ba*, or *Abhidharmakośa kārikā*.

13. *sPyod.jug: Byang.chub sems.dpa'i spyod la 'jugs.pa*. or *Bodhisattva caryāvatāra*, it is also known as the *Bodhicaryāvatāra*, and was written by Śāntideva.

14. These stories are found in the *Avatamsaka Sūtra*.

15. *rGyal.po.la. gtam bya.ba rin.po.che'i phreng.ba*, or *Rāja parikathā ratnāvalī*.

16. *bsLab.pa kun.las btus*, or *Śikṣhā samuccaya*.

17. *Theg.pa chen.po'i mdo sde'i rgyan.gyi tshig le'ur byas.pa,* or *Mahāyāna sūtrālankāra kārikā.*

18. *bsGom.rim,* or *Bhāvanā krama,* was written by the Indian master Kamalaśīla, who lived in the eighth century and who helped to establish Buddhism in Tibet.

19. The three collections of scripture, or Tripiṭaka, are the collections of moral discipline (vinaya), discourses (sūtra), and higher philosophy (abhidharma). The twelve categories of the Buddha's speech are: prose, mixed prose and verse, exposition, verse, solemn utterances, introductory literature, legends, life histories, birth stories, extensive explanations, marvelous phenomena, and instructions.

20. The three trainings are moral conduct, transic absorption, and wisdom.

21. The two kinds of enlightenment thought are the relative and ultimate enlightenment thoughts, which are described later in the text.

22. Hārītī was a demoness who terrorized a village by eating the children. The Buddha subdued her and promised that he and his monks would always dedicate a share of their food to her so that she could feed herself and her own children and would thus have no need to steal and eat others' children.

23. *S'es.rab kyi pha.rol.tu phyin.pa'i man.ngag gi bstan.bcos mngon.par rtogs.pa'i rgyan zhes.bya.ba'i tshig le'ur byas.pa,* or *Abhisamayālankāra nāma prajñāpāramitopadeśa śastra kārikā.*

24. *'Phags.pa dam.pa'i chos dran.pa nye.bar gzhag.pa,* or *Ārya saddharmānusmṛtyupastāna.*

25. *bShes.pa'i spring.yig,* or *Suhṛlleka* (*The Letter of a Friend*), was written by great Indian saint Nāgārjuna.

26. *sLob.ma.la springs pa'i spring.yig*, or *Śiṣhyalekha*, was written by Candragomin.

27. "*Phags.pa rgya.cher rol.pa zhes.bya.ba theg.pa chen.po'i mdo*, or *Ārya lalitavistara nāma mahāyāna sūtra*.

28. '*Phags.pa drang.srong rgyas.pas zhus.pa zhes.bya.ba theg.pa chen.po'i mdo*, or *Ārya ṛṣhivyāsa paripṛcchā nāma mahāyāna sūtra*.

29. The god surveys the place where he was previously born, the place where he presently resides, and the place where he will next be born.

30. *Chos mngon.pa'i mdzod.kyi 'grel.bshad*, or *Abhidharmakośa ṭīkā*.

31. *bsTan.bcos bzhi.brgya.pa zhes.bya.ba'i tshig le'ur byas.pa*, or *Catuhśataka śastra kārikā nāma*, was written by Āryadeva.

32. '*Phags.pa lhag.pa'i bsam.pa bskul.pa zhes.bya.ba theg.pa chen.po'i mdo*, or *Ārya adhyāśaya samcodana nāma mahāyāna sūtra*.

33. *DBu.ma.la. 'jug.pa'i tshig le'ur byas pa*, or *Madhyamakāvatāra kārikā nāma*, was written by Candrakīrti.

34. '*Dul.ba lung bla.ma'i bye.brag lung zhu.ba'i 'grel.ba*, or *Vinayottarāgama viśeṣhāgama praśna vṛtti*.

35. Our teacher refers to the Buddha of this present time, the Buddha Śākyamuni.

36. This example refers to a folktale in which a hare was drinking water from a pond when a branch fell off a nearby tree and plunged into the water. Frightened by the unexpected sound and not examining its source, the hare thought it came from some

ferocious beast that was going to attack and eat him. Running through the forest, he told all the other animals along the way not to go to the pond for water because of the beast. So all the other animals also became frightened and ran in the opposite direction from the pond. However, one lion heard what was going on. Having gone down to the pond, he thoroughly examined the area to discover that no monstrous beast was there and that the sound of "chal" was only caused by a branch hitting the water.

37. Sakya Pandita Kunga Gyaltshen (Sa.skya pan.di.ta kun.dga' rgyal.mtshan), 1182-1251, was the Sixth Patriarch of the Sakya tradition and also the most renowned. Having become known as the greatest scholar ever to arise in Tibet with his writings on logic, moral discipline, philosophy, grammar, music, the arts, tantra, and other fields, he was invited to China (then under the rule of the Mongols) and established Buddhism in the court of the Mongol emperors.

38. Karmabhūmika refers to the fact that in this world the result of an action can mature in this very lifetime.

39. This is literally translated as "death dharma," which is any practice that is certain to bring benefit to one in one's next life.

40. *Mya ngan bsal ba,* or *Śoka vinodana,* was written by Aśvaghoṣha.

41. *sKyes.pa'i rabs.kyi rgyud,* or *Jātaka mālā.*

42. *Ched.du brjod.pa'i tshoms,* or *Udāna varga.*

43. *'Phags.pa rgyal.po.la gdams.pa zhes.bya.ba theg.pa chen.po'i mdo,* or *Ārya rājāvavādaka nāma mahāyāna sūtra.*

44. *Las.rgyas tham.pa,* or *Karmaśataka.*

45. *'Phags.pa nges.pa dang mi.nges.par 'gro.ba'i phyag.rgya la 'jug.pa zhes.bya.ba theg.pa chen.po'i mdo,* or *Ārya niyata aniyata gati mudrā avatāra nāma mahāyāna sūtra.*

46. Visible results refers to results that one experiences in this life.

47. 'Phags pa byams.pa'i seng.ge'i sgra chen.po zhes.bya.ba theg.pa chen.po'i mdo, or Ārya maitreya mahāsimhanāda nāma mahāyāna sūtra.

48. 'Phags.pa 'dul.ba rnam.par gtan.la dbab.pa nye.bar 'khor gyis zhus.pa zhes.bya.ba theg.pa chen.po'i mdo, or Ārya vinayaviniścaya upāli paripṛcchā nāma mahāyāna sūtra.

49. This example refers to one of the *Jātaka* stories. The Buddha was born in that lifetime as a ship captain who killed one of his own sailors, known as *Mi.nag mDung thung can*, who was planning to kill the 500 traders who were traveling on that ship. To save those 500 men, as well as to save the sailor from committing such a great nonvirtuous deed, the captain killed the sailor.

50. The four defeats are the four main vows of a monk or nun, the breaking of which causes a monk or nun to lose his or her vows. These are killing another person, stealing, sexual intercourse, and lying (in regard to achieving some result of practice which one has not actually achieved).

51. 'Phags.pa byang.chub sems.pa'i spyod yul gyi thabs kyi yul la rnam.par 'phrul.ba bstan.pa zhes.bya.ba theg.pa chen.po'i mdo, or Ārya bodhisattva gocara upāya viṣhaya vikurvāṇa nirdeśa nāma mahāyāna sūtra.

52. 'Phags.pa shes.rab.kyi pha.rol.tu phyin.pa sdud.pa tshigs.su bcad.pa, or Ārya prajñāpāramitā sañcaya gāthā.

53. 'Phags.pa shes.rab.kyi pha.rol.tu phyin.pa rdo.rje gcod.pa zhes.bya.ba theg.pa chen.po'i mdo, or Ārya vajracchedikā nāma prajñāpāramitā mahāyāna sūtra.

54. Ordinary beings are those with whom one has no active relation or connection, so that one possesses a basic indifference toward them.

55. *'Phags.pa bzang.po spyod.pa'i smon.lam gyi rgyal.po*, or *Ārya bhadracaryā praṇidhāna rāja*.

56. *'Phags.pa chos yang.dag.par sdud.pa zhes.bya.ba theg.pa chen po'i mdo*, or *Ārya dharma samgīti nāma mahāyāna sūtra*.

57. *Tshad.ma rnam.'grel gyi tshig le'ur byas.pa*, or *Pramāṇa vārttika kārikā*, was written by Dharmakīrti.

58. *'Phags.pa khyim.bdag dpas.byin gyi zhus.pa zhes.bya.ba theg.pa chen.po'i mdo*, or *Ārya vīradattagṛhapati paripṛcchā nāma mahāyāna sūtra*.

59. The first stage, obtained through an intention, refers to the person who has still not realized emptiness, but who still meditates on the enlightenment thought with great intent and faith. The second, pure aspiration, refers to those bodhisattvas of the first to the seventh bhūmis who faultlessly possess good thoughts and aspirations for others. The third, full ripening, refers to those bodhisattvas on the eighth to tenth bhūmis who possess wisdom without making any effort, just like the result of fully ripened karma arises without any effort. The fourth, devoid of obscurations, refers to the stage of Buddhahood.

60. The twenty-two examples are: like the earth, like gold, like the moon, like fire, like a treasure, like the source of jewels, like an ocean, like a diamond, like Mount Sumeru, like medicine, like a spiritual friend, like a gem, like the sun, like a song, like a king, like a treasury, like an elephant, like a pack animal, like a water spring, like a pleasant sound, like a river, and like a cloud.

The twenty-two assistants are: endowed with intention, thought, aspiration, application, giving, moral conduct, patience, diligence, meditation, wisdom, skillful means, prayer, power, transcendental wisdom, four beliefs, two accumulations, thirty-seven factors of enlightenment, compassion and insight wisdom, dharani and self-reliant knowledge, the four complete teachings (of impermanence, suffering, selflessness and peacefulness of Nirvāṇa), the only path, and the Dharmakāya (body of truth).

The twenty-two examples and the twenty-two assistants are in a direct corresponding relationship to each other. For example the first example of like the earth and the first assistant of endowed with intention is explained as follows: 'Just as grass and trees grows and increase in dependence upon the earth, so virtues grow and increase in dependence upon the enlightenment thought endowed with intention.'

61. *'Phags.pa byang.chub sems.dpa'i sde.snod ces.bya.ba theg.pa chen.po'i mdo*, or *Ārya bodhisattva piṭaka nāma mahāyāna sūtra*.

62. The three vehicles refers to the Śrāvakayāna, Pratyekabuddhayāna, and the Bodhisattvayāna. The first two are classified within the Hinayāna school, while the latter is classified under the Mahāyāna. The Vajrayāna school is not classified separately, but is found within the Mahāyāna school.

63. Two purposes refers to accomplishing the benefits for oneself and for others. The fully Enlightened Ones do this by accomplishing the Dharmakāya for the sake of themselves and the Rūpakāya (which consists of the Sambhogakāya and Nirmāṇakāya) for the sake of others.

64. This is found in the *mDo mdzangs blun*, which has been translated into English by Stanley Frye under the title, *Sūtra of the Wise and Foolish*, Library of Tibetan Works and Archives, Dharamsala, 1981.

65. *'Phags.pa dkon.mchog sprin ces.bya.ba theg.pa chen.po'i mdo*, or *Ārya ratna megha nāma mahāyāna sūtra*.

66. *DBus dang mtha' rnam.par 'byed.pa*, or *Madhyānta vibhanga*.

67. *'Phags.pa chos thams.cad kyi rang.bzhin mnyam.pa.nyid rnam.par spros.pa ting.nge.'dzin gyi rgyal.po zhes.bya.ba theg.pa chen.po'i mdo*, or *Ārya sarva dharma svabhāva vipañcita samādhirāja nāma mahāyāna sūtra*.

68. When one sneezes, at that moment no thoughts arise in one's mind.

69. The general posture of meditation as well as the various recitations and prayers have been stated earlier in the text in the 'refuge' section.

70. *'Phags.pa 'jam.dpal rnam.par 'phrul.pa'i le'ur zhes.bya.ba theg.pa chen.po'i mdo*, or *Ārya mañjuśrī vikurvāṇa parivarta nāma mahāyāna sūtra*.

71. *Theg.pa chen.po'i rgyud bla.ma'i bstan.bcos*, or *Mahāyānottara tantra śastra*.

72. *'Phags.pa lang.kar gshegs.pa'i theg.pa chen.po'i mdo*, or *Ārya lankāvatāra mahāyāna sūtra*.

73. *Byang.chub sems kyi 'grel.pa*, or *Bodhicitta vivarana*, was written by Nāgārjuna.

74. *Rigs.pa drug.cu.pa'i tshig le'ur byas.pa zhes.bya.ba*, or *Yuktiśaṣhtikā kārikā nāma*, was written by Ārya Nāgārjuna.

75. *Nyi.shu.pa'i tshig le'ur byas.pa*, or *Vimśaka kārikā*, was written by Ācārya Vasubandhu.

76. *'Phags.pa mkha'.'gro.ma rdo.rje gur zhes.bya.ba'i rgyud.kyi rgyal.po chen.po'i brtag.pa*, or *Ārya ḍākinī vajrapañjara mahātantra rāja kalpa nāma*.

77. *'Phags.pa shes.rab.kyi pha.rol.tu phyin.pa brgyad stong.pa*, or *Ārya Aṣhṭasāhaśrikā prajñāpāramitā*.

78. *rNam.par snang.mdzad chen.po mngon.par rdzogs.par byang.chub.pa rnam.par sprul.ba byin.gyis rlob.pa shin.tu rgyas. pa mdo.sde'i dbang.po rgyal.po zhes.bya.ba'i chos.kyi rnams grangs*, or *Mahāvairocanābhisambodhi vikurvatī adhishtāna vaipulya sūtra indrarājā nāma dharma paryāya*.

79. *Ye.shes snying.po kun.las btus.pa zhes.bya.ba*, or *Jñānasāra Samuccaya nāma*, was written by Āryadeva.

80. *'Phags.pa 'od.srung gi le'u zhes.bya.ba theg.pa chen.po'i mdo*, or *Ārya Kāśyapa parivarta nāma mahāyāna sūtra*.

81. *'Phags.pa yab dang sras mjal.ba zhes.bya.ba theg.pa chen.po'i mdo*, or *Ārya pitāputra samāgama nāma mahāyāna sūtra*.

82. *'Phags.pa gang.pos zhus.pa zhes.bya.ba theg.pa chen.po'i mdo*, or *Ārya pūrṇa paripṛcchā nāma mahāyāna sūtra*.

83. Cessation refers to the Śrāvaka's Nirvāṇa, which is only the cessation of suffering and the cause of suffering.

84. "The unexamined alone is pleasing" refers to the idea that for the sake of the functioning of karma and of accomplishing the path within the relative truth, one should not examine the existence or cause of origination of all phenomena. This excerpt is found in Aśvaghoṣha's *Don dam chang.chub kyi sems bsgom. pa'i man.ngag*, or *Paramārtha bodhicitta bhāvanā krama varṇa samgraḥ*.

85. This verse is found in the *Ting.nge 'dzin rgyal.po mdo*, *Samādhi rāja sūtra:*

> The magicians create a variety of magical forms,
> such as horses, elephants, carts, and the like.
> In whatever form they appear, still they do not
> (truly) exist. So, one should know all phenomena
> to be the same.

86. This refers to rebirth within the realm of form.

87. *rDo.rje theg.pa'i mtha' gnyis sel.ba zhes.bya.ba*, or *Vajrayāna koṭi dvayāpoha nāma*.

88. The Great Translator is Rinchen Zangpo (Rin.chen bzang. po).

89. *'Phags.pa dkon.mchog brtsegs.pa chen.po'i chos.kyi rnam. grangs le'ur stong phrag brgyas.pa*, or *Ārya mahāratnakūta dharma paryāya śatasāhasrikā grantha*.

90. Pha.wang stones are stones found in Tibet that are naturally square in shape. When broken, the pieces are also square in shape.

Outline of the Beautiful Ornament of the Three Visions

The Preliminaries

I. Introduction
II. Faith
III. Refuge

A. The causes of taking refuge
B. The object of taking refuge
C. The procedure for taking refuge
D. The benefits of taking refuge
E. The precepts of taking refuge

The Main Teaching

I. The instructions on the impure vision to produce renunciation

A. The instructions on the faults of worldly existence to produce renunciation

1 The suffering of suffering
a. The suffering of the hells
   1. The eight cold hells
   2. The eight hot hells
   3. The neighboring hells and minor hells
b. The suffering of the hungry ghosts
   1. External obscurations
   2. Internal obscurations
   3. The obscuration of obscurations

    c. The suffering of the animals
       1. Those who dwell in outer oceans
       2. Those who dwell in the darkness between continents
       3. Those who are scattered in the higher realms
2 The suffering of change
    a. The general suffering of change
    b. The suffering of human change
       1. The suffering of birth
       2. The suffering of old age
       3. The suffering of disease
       4. The suffering of death
    c. The suffering of the gods' and demigods' change
3 The suffering of conditional phenomena
    a. The suffering that activities are never ending
    b. The suffering of not being satisfied by desire
    c. The suffering of never being wearied of birth and death

B. The instructions on the difficulty of obtaining the prerequisites to evoke diligence

1 The difficulty of obtaining this human body endowed with the prerequisites
    a. The difficulty of obtaining a human body from the viewpoint of cause
    b. The difficulty of obtaining a human body from the viewpoint of number
    c. The difficulty of obtaining a human body from the viewpoint of nature
2 The great benefit of this body which has been obtained
3 The prerequisites obtained will not last long
    a. The reflection on impermanence has inconceivable benefits
       1. It checks attachment for things
       2. It is a goad that stimulates vigor
       3. It is an antidote to suffering
       4. It is a helper in realizing emptiness, the ultimate truth
    b. How to contemplate impermanence

1. Reflect on the certainty of death and thus relinquish grasping at permanence
   a. Death is certain because, having been born, one does not have the power to remain
   b. Death is certain because the body is insubstantial
   c. Death is certain because life is not permanent
2. Reflect on the uncertainty of the time of death and thus shorten the range of one's plans
   a. There is no certainty about the time of death because there is no fixed life span
   b. There is no certainty about the time of death because the causes of death are manifold
      i. Body and life are easily separated
      ii. The Lord of Death has no love
      iii. There are many hostile forces, diseases, and malignant spirits
   c. There is no certainty about the time of death because the causes of life are few
3. Reflect that nonreligious activities are not beneficial, and thus practice the holy Dharma
   a. The holy Dharma should be practiced because food and wealth are useless
   b. The holy Dharma should be practiced because kinsmen and associates are useless
   c. The holy Dharma should be practiced because eloquence and power are useless

C. The instructions on virtuous and nonvirtuous deeds and their results to clarify what is to be accepted and what is to be rejected

1 Produce the desire to discard nonvirtue by reflecting on nonvirtuous deeds and their results
a. Nonvirtuous deeds
b. The results of nonvirtuous deeds
   1. The ripened result
   2. The result similar to its cause
      a. Experience similar to its cause
      b. Action similar to its cause
   3. The result of ownership
c. Discarding nonvirtuous deeds

2 Produce the desire to practice virtue by reflecting on virtuous deeds and their results
a. Virtuous deeds
b. The results of virtuous deeds
   1. The ripened result
   2. The result similar to its cause
      a. Experience similar to its cause
      b. Action similar to its cause
   3. The result of ownership
c. Performing virtuous deeds

3 Transform neutral deeds into virtues by reflecting on them
a. Neutral deeds are fruitless
b. Neutral deeds have no results
c. Transforming neutral deeds into virtues

II. The instructions on the vision of experience to produce noble aspirations

A. Meditate until the common experience arises in one's mindstream
1 Loving kindness, the desire to benefit other beings
a. Loving kindness for one's mother
   1. Think of one's mother
   2. Think of her kindness
      a. Think of her kindness in giving one's body and life
      b. Think of her kindness in giving instructions of acceptance and rejection
      c. Think of her kindness in bearing hardships in order to bring one up
   3. Think of the need to repay her kindness
b. Merge that meditation with other relatives
c. Merge that meditation with ordinary beings
   1. Meditate on neighbors and the like
   2. Meditate on one's enemies
   3. Meditate on all sentient beings

2 Compassion, the desire to destroy the suffering of others
a. Compassion in reference to sentient beings

    b. Compassion in reference to the Dharma
    c. Compassion in reference to no object

3 The enlightenment thought, the desire to gain Buddhahood for the sake of others
  a. The wishing enlightenment thought, the desire for the result for the sake of others
  b. The entering enlightenment thought, the training on the path for the sake of the result
    1. Equality between self and others
    2. Exchanging self for others
    3. Training in the conduct of equality and exchanging
      a. Training in the general conduct of the Bodhisattvas
      b. Training in the six Perfections to ripen oneself
        i. The defining characteristic of the six Perfections
        ii. The method for accomplishing the six Perfections
          • The four qualities to be practiced
          • The seven attachments to be discarded
        iii. The benefits of the six Perfections
      c. Training in the four practices of gathering to ripen others
        i. Giving
        ii. Speaking pleasantly
        iii. Purposeful conduct
        iv. Acting with a harmonious purpose
  c. The ultimate enlightenment thought, the combination of calm abiding and insight wisdom
    1. The nature of the ultimate enlightenment thought
    2. The methods for producing the ultimate enlightenment thought in the mind
    3. The manner in which to practice whichever method has been taught
      a. Calm abiding
        i. The five faults and eight antidotes (or corrective measures)
        ii The nine placements of the mind
        iii. The five experiences of meditation
      b. Insight wisdom
        i. Recognize the nature of appearances

      ii. Keep the mind in the state free from conceptual extremes
      iii. Develop the unshakable understanding that the nature of mind is inexpressible
    c. The merging of calm abiding and insight wisdom

B. Meditate with unshakable understanding that an extraordinary experience in the Vajrayāna path will arise

III. The instructions on the pure vision to produce enthusiasm

A. The ornamental wheel of the inexhaustible enlightened body
B. The ornamental wheel of the inexhaustible enlightened voice
C. The ornamental wheel of the inexhaustible enlightened mind

Colophon

Bibliography

Batchelor, Stephen, trans., *A Guide to the Bodhisattva's Way of Life* (a translation of Śantideva's *Bodhicaryāvatāra*). Dharamsala, India: Library of Tibetan Works and Archives, 1979.

Bhattacharya, Vidhushekkhara, ed., *Bodhicaryāvatāra*. Calcutta: The Asiastic Society, 1960.

Jamspal, Lozang, Ngawang Samten, and Peter Della Santina, trans., *Nāgārjuna's Letter to King Gautamīputra* (a translation of Nāgārjuna's *Suhṛllekha*). Delhi: Motilal Banarsidass, 1978.

Ngulchu Thogmed, *Byang.chub sems.dpa'i spyod.pa.la 'jugs.pa'i rtsa.ba dang 'grel.ba legs.par bshad.pa'i rgya.mtsho zhes.bya.ba bzhugs.so* (Śantideva's *Bodhicaryāvatāra* along with a commentary by Ngulchu Thogmed [dNgul.chu Thogs.med]). Sarnath, Varanasi: Sakya Student's Union, 1982.

Sangpo, Khetsun, *Biographical Dictionary of Tibet and Tibetan Buddhism*, Vols. X and XI, The Sa-skya-pa Tradition. Dharamsala, India: Library of Tibetan Works and Archives, 1979.

Suzuki, Daisetz T., ed., *The Tibetan Tripitaka*, Peking Edition, Catalogue and Index. Tokyo: Suzuki Research Foundation, 1962.

Trizin, Sakya (H.H. Sakya Trizin) and Ngawang Samten Chophel, trans., *A Collection of Instructions on Parting From the Four Attachments*. Singapore: The Singapore Buddha Sasana Society, Sakya Tenphel Ling. 1982.

Index

Afflictions xv-xvi, xxi, 6, 8, 20, 36, 38, 45, 52, 55, 65-6, 69, 72-3, 85, 87, 104, 105, 108, 120-1, 128-9, 152, 170-2, 177, 192, 210
Aggregates 48, 53, 87, 129, 176-7, 193, 210
Anger 5-7, 25, 33, 90, 93, 101, 121, 124, 152-3, 161
Animals 21-2, 36-8, 46, 53, 57-8, 59, 90, 96, 125, 178, 222
Antidotes 67, 98, 162-4, 166-7, 170, 189, 192, 204, 223, 226
Alertness 14, 25, 54, 104, 163, 167, 170, 204
Ārya Deva 111, 157, 213, 219
Aspiration xvii, 10, 12, 14, 22, 25, 97, 120, 141, 216, 224
Attachment xvii, 20-1, 36, 46, 48-51, 58, 81-2, 98, 144, 153-4, 158-61, 169, 197, 222
Avarice 34-6
Awareness 107

Birth 40, 43, 47-8, 52-4, 58, 63, 66, 72, 85, 109, 129, 132, 190, 222
Bodhisattva 8, 11, 25, 69, 108, 111, 122, 142, 145, 151-2, 197, 225
Buddha 10-12, 17, 25, 39, 55-61, 65, 97, 100, 108, 110, 112-7, 125, 131-3, 136-7, 157, 185, 191, 198-200, 201-5, 210, 212, 215-6, 225

Calm Abiding 156-71, 195-7, 225-6
Calumny 88-92
Candra Gomin 213
Candra Kīrti 115, 126, 176, 213
Cessation 11, 186, 192, 219
Cittamātra 157, 188
Conceptual Extremes 157, 174, 184-97
Conceptualizations 157, 170, 173, 188
Conditional Phenomena 48-55
Confession 94
Corrective Measures 162, 226
Consciousness 106, 157, 165, 168-70, 176-8, 181-3, 187, 194-6, 210
Covetousness 88-92

Death 40-48, 66-87, 105, 107, 190, 210, 222-3
Death, Lord of 26, 27, 72-3, 77-8, 80, 82, 84, 85, 190, 223

Deeds (*see* Karma)
Delusion 36-8, 47, 88, 90, 95, 173-5, 193-4
Demigods 44-5, 96, 178, 222
Desire xvii, xix, 38, 48, 50-1, 53-4, 67, 81, 88, 90, 95, 159, 210, 222
Dharma 4, 11, 13, 36, 38, 53, 60, 63-4, 67, 68, 74-5, 80-6, 96, 101, 110, 117, 120, 124, 128, 155-6, 160, 181, 193, 198, 202-3, 214, 223, 225
Dharma, phenomena 171, 174
Dharmadhātu 181-2, 196
Dharmakāya 10, 105, 135, 216, 217
Dharma Kirti 181, 216
Diligence 20, 162, 169, 216, 222
Disease 40, 42-3, 47, 66, 190, 222

Effort 152, 154, 162-3
Emptiness 2, 67, 97, 132, 157, 170-3, 183, 187-9, 191-5, 216, 223
Enlightened One 2, 6, 8, 10-12, 16-7, 61, 163, 217
Enlightenment 61, 63, 110, 114, 131, 162, 171-3, 191, 197, 203, 210
Enlightenment Thought 85, 107, 112, 119, 132-51, 193, 198, 212, 216, 225
  entering 134, 138-51, 225
  relative 132, 134, 212
  ultimate 132, 134, 157, 212, 225-6
  wishing 134-8, 225
Equanimity 164-6, 170

Faith 4-8, 9-10, 60-1, 111, 162, 216, 221
Fear 5-7, 8-9

Gathering, four means of 151, 154-6, 225
Giving 101-2, 114, 151-5, 171, 216
God 194
Gods 21, 38, 44-8, 53, 59, 64, 96, 136, 178, 210, 213, 222

Happiness 21, 28, 38, 45, 47, 48, 54-5, 85, 113-25, 128, 138-51, 183
Harsh Speech 88-92
Hatred 33, 88, 95, 101, 121, 161, 169, 210
Heaven (*see* Realms of desire, form and formlessness)
Hell 6, 21-33, 46, 53, 90, 221
Hīnayāna 10, 114, 157, 217
Human Body, difficulty to obtain 55-67
Hungry Ghost 21, 33-6, 46, 53, 90, 221

Idle Speech 88-92
Ignorance 5-7, 37, 90, 128, 132, 169, 210
Impernmanence 66-87, 216, 222
Impurity 169, 179

Inexpressible 174, 188-97, 226
Insight Wisdom 157-8, 171-97
Insubstantial 69-71, 186-7, 223
Interdependent Origination 169

Jetsun Dagpa Gyaltsen xiv, 3, 20, 21, 39, 40, 52, 55, 113, 160, 186, 188, 189, 208, 211

Karma 4, 26-7, 30, 33, 36, 38, 48, 52, 58, 59, 63-4, 67, 70, 78, 87-111, 120, 128-31, 216, 219
Killing 88-92

Lam Dre xiv-xv, xvii, 25, 208
Laziness 153, 162-3
Liberation, personal (Nirvāṇa) 20, 47, 53-4, 63, 67, 97, 105, 113-4, 134, 136-8, 152, 154, 157, 172, 182, 189, 198, 204
Loving Kindness 112-25, 169, 224-5
Lying 88-92

Mādhyamaka 187-8
Mahāyāna xiii, xiv, xvi, 10, 114, 124-5, 134, 157, 183, 192, 217
Mañjuśhri 180
Malice 88-92
Māra 2, 5, 106, 107, 172, 210
Meditation xvi, xvii, 2, 9, 105, 152, 154
  equality of self and other 140-3
  exchanging self for other 143-51
  placement of mind in 157-71
Merit 5, 9, 10, 13-4, 16, 46, 70, 78, 97, 99-102, 114-5, 132, 135, 146, 173, 192, 201
Method 148, 171-3, 192, 211
Mind 4, 14, 86, 88-90, 103, 147, 157-71, 173-97, 201-4, 211, 226
  clarity of 169
  primordial 157-8, 193
Mindfulness 14, 25, 54, 86, 104-5, 163, 165-6, 170
Miserliness 34-6, 153
Moral Conduct 152, 154, 159, 212
Morality 56-7, 102, 152
Mother's Kindness 116-9

Nāgārjuna 13, 142, 157, 189, 212, 218
Name 174-6, 189-91, 193
Neutral Deeds 103-7, 224
Nirvāṇa (*see* Personal Liberation) 21, 69, 73, 113, 134, 151, 157, 173, 182-3, 189, 200, 204, 216, 219

INDEX ■ 230

Noble Assembly 11, 13
Nonvirtuous Deeds 87-95, 99, 223-4

Old Age 40-2, 49, 66, 190, 222
Omniscience xvii, 12, 13, 63, 66, 97, 192

Path iii, iv, vi, 2-3, 11-12, 64, 105, 111, 112, 114, 125, 150, 172, 188, 197, 199, 204, 216
Path Including Its Result (Lam Dre) xii-xvii, 2, 3, 25, 179, 208, 210-11
Patience 5, 114, 152, 154, 216
Perfections 112, 151-4, 171, 199, 225
Pratyekabuddha 69, 113, 114, 136, 172, 217
Prayer 7, 9, 13, 119, 122, 123, 126, 129, 138, 216
Preceptor 6, 7, 10-15, 54, 98, 100, 119, 177
Precious Gems 54
Prerequisites 55-66, 93, 96, 222
Pride 4, 82, 149, 170

Realm xvi, 21, 44, 55
   formless 21, 46, 191, 196
   higher 38, 45, 47, 48, 55-6, 57, 63, 64, 91-4, 96
   human 40
   lower 22, 38, 40, 41, 55, 57, 90, 91-4, 111, 160
   of desire 21, 28, 45, 48, 166, 178, 185, 190
   of form 21, 46, 190, 219
Refuge 9-17
Relative Truth 148, 190, 219
Root Treatise of the Vajra Verses xiii, xv, 20, 87, 112, 201, 207, 208

Sachen Kunga Nyingpo xii, xiv, 3, 208, 210-11
Sakyapa xi-xv, 208
Sakya Pandita 102, 103, 104, 134, 154, 180, 190, 192, 208, 214
Śākyamuni xi, 145, 213
Saṃsāra (*see* Worldly Existence) xvii, 157, 169, 173, 182, 183, 189, 200, 203
Sangha xvi, 11, 99, 100
Śāntideva 211
Self 128-32, 139, 141, 144, 148, 157, 158, 171, 173-7, 193
Selflessness 156, 172, 173-83, 214
   of phenomena 177-83
   of the person 173-7
Sentient Beings xv, xvi, 12, 20, 55, 109, 113-6, 121-5, 126-7, 128-30, 141, 159, 191, 204
Sexual Misconduct 88-92
Śrāvaka 102, 111, 113, 114, 136, 157, 173, 192, 217, 219
Stealing 88-92

Suffering
   of change 38-48
   of conditional phenomena 48-55
   of suffering 21-38

Transic Absorption xv, xvi, 2, 112, 161, 162, 163, 166, 167, 170, 172-3, 196, 197, 212
Triple Gem (Three Jewels) xvi, 4, 5, 7, 10-17, 80, 98, 99, 107, 198
Truth (see Relative, Ultimate) 4-5, 59, 152

Ultimate Truth 67, 128, 134, 148, 171-97, 223
Unhappiness 48, 141, 167

Vajrayāna xii, xiii, xiv, 3, 112, 197-200, 204-5, 208, 211, 217, 226
Vehicle 63, 101, 114, 137, 138, 153, 198, 217
   cause 199
   perfection 199
   result 199
View xvii, 10, 128, 132, 159, 172, 177
   right 111, 159, 190
   wrong 46-7, 59, 88-92, 98, 101
Virtuous Deeds 87, 95-103, 223-4
Virūpa xii-xiv, 20, 120, 125, 181, 208, 210
Vision xv-xvii, 211
   impure 20-111
   of experience 112-200
   pure 201-5

Wisdom (see Insight Wisdom) 14, 16, 91, 97, 152, 153, 154, 156, 171-3, 187, 189, 192, 196, 201, 203, 204, 210, 212, 216
Worldly Existence (see Samsāra) 9, 10, 11, 17, 20-1, 24, 39, 42, 47-8, 50, 53-5, 105, 131, 132, 136, 139, 152, 160, 163, 172, 189, 193-4, 214, 221

Yogacarya 183-4

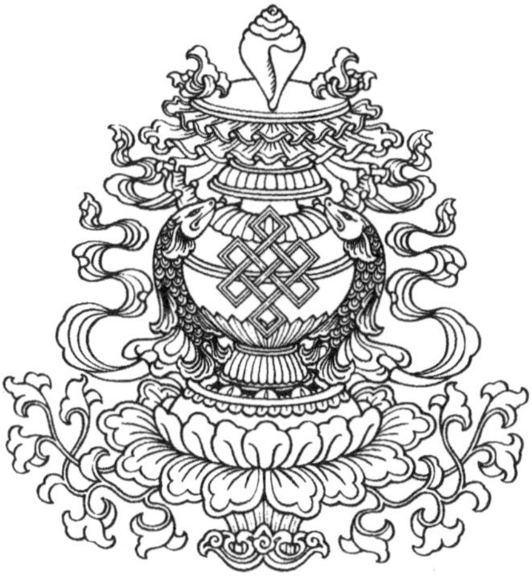